Children's Transitions in Everyday Life and Institutions

Transitions in Childhood and Youth

Series editors: Marilyn Fleer, Mariane Hedegaard and Megan Adams

The series brings together books that present and explore empirical research and theoretical discussion on the themes of childhood and youth transitions. Special attention is directed to conceptualizing transitions holistically so that societal, institutional and personal perspectives are featured within and across books. Key to the series is presenting the processes of transitions between practices or activities and their relationship to the person, in contexts such as, intergenerational family practices, the processes of care, a person's development, the learning of individuals, groups and systems, personal health, labour and birthing and aging. All books take a broad cultural-historical approach of transitions across a range of contexts and countries and when brought together in one place make an important contribution to better understanding transitions globally. Books in the *Transitions in Childhood and Youth* series offer an excellent resource for postgraduate students, researchers, policy writers and academics.

Forthcoming in the series:

Supporting Difficult Transitions: Children, Young People and their Carers, edited by Mariane Hedegaard and Anne Edwards

Children's Transitions in Everyday Life and Institutions

Edited by
Mariane Hedegaard and Marilyn Fleer

BLOOMSBURY ACADEMIC
LONDON • NEW YORK • OXFORD • NEW DELHI • SYDNEY

BLOOMSBURY ACADEMIC
Bloomsbury Publishing Plc
50 Bedford Square, London, WC1B 3DP, UK
1385 Broadway, New York, NY 10018, USA

BLOOMSBURY, BLOOMSBURY ACADEMIC and the Diana logo
are trademarks of Bloomsbury Publishing Plc

First published in Great Britain 2019
Paperback edition published 2020

Cover design: Joshua Fanning
Cover image: © Bec Parsons/Thinkstock

A catalogue record for this book is available from the British Library.

A catalog record for this book is available from the Library of Congress.

ISBN: HB: 978-1-3500-2145-7
         PB: 978-1-3501-7519-8
         ePDF: 978-1-3500-2147-1
         eBook: 978-1-3500-2146-4

Series: Transitions in Childhood and Youth

Typeset by Integra Software Services Pvt. Ltd.

To find out more about our authors and books visit www.bloomsbury.com
and sign up for our newsletters.

Contents

Notes on Contributors

Megan Adams is Senior Lecturer in the Faculty of Education at Monash University. As a qualified teacher, Megan has extensive experience in Australian and international educational contexts ranging from pre kindergarten to the tertiary level. Megan's specific research focus is on internationally mobile families with young children. In addition her interests are pedagogy, curriculum and inclusive education.

Karin Aronsson is Professor Emeritus at the Department of Child and Youth Studies, Stockholm University, Sweden. Before that, she was Professor of Child Studies at Linköping University, Sweden. Her research is focused on asymmetries, affect and multiparty participation in social interaction. Much of her work involves institutional settings, such as schools, health clinics and intermediate areas between the private and public. She primarily publishes in international journals and serves on several editorial boards: *Applied Linguistics, Journal of Language and Social Psychology, Research on Children and Social Interaction* and *Text & Talk*.

Paula Cavada-Hrepich is a postdoctoral researcher in the Department of Communication and Psychology at Aalborg University, Denmark. Her recent research has centred on the transition to the first year of primary school from the children's perspective in Chile and Denmark. Her latest publication is 'Children's resistance in the emergence of learning as leading activity: Playfulness in the transformation of spaces of participation' in *Resistance in Everyday Life: Constructing Cultural Experiences* (2017). Currently, she is participating in three different research projects studying the transition to a new educational system of newly arrived children in Denmark, the collaboration towards learning between parents and preschool institutions, and representations of justice in the school of Danish pupils. She is Associated Researcher at the Niels Bohr Centre for Cultural Psychology at Aalborg University and at the Center for Advanced Research in Education at University of Chile, Chile.

Anamika Devi is a current PhD student in the Faculty of Education, Monash University, Australia. Her research and teaching interests focus on play and pedagogy in diverse cultural contexts, adults' support of children's learning and development in different settings, intentional teaching, STEM, and the cultural-historical perspective on play. Her most recent journal article (co-author with Marilyn Fleer and Liang Li) is '"We set up a small world": Preschool teachers' involvement in children's imaginative play' in the *International Journal of Early Years Education*. She is a member of the International Society for Cultural and Activity Research (ISCAR) and a member of Early Childhood Australia (ECA).

Marilyn Fleer holds the Foundation Chair of Early Childhood Education and Development at Monash University, Australia, and was awarded the 2018 Kathleen Fitzpatrick Laureate Fellowship by the Australian Research Council. She was a former President of the International Society of Cultural-historical Activity Research (ISCAR). Currently she holds the position of Honorary Research Fellow in the Department of Education, University of Oxford, and a second Professor position in the KINDKNOW Centre, Western Norway University of Applied Sciences.

Lucas Gottzén is Professor of Child and Youth Studies at Stockholm University, Sweden. Positioned at the intersection between child and youth studies and critical studies of men and masculinities, he has explored gendered and generational aspects of family life; affect, embodied action and identity making of children, youth and violent men. He has published in a variety of journals, including *Children's Geographies, Gender & Society, Journal of Youth Studies* and *Men and Masculinities*. He is editor of the forthcoming *Routledge International Handbook of Masculinity Studies* (with Ulf Mellström and Tammy Shefer).

Mariane Hedegaard is Professor Emeritus in Developmental Psychology at the University of Copenhagen, Denmark. She is doctorate honoris causa at the University of Pablo Olavide in Seville, Spain and she holds a senior research fellowship at the Department of Education, University of Oxford, UK. Mariane has authored and co-edited twenty-five books, of which eleven are in English. These include *Radical-local Teaching and Learning*; *Vygotsky and Special Needs Education*; *Motives in Children's Development*; *Learning, Play and Children's Development*; and *Children, Childhood and Everyday Life*. She has also written a number of articles in journals such as *Mind, Culture and Activity*; *Outlines: Critical Social Studies*; *Culture & Psychology*; and *Learning, Culture and Social Interaction*.

Dorte Kousholt is Associate Professor at the Danish School of Education, Aarhus University, Denmark. Her research interests concern children and families' everyday lives, and children's communities in and across different institutional contexts and parenthood. She has carried out ethnographic research following children across various contexts of their everyday lives. Dorte has published articles on children's everyday life across contexts and children's communities, parental cooperation, family life, and collaborative methodology, including 'Researching family through the everyday lives of children across home and day care in Denmark' (2011) and 'Collaborative research with children: Exploring contradictory conditions of the conduct of everyday life' (2016).

Liang Li is Senior Lecturer in the Faculty of Education at Monash University, Australia. Her research interests focus on play and pedagogy, child development, the cultural world of infant-toddlers, family study, early childhood teacher education, and visual methodology. She publishes nationally and internationally: research collaborations with Avis Ridgway and Gloria Quinones resulted in co-authorship of *Early Childhood Pedagogical Play: A Cultural-Historical Interpretation Using Visual Methodology* (2015) and a co-edited book, *Studying Babies and Toddlers: Relationships in Cultural Contexts* (2017).

Judith MacCallum is Associate Professor at the School of Education, Murdoch University, Australia. Drawing on sociocultural perspectives, her research uses qualitative and quantitative methods to investigate learning and development. In the context of schools and communities, she has focused on motivational change and development, collaborative learning, mentoring of young people and teacher professional learning.

Veronica Morcom is Honorary Research Associate at Murdoch University, Australia, and an experienced level three primary classroom teacher. She has conducted longitudinal research within school communities to examine the values underpinning collaborative classrooms and negotiating classroom social practices to support student and teacher learning and motivation.

Kasper Munk is a doctoral student at the Department of Education, University of Oxford, UK. His research focuses on professional decision making and learning. His doctoral research explores the external conditions, both cultural and material, of teachers' enactment of in-the-moment professional decisions in school classrooms. Kasper is a psychologist by training from the University of Copenhagen, Denmark, where he also worked closely with Mariane Hedegaard on the topic of professionals' proactive engagement with the conditions of their pedagogical work. His current interests include the potential and pitfalls of using new technologies in professional education. Kasper's article 'Motive orientations at work' can be found in *Learning, Culture and Social Interaction.*

Jennifer A. Vadeboncoeur is Professor in Human Development, Learning and Culture in the Faculty of Education at the University of British Columbia, Canada. She has conducted ethnographic research with youth and educators in alternative programmes in the United States, Australia and Canada. Her research in Canada continues to examine the longitudinal trajectories of young people after they complete their high school diploma, including transitions between work, family and post-secondary education institutions. Her current research also includes studies with young people as they create imagined schools *for* education, and longitudinal investigations of the imaginative play of young children and how imaginative play changes over time, space and relationship. Recent publications include *Vygotsky and the Promise of Public Education* (2017) and 'Creativity as a practice of freedom: Imaginative play, moral imagination, and the production of culture' (with A. Perone and N. Panina-Beard) in *The Palgrave Handbook of Creativity and Culture Research* (2016).

Ditte Winther-Lindqvist is Associate Professor of developmental psychology at Aarhus University, Danish School of Education, Denmark. Positioned at the crossroads of cultural historical developmental psychology and existential phenomenology, she has explored children's play and development, and child and youth identity development during different kinds of transitions. Among Ditte's latest work is an entry in *Oxford Bibliographies*: 'Early Childhood Education and Care (ECEC) in Denmark' (together with Lone Svinth). She also has a chapter on 'Social identity in transition', in the book *Children, Childhood and Everyday Life* and a chapter on 'Playing games with rules in early child care and beyond', in the forthcoming *Cambridge Handbook of Play: Developmental and Disciplinary Perspectives.*

Acknowledgements

Chapter 4

We are grateful to the families of Vissy, Margie and Zeb. Megan Adams acknowledges and thanks the scholarship contributions made by the Australian Postgraduate Association. Some of the ideas build upon those in Megan's unpublished doctoral thesis.

Chapter 9

The study reported in this chapter was supported through an Australian Research Council Discovery Grant (ARC DP140101131). Sue March acted as the senior research assistant. Her contribution to expertly supporting the teachers' implementation of the teaching programme was important to the success of the research. Previous ARC outcomes also framed what took place in the project. The research assistance of Taj Johora and Junqian Ma and data scribing and organizing by Freya Fleer-Stout, Madeleine Holland and Ainslie Holland is acknowledged. Last but not least, is the contribution of the two lead teachers who actively constructed an innovative teaching programme, and who were prepared to continually develop their programme over the course of the two years. The teachers' full engagement in the project and their willingness to contribute to new practices was key for the success of the research. Special mention of Rebecca Lewis in her reading of cultural-historical theory through her own PhD studies, and her willingness to implement a playworld approach, is made.

Chapter 10

The first author would like to thank all teachers, parents and children who participated in the study. Acknowledgement is extended to the Australian Post Graduate Scholarship (APA) for giving financial support and the Department of Education and Early Childhood Development (DEECD) (approval number- 2014_002482) and Monash University Human Research Ethics Committee (MUHREC) (approval number- CF14/2673-2014001452) for giving the approval to conduct this research. Thank you to the editors and reviewers of the book for providing valuable feedback on this chapter.

Children's Transitions in Everyday Life and Institutions: New Conceptions and Understandings of Transitions

Mariane Hedegaard and Marilyn Fleer

Introduction

Children's transitions into different institutions, such as when starting school, has always been an important topic in research and something that is of great interest to families as they support the transitioning child into the different institutions they attend and life course events they experience. Many have written on this topic and have made important contributions to understanding how children's transition impacts on well-being (e.g., Cavada, 2016; McLelland & Galton, 2015) and is being experienced in different countries (e.g., Ballam, Perry & Garpelin, 2017a), in different institutions (e.g., Wilder & Lillvist, 2017), and during different life course events (e.g., De Gioia, 2017). What has been common to most of the writing on this topic, has been the theoretical work of Uri Bronfenbrenner: in particular his early work on ecological theory (Bronfenbrenner, 1979) and his later work on a bio-ecological model of child development (Bronfenbrenner & Morris, 2006) have framed how researchers have come to understand children's transitions in everyday life and into different institutions.

A great deal has been learned through these studies about how children experience transitions. In declaring an ecological or a bio-ecological model of child development, researchers have theorized their results in relation to the systems in which the children are found (Dockett, Griebel & Perry, 2017). Results have been explained through detailed descriptions of how societies shape the ways in which a child experiences the institutions that they attend and how their pathway into these institutions during moments of transition are experienced

(Dockett & Einarsdottir, 2017). We now know a great deal about how systems frame and create institutional conditions for children from this important work (Ballam, Perry & Garpelin, 2017b).

We have also seen a merging of theoretical traditions to support deeper theorization and research on transitions. For example, Pollard (Lam & Pollard, 2006; Pollard & Filler, 1996) has integrated Bronfenbrenner's social constructivist approach with Vygotsky's dialectic approach and, through this, has foregrounded the child's role in creating conditions for their own learning. Through a series of case studies he followed children from four to seven years of age, studying how children themselves contributed to their own learning conditions as they entered into a new institution. Important theoretical work has also been undertaken in relation to young people and adults in this respect (see Stetsenko, 2017), but more needs to be known about children's agency and perspectives in creating conditions during their transition for their own learning and development.

In this book, the contributors have all drawn upon Vygotsky's cultural-historical theory of transition, seeing it as central for understanding child development. Transition in children's life course takes place when a child enters a new practice with new demands (Bozhovich, 2009; Elkonin, 1999; Vygotsky, 1998). This may lead to tensions and in some cases crises may result in ruptures, which means that earlier competences and motives disappear, and become integrated and subordinated in relation to other competences and motives. This book orients the reader to this perspective, while also drawing attention to how transition can be conceptualized as taking place when children move between everyday practices and everyday settings (Hedegaard, 2016; Hedegaard & Fleer, 2013). These everyday transitions are not conceptualized as ruptures, though they may lead to tension, but are viewed as important for children's development. This perspective foregrounds the need for children and their carers to be conscious of the differences in activities in the different settings.

By going beyond a bio-ecological model of transition, we show in this chapter and throughout the pages of this book, how children contribute to their own transitions through their motive orientation to new institutional practices before entering into them. We also show how demands and intentional interaction during the new activities shapes their own conditions. Rather than seeing transitions as problematic, we argue in line with Vygotsky's theory of development that transitions can give new and important conditions for children's development. By taking this agentic stance, we argue that new insights into transitions can be gained. This is in keeping with Stetsenko's (2017) life course work on what she has called a transformative activist stance. Stetsenko introduces a dialectically recursive and dynamically co-constitutive approach to development in which 'people can be said to realize their own development *in the agentive enactment of changes that bring the world, and simultaneously their own lives, including their selves and minds, into reality*' (p. 31, original emphasis). In this reading of agency, development is a transformative process where histories and future enactments are recursively constituted. This conceptualization of development is not biologically deterministic, or viewed as a progressive transition of the child into a cultural community, but rather it conveys a sense that 'development is about participating yet is also, and even more critically, to *contributing* to transformative communal practices' (p. 34). Captured in her concept of activism, her work (like the chapters in this book), gives different insights into the concept of transition to that which is currently foregrounded in the literature. Likewise, the contributors to this book draw upon different theoretical tools – notably, cultural-historical concepts.

A cultural-historical conception of transitions

What is central for a cultural-historical perspective on development is the periodization of children's development that is connected to their transition from one institutional practice to the next. In understanding these transitions, Vygotsky described critical periods related to change in external conditions. According to this theory, periods in children's development have three phases: 1) a stable phase, 2) a critical period with ruptures that leads to 3) a new constructive period of neo-formation. In the critical period, a child becomes relatively difficult in comparison with how they previously entered into the practice traditions in everyday life. There is disintegration and ruptures of what has been formed in the preceding stages. During these critical periods the child does not so much acquire, but loses what s/he has acquired earlier. Neo-formations serve as the basic criterion for driving children's development from one age period to another.

Analysing a child's entry into new practice traditions in Vygotsky's theory is left at the institutional level (e.g., school or home) and not necessarily across different institutions or at the societal level. In drawing upon Hedegaard's (2014) model of transition (Figure 1), this dimension is captured as the child's movement occurs between the different institutions s/he attends in the context of societal values. In relation to this we also have to conceptualize, for example, when a child starts school, s/he could also be going to after-school care, to different clubs or after-school events, while actively participating in known home practices (Hedegaard & Fleer, 2013). From this perspective, researchers who have contributed to this book have paid close attention to the child's intentions, as s/he enters into the different institutions (zigzagging), while also examining how societal expectations are realized at the institutional level through rules, values, policies, funding etc.

To fully understand the conditions for children's lives one has to identify the institutional practices a child participates in. Also needed is a close study of the activities that dominate within institutional practices, where the demands that practices put on children, the possibilities these give for activities and how children act in these activities, can then be understood. Children's learning and development in families, kindergarten and school takes place through children's engagement in these activities, but children also recreate activities in specific activity settings, alone or together with other people (i.e., parents, siblings, teachers and classmates). New demands and new motives arise from entering a new institution or when moving between several institutions over the same period, such as home and kindergarten or home, school and day care.

The focus in this book is on children's transition between institutions, such as starting day care, leaving the safety of home for several hours to enter day care, or moving from home to school every day for many years. Changing participation from one activity to another is the central aspect, because both demands and motives changes through this transition. Transition between activity setting also take place in the same institution, as when a child in school moves from one subject class to another, or when a child in kindergarten moves through the daily schedule of the different activity settings, such as arrival time, play time, lunch and outdoor activities. Transition is a key concept for understanding development: both in relation to possible developmental trajectories and in relation to daily transition between the different communities in home, day care and school.

In Figure 1, the relation between societal conditions, traditions and values, institutional practice with its activity settings, and a child's activities, are depicted. This is a model of the general structural relations that may be used to analyse children's learning and development. In concrete terms, the dynamic between these relations are the centre of our focus, as we will illustrate by following children in different settings and different activities as they transition between them.

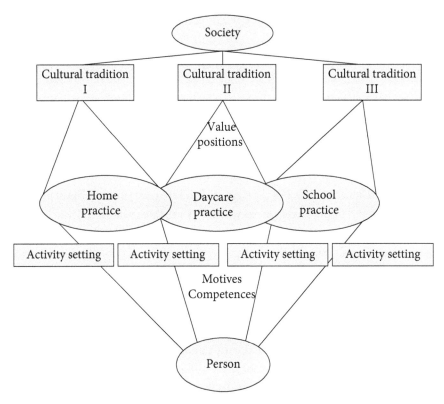

Figure.1 Illustration of the relations between society–practice and persons with cultural traditons and activity settings as mediating links

This model frames how the book has been organized, and through this, shows how the concepts in this model contribute to analysing the transitions discussed in the specific chapters.

Different dimensions of transition are illustrated through the different chapters, where authors have primarily referenced concepts shown in Figure 1, and where the content of the chapters collectively contribute to a new way of understanding transitions.

The book is organized into two sections. The first section contains chapters that view transitions and what it means for children's development from a societal perspective. The second section contains chapters that depict transitions from the children's perspective as it takes place through moving between different activities, where children become aware of different ways of interacting. Together, the two sections explicate a cultural-historical conception of transitions, while at the same time introducing new insights and understandings through this reading of transitions.

Part 1: Societal trajectories: Children's life courses

Transitions in children's life courses are related to the possible trajectories that a society provides (Hedegaard, 2012; Hundeide, 2005; Rogoff, 2003). For children in most societies these societal trajectories imply compulsory schooling; in some places though, other trajectories dominate where children are expected to participate in work from a very early age (Hundeide, 2005; Rogoff, 2003). In contrast to this, in several Western societies there are trajectories that provide opportunities and create expectations for children's participation in childhood education from a very early age. In Danish society, it is expected that children start in nurseries at around one year old and in the kindergarten when they are three years old. Participation in kindergarten practice is not obligatory but is advocated by the state and 98 per cent of Danish parents choose this possibility for early childhood care and education. Transition in children's life courses from an early age is central to their development, because the new institutions they participate in orient children to new demands and new motives that are essential to becoming citizens in society.

Entering school is obligatory in most nations, and many people who care for children (parents, grandparents and early childhood teachers) see schooling as a way of gaining social status in society (Wong & Fleer, 2012) and to develop the competences needed to participate in their community (Hedegaard & Fleer, 2013; Rogoff, 2003). In nearly all societies, transition to school is not an event that children can avoid; it is a must for being a child today. Transition to school may be something children are oriented to in many countries long before they start school. Both in narratives about being a child and in everyday practice children are confronted with the event of starting school, and by the activities that take place in early childhood education. It is common for many young children when meeting a new adult and being introduced to the family to be asked: 'Are you going to school?' or, 'When do you start to go to school?'

In the following excerpt of two girls playing at going to school, we can see how children start to have ideas about the pending school demands that leads both to excitement at what is happening and to anxiety about managing these new demands.

A morning setting in January, in The Oak Tree kindergarten

There are activities going on at three of the tables in the room. Two pedagogues sit together at one of the tables with some of the youngest children, who are drawing. At the largest table, two girls, Else and Laila (both five years) are playing with small dolls. They have two extendable doll's houses. They move some dolls between the houses and talk.

Laila says, 'We need to relax' and 'When are we going to school?'

Else: 'Oh, why should I be late? I do not want to. Princesses come in time!'

Laila: 'You are right in time to get to school, no one is there yet!'

Laila make her voice brighter and says: 'The prince must also attend school (she moves a character who is a man in armour on horseback).'

Between the two girls are now collected seven dolls.

The girls then negotiate with a boy about the exchange of a toy aeroplane for more figures for their doll's houses. They go with him to another room to get the figures.

Coming back, Else says to Laila: 'Come on, now we will play.' She takes Laila's hand and leads her back to the table.

The girls move the figures around. Laila mentions the word 'detention'.

Else: 'We should not be in detention, because we were so decent and did everything the teacher said.'

What this example shows is that children may be oriented to activities in school practice that they only vaguely know. The two girls have expectations of what is going to happen; expectations that are mixed with excitement and anxiety about what is expected of them, rather than towards what they will learn.

Hedegaard and Munk (Chapter 2) question this orientation, which is already seen in kindergarten. Their project contains a critique of the conditions that the Danish government creates for preschool children and teachers with demands for learning activities in kindergarten that orient them to school learning, instead of involving them in play activity where they may create competences of imagination and planning that children need when at school, undertaking abstractions in literacy and oral activities. The schoolification of early childhood education is increasingly being seen in many Western countries, where governments are placing great demands upon teachers for a more formalized programme to improve the academic outcomes of children (see Fleer & van Oers, 2018). In discussing this problem in Denmark, Hedegaard and Munk argue that orienting children towards school learning instead of learning to play excludes children from acquiring foundational life competences of social interaction and emotional imagination, competences that kindergartens have traditionally provided as part of their practice.

Transition from one institutional practice to another, such as leaving kindergarten and entering school, leads to a restructuring of children's relation to their environment that may result in some kind of crisis. Since most children enter into these crises they should not be seen as harmful but as part of growing up in a culture. Vygotsky (1998) and Elkonin (1999) describe what happens to children through this transition as crises because the child's way of relating to his or her environment does not fit with the new demands. A kind of destruction or restructuring of the child's competences and motives has to take place leading to new competences and motives. Depending on how the environment is created, these crises will be more or less obvious during the child's transition. The crises in one institution, such as home, may be the result of new demands when a child is entering school. Hedegaard (2018) describes how a family has small daily crises created by a child entering school. Emil, a six-year-old boy in a family with four children, has just started in the transition class in school, class zero. Through a description of conflicts that Emil creates in his everyday activities we can follow how his relationship with his parents and siblings changes and that these changes imply minor crises that in many ways are created intentionally by the child, because he is oriented towards a new position in the family by going to school. Emil and his siblings are followed through visits to their home and school over eight months. During the first visit the observer participates in a setting where his sisters are doing homework supported by their mother. In this setting Emil intentionally provokes his mother by threatening to erase his older sister's maths homework. He also empties his mother's purse, and he talks provokingly loud and puts his legs on the homework table. The mother in a calm voice tells Emil to stop teasing his sister and to take his legs off the table, and she allows him to play with her purse and ignores his loud speech. A month later we again visit the family and participate in a homework setting where the two oldest children are doing their homework with their mother supporting them. In this situation Emil demands that his mother also help him with homework. Since he does not have any homework when attending the transition class in school, he asks his mother to create homework tasks for him. She then writes some letters and Emil has to say the name of the letter and give examples of words that start with this letter. His two older sisters also become engaged and try to help him by pointing to objects that begin with the letter their mother gave him. In the end, all three children are competing for the mother's attention for their different homework tasks. And when the father comes home they all complain to him that they have a headache because it is too noisy and they cannot work (that requires getting their mother's full attention and help). There are crises in both situations but we can follow how the relationship changes from Emil being outside the homework situation to becoming an insider in the second homework situation. In half a year, he becomes a legal member of the homework group. The crisis in the homework setting disappears after the Christmas holidays because one of his sisters finds a schoolmate she can do homework with, and the family's homework situation thereby changes.

To follow how demands and motives may interact in the child's everyday social situation Hedegaard (2012) has used the concept of activity setting (see Figure 1). An activity setting is seen as guided by the expectations of a practice, and can be found in everyday institutional practices in society, as we saw in the excerpt from Else and Laila's play setting or Emil's homework setting.

How someone's different motives and demands become coordinated in such a setting may lead to changes in both the person's activities and the setting and thereby, in the long run, may also change the practice traditions.

To understand children's learning and development in a specific setting (i.e., a homework setting), one has to see them in this setting (i.e., their family) but also as participants in several other institutions, and how practice in one institution crosses over and influences children's activities in another institution. To understand a schoolchild's social situation at home one also has to conceptualize how school practice influences home practice and puts demands on children's everyday activities in cooperation with parents and siblings. Consequently, for children's everyday activities at school one has to conceptualize how home practice influences children's activities in school.

In Danish society, the crises that result from transitions are not seen as important for children's development. On the contrary, the way the government has designed the system for transition from kindergarten to school has made conditions for transition to school as smooth as possible. Ditte Winther-Lindqvist (Chapter 3) questions the Danish strategy from a theoretical understanding that development should be seen as qualitative changes through different age periods where this change implies some sort of rupture. She criticizes the general tendency in the Danish – as well as in an international context (Dockett & Einarsdottir, 2017) – to regard school transition as a problem for the child. Unfortunately, as Winther-Lindqvist argues, this 'danger-rhetoric' has led to a practice where differences between day care and primary school are minimized and the transition is organized into a step-by-step process with a lengthy preparatory period, because of the concern that the school transition is thought to be mainly problematic.

Conversely, disruption may be difficult when it does not follow the societal practice of transitions, as is illustrated by Adams and Fleer (Chapter 4). Children from expatriate families enter a new institution in midterm, where established routines and social practices are already in place. These are different kinds of conditions for children to enter than when they all start school at the same time, and these conditions may create difficulty for some children. Adams and Fleer's study shows how children handle this transition into established practices in different ways. Activity settings of free play appear to make visible what matters to the children in such a transition, as well as supporting them to adapt to the rules and roles of the new practice. In this way, free play time acts as a resource for supporting children's transition midway through a school year.

Opportunity for play has also been found to be a valuable resource for children's transition in schools in Chile in a study by Paula Cavada-Hrepich (Chapter 5). Seen from the children's perspective, playfulness acts as a resource for children in meeting the demands of new classroom activities. Cavada-Hrepich's study demonstrates how children's playfulness is used as a resource in the processes of meaning making, and repositioning children to engage with and fulfil the new demands they meet in a new classroom practice. The use of this resource changes when children are transitioned from kindergarten class to first grade as the first year of primary school becomes more individually oriented, more structured and rule-bound, and children's use of playfulness becomes more oriented to resolving the task of being 'a student' or 'schoolchild'.

MacCallum and Morcom (Chapter 6) in an intervention research study directly created support for children's transition. The children were offered opportunities to becoming agentive in the classroom using four experimental practices: the daily social circle, a model for making classroom agreements, weekly classroom meetings and sociograms. In fourth grade, after the experiment was finished, the children's evaluations showed that the daily social circle was the tool they appreciated the most and they missed this when in fourth grade.

As MacCallum and Morcom found, these social circles were useful as a resource for some children as they transitioned from one year level into another, just as the free play time was used by the expatriate children in Adams and Fleer's study (Chapter 4). Children's participation in social circles gave insights into the demands made upon them as they transitioned between different classroom practices and activity settings, but also how children were oriented to these demands. Like other studies on transitions in this book, the social circles afforded a level of awareness by children about the differing practices across year levels and within activity settings where the child's relations with each other changed.

Part 2: Transition between daily practices and everyday activity settings

Transitions between activities when viewed as directed forward as societal trajectories of practice, may also be seen as a zigzag of transitions when a child moves regularly between different institutions, because the child participates in several different practices in the same day or week. Transition may be described as a societal trajectory through different practices. This transition can be pictured either as horizontal (Hedegaard's model, this chapter) or as vertical (i.e., children moving from day care and entering kindergarten (Kousholt, Chapter 7 and Winther-Lindqvist, Chapter 3).

When following the children's intentions in the different institutions in which they participate, it is possible to examine transitions in relation to the child's changing relations with others. Berger and Luckman's (1966) concept of primary and secondary socialization points to the change in children's conception of their relationship to other persons when moving from home into school or going from one primary grade to the next in the subsequent year. Children thereby enter into a new kind of relationship with the new care-persons or teachers. Such new relations give the children the opportunity to become aware of these new relations. When children gain experience of a new social situation by entering the institutional practice of school, they may be able to use this new experience to contrast and reflect on their social situation. Secondary socialization takes place much earlier in Western societies today than in 1966, when Berger and Luckman first formulated their concepts, because children enter into new institutions much earlier. Today this secondary socialization happens for many children when they start day care, because of the contrast they may experience between home and kindergarten, and the respective demands and possibilities available. We argue that this is a double socialization, because children are socialized into participating in activities at home and at the same time these children participate in the same type of activity in kindergarten, such as putting on their clothes or having a meal, but the demands for how to act may be quite different. Children thereby start to reflect on their relations to other persons and the contrast between the different social situations. Focusing on the child's social situation requires a search for the child's perspective – which means an interpretation of a child's motive orientation in the different activity settings the child participates in during everyday life and how the child's motive orientation relates to the demands that the child meets while participating in different settings.

Kousholt (Chapter 7) argues that understanding the importance of transitions in children's everyday life for learning and development can be gained through following the child's perspective. It is important, she argues, to see children as active in conducting their everyday life across the different settings and to look for both the continuity and the discontinuity in children's active effort of moving between the different practices and contexts. Children's conduct in their everyday life across different institutions has to be seen as a shared process between a child and the different communities that the child participates in, such as home and day care.

Making the transition every day from one practice to another, a child meets different demands but also becomes oriented in different ways, guided by the objectives of the specific practices that give room for specific activities within them. The daily activities in different institutions may be different both in form and content. At home the leading objective is care of the children, and in school the leading objective is related to subject matter. In school, care is also an important objective, but is subordinated to learning. At home, learning may also be an objective, but it is usually subordinated to the prime objective of caring for children. In day care or kindergarten the leading objective is both care and learning, where the care may orient children into becoming independent of adult help and the learning may ideally be directed towards the child's learning to care for other people, both socially and emotionally.

The contrasts between the different activities at home, in kindergarten and school become a foundation for children to differentiate between what matters and is important in one context or another. When taking the child's perspective this foregrounds what matters for children themselves in the different contexts.

To differentiate between what matters in one context and what matters for the child may also be a consequence of the movement between different institutions. This differentiation can be related to Leontiev's (1978) discussion of children's development of motives and formation of consciousness. Moving between different practice traditions where children meet different demands, for instance about how to relate to adults, may create contrasts that allow a child to understand what s/he wishes and what makes sense for him or her, as well as what is different from what is expected in the actual practice setting. The child will thereby gradually develop a sense of what is personal and what is shared, between sense and meaning. What is meaningful and valued in one context is not always meaningful and valued in another context. For example, Gottzén and Aronsson (Chapter 8) have drawn attention to how meanings from different practices are raised in the family through discussions at the dinner table, where the objective meanings of school knowledge have different connotations for the parents and for the children. There is a latent conflict between the parents and the children's values during the discussion of the knowledge that children have acquired in school about evolution and the parents' values and religious beliefs. The study demonstrates that both children and adults change and gain new insights and the adults modify their views. This result illustrates that the individual and their environment have to be seen as a unity, and that learning takes place through changes in this unity. These changes occur through a person's motives and values, as well as through the respective demands that arise within the specific activity settings, such as dinner time.

When we start to study more closely the transitions that may take place within an activity, as in children's play, where they move between the different spheres of reality, planning and imagination, children's intentional orientation becomes the key to analysing the unity and the conflicts.

Transitions within activity settings can also be created through collective imaginary situations in playworld settings. Fleer (Chapter 9) analyses this unity through her playworld project where teachers and children collectively create imaginary situations through an engineering playworld (Lindqvist, 1995). Within the activity setting of the playworld, there are many microgenetic transitions in the play, as the teachers enter the play and take a role in the imaginary playworld that is collectively built over time between teachers and children. As with the concept of double socialization, Fleer examined how teachers, when playing together with children, transitioned between their real role as teachers and their play role as characters in a collectively developed playworld. Fleer's research shows how new conditions for children's development are created, as can be seen when children become aware of their own role as players, at the same time as realizing their own expectation of their teachers – as teachers rather than as players. The study found that when adults took on a role in the play, children changed their relations with their teachers from that of a real role to a play role, but this was not always straightforward. The contradictions between the real roles and play roles of teachers created new developmental conditions for children. Through studying the children's intentions within activity settings, it becomes possible to see how children transition within the playworld, and to acknowledge that this acted as a positive force for their development.

How teachers draw upon play to orient their children to learning is an important topic for transition research in a time of changing societal expectations of increased cognitive competence. In studying children's intentions as they move across the activity setting of free play time and a learning activity, Devi, Fleer and Li (Chapter 10) have shown how children's motive orientation for play can be disregarded by teachers in their quest to meet the institutional demands for improved learning outcomes (Fleer & van Oers, 2018). As with studies in Denmark by Hedegaard and Munk (Chapter 2) and Winther-Lindqvist (Chapter 3), the schoolification agenda in Australia has changed the practice traditions in preschools. The ruptures experienced by children as they transition across activity settings are often not visible to teachers who are seeking to orient children to learning. What this means for children as they transition from a free play activity setting to a table-based learning activity setting is important for understanding how children's conditions for their development are changing. Here the different value positions and societal expectations are realized in institutional practices, and made concrete for children through how they participate in the activity settings. This relational model of transitions is theorized in Hedegaard's model of children's development as shown in Figure 1, where following the child's intentions is crucial for understanding the societal, institutional and personal relations. Together, these provide new insights into the contribution that transitions in everyday life make to children's development.

Following the intentions of children was also a focus in the study by Vadeboncoeur (Chapter 11), who analysed the imaginative play of twin children at home, introducing moral imagining as a concept to explain the creation of relationships and relational histories in play. Like Fleer (Chapter 9), Vadeboncoeur shows how transitions within activity settings can also be full of potential contradictions – rules of play, and the rules of the practice tradition – as was shown when soft toys were brought to the dinner table and the children continued to play, despite the parents' practice tradition for mealtimes to be focused on eating. Vadeboncoeur describes the demands of the practice traditions as necessitating shifts in imaginative play that may lead to negotiation, as well as dissolution or termination of play. In this chapter, Vadeboncoeur shows that analyses of how children's play changes can provide insights into transitions, and like other chapters, she offers new understandings. What is illustrated in this chapter is participant's moral imagining through transitions within, between and from imaginative play.

Conclusion

In drawing upon a cultural-historical conception of transition, where societal, institutional and personal perspectives are foregrounded in the analytical frame, it was possible to determine that transitions should not always be problematized.

In fact, transitions should be viewed as the changing conditions that create new possibilities for children's development. In being positioned as a schoolchild (Bozhovich, 2009), the child has a new social position in their family and in their community. Being a schoolchild is important and socially valued in most Western communities. Through transitioning into school, the child is oriented towards schoolwork, and this creates new conditions and builds different kinds of competence for a child. Gaining competence as a schoolchild affords a different relationship with others, as well as giving the child agency because of their new competences, such as being able to read, which in turn allows them to participate in the institutions in different ways. This agentic and positive reading of transitions speaks differently to the existing literature. Furthermore, this orientation to transitions research is timely, given the increased societal expectations in some Western countries for greater cognitive outcomes in preschools.

In a more positive and agentic conception of transitions it becomes possible to show how a child contributes to and shapes their own transition. Through following children's intentions in the various activity settings and as they transition within and across activity settings (Hedegaard, 2012), it becomes possible to bring into focus the numerous transitions that children participate in not just when starting school, but throughout their everyday lives within different institutions. Previous research framed from an ecological or bio-ecological perspective has not paid attention to the myriad of microgenetic transitions that children experience within activity settings. This chapter and those that follow, show how children in different activity settings of free play time, playworlds, social circles and mealtimes, orient themselves to transitions within these activity settings.

Analysing activity settings with the concept of demands, motive orientation and children's intentions, gives a new theoretical reading of transitions. In this reading, it becomes possible to analyse how children are shaped by, as well as how they shape their own transitions. It is through paying attention to children's intentions within activity settings that we begin to see how they contribute to their own developmental conditions. This dynamic reading of transitions is not something that is within the person or something that affects the person, but rather is a relation between the person and the activity setting. This is a new theoretical contribution to the literature on transitions.

We have also argued that a form of double socialization occurs during transitions, because children can experience the same activity setting in different institutions, but how the practices are organized may be different. That is, children undertake the same activity of getting ready for a rest or for a meal in the home and then again in a childcare setting, but when the practice traditions are different, the child participates and acts in the activity setting differently. This allows for the possibility of becoming more aware of the activity settings and how they are being experienced differently. Once again, these insights are realized because the researcher follows the child's intentions and notices what they are being oriented towards and how their relations with the people in the activity setting change or are different. But at the same time, analysing how the child contributes differently in the different activity settings is also important. This new cultural-historical reading of transitions allows us to theorize how children contribute to their own developmental conditions within the everyday lives of the institutions that they attend.

Consequently, a cultural-historical reading of transitions as we theorize in this chapter, foregrounds activity settings and conceptualizes possible double socializations, and this makes it possible to better understand the developmental conditions of children because it brings forth the many different transitions and developmental conditions in everyday life within institutions. This is a new perspective and uniquely contributes to empirical and theoretical work on transitions.

Theorized from a cultural-historical perspective, the illustrative studies of the agentic child who contributes to, and is shaped by the myriad of transitions across institutions (Section 1), and within activity settings (Section 2), is a new perspective on how transitions can productively contribute to children's development over their life course.

References

Ballam, N., B. Perry & A. Garpelin (2017a), 'International perspectives on the pedagogies of educational transitions', in N. Ballam, B. Perry & A. Garpelin (eds), *Pedagogies of educational transitions: European and antipodean research* (pp. 1–14). Switzerland: Springer International Publishing.

Ballam, N., B. Perry & A. Garpelin (eds) (2017b), *Pedagogies of educational transitions: European and antipodean research*. Switzerland: Springer International Publishing.

Berger, P. L. & T. Luckmann (1966), *The social construction of reality: A treatise in the sociology of knowledge*. Garden City, NY: Doubleday.

Bozhovich, L. I. (2009), 'The social situation of child development', *Journal of Russian and East European Psychology*, 47(4), 59–86.

Bronfenbrenner, U. (1979), *The ecology of human development: Experiments by nature and design*. Cambridge, MA: Harvard University Press.

Bronfenbrenner, U. & P. A. Morris (2006), 'The bioecological model of human development', in W. Damon & R. M. Lerner (eds), *Handbook of child psychology, Vol. 1. Theoretical models of human development* (pp. 93–102). New York: Wiley.

Cavada, P. (2016). Starting first-year primary: Children's transition in classroom learning activities. Ph.D thesis. University of Copenhagen, Faculty of Social Sciences, Department of Psychology.

De Gioia, K. (2017), 'Giving voice to families from immigrant and refugee backgrounds during transition to school', in S. Dockett, W. Griebel & B. Perry (eds), *Families and transition to school* (pp. 37–50). Switzerland: Springer International Publishing.

Dockett, S. & J. Einarsdottir (2017), 'Continuity and change as children start school', in N. Ballam, B. Perry & A. Garpelin (eds), *Pedagogies of educational transitions: European and antipodean research* (pp. 133–140). Switzerland: Springer International Publishing.

Dockett, S., W. Griebel & B. Perry (eds) (2017), *Families and transition to school*. Switzerland: Springer International Publishing.

Elkonin, D. B. (1999), 'Toward the problem of stages in the mental development of children', *Journal of Russian and East European Psychology*, 37(6), 11–30.

Fleer, M. & B. van Oers (2018), 'International trends in research: Redressing the north-south balance in what matters for early childhood education research', in M. Fleer & B. van Oers (eds), *International handbook of early childhood education, Volume 1* (pp. 1–30). Dordrecht: Springer.

Hedegaard, M. (2012), 'Analyzing children's learning and development in everyday settings from a cultural-historical wholeness approach', *Mind, Culture, and Activity*, 19(2), 127–138.

Hedegaard, M. (2014), 'The significance of demands and motives across practices in children's learning and development: An analysis of learning in home and school', *Learning, Culture, and Social Interaction*, 3, 188–194.

Hedegaard, M. (2016), 'Imagination and emotion in children's play: A cultural-historical approach', *International Research in Early Childhood Education*, 7(2), 57–72.

Hedegaard, M. (2018), 'Children's creative modelling of conflict resolutions in everyday life as central in their learning and development in families', in M. Hedegaard, K. Aronsson, C. Højholt & O. Skjær Ulvik (eds), *Children, childhood and everyday life, 2nd edition* (pp. 55–74). Charlotte, NC: Information Age Publishing.

Hedegaard, M. & M. Fleer (2013), *Play, learning and children's development: Everyday life in families and transition to school*. New York: Cambridge University Press.

Hundeide, K. (2005), 'Socio-cultural tracks of development, opportunity situations and access skills', *Culture Psychology*, 11, 241–261.

Lam, M. S. & A. Pollard (2006), 'A conceptual framework for understanding childen as agents in the transition from home to kindergarten', *Early Years*, 26, 123–141.

Leontiev, A. N. (1978), *Activity, consciousness, and personality*. Englewood Cliffs, NJ: Prentice-Hall.

Lindqvist, G. (1995), 'The aesthetics of play: A didactic study of play and culture in preschools'. Acta Universitatis Upsaliensis. Uppsala Studies in Education 62. Stockholm/Sweden: Almqvist & Wiksell International.

McLellan, R. & M. Galton (2015), *The impact of primary-secondary transition on students' wellbeing*. Cambridge University. A Nuffield Foundation report.

Pollard, A. & A. Filler (1996), *The social world of children's learning*. London: Bloomsbury.

Rogoff, B. (2003), *The Cultural Nature of Human Development*. New York: Oxford University Press.

Stetsenko, A. (2017), *The transformative mind*. New York: Cambridge University Press.

Vygotsky, L. S. (1998), *Child psychology: The collected works of L.S. Vygotsky, vol. 5*, trans. M. J. Hall & R.W. Rieber (ed. English translation). New York: Kluwer Academic and Plenum Publishers.

Wilder, J. & A. Lillvist (2017), 'Collaboration in transitions from preschool: Young children with intellectual disabilities', in N. Ballam, B. Perry & A. Garpelin (eds), *Pedagogies of educational transitions: European and antipodean research* (pp. 59–74). Switzerland: Springer International Publishing.

Wong, P-L., & M. Fleer (2012), 'A cultural-historical study of how children from Hong Kong immigrant families develop a learning motive within everyday family practices in Australia', *Mind, Culture, and Activity*, 19(2), 107–126, oi.org/10.1080/10749039.2011.634941

Part 1

Societal Trajectories: Children's Life Courses

2

Play and Life Competences as Core in Transition from Kindergarten to School: Tension Between Values in Early Childhood Education

Mariane Hedegaard and Kasper Munk

Children's development takes place through participation in different institutional practices

From a cultural-historical perspective, children's development can be seen as a life course through qualitatively different institutions (Elkonin, 2005; Hedegaard, 2012; Hundeide, 2005; Rogoff 2003; Vygotsky, 1998). The transition from kindergarten to school marks a qualitative change in children's life course development. It is through the change in institutional activity settings that children meet new demands, such as spending longer at school than kindergarten. Kindergarten and school create different learning settings because their objectives, practice traditions and activity settings are different; these differences give different possibilities for activities with different demands on the participants. The transition from kindergarten to school is smoother for some children than for others, but for all it will involve some kind of rupture, since school implies a new practice with new traditions and activity settings. When moving to school, children themselves may express expectations of change (Hviid, 2012; White & Sharp, 2007). The transition means that children meet new demands and have to develop new motives and competences that will reorient their relation to other persons and their surroundings (Hedegaard, 2012; Winther-Lindqvist, 2012).

The problems addressed in this chapter are how new societal demands on practice have made it difficult to keep play as a central activity in kindergarten and how professionals have to find a way forward for preparing children for school practice that aligns with the time-honoured custom of play in kindergarten.

In our study, we took our departure point from the new educational agendas in Denmark that have created tensions for both kindergarten and school practices. Together with two kindergarten leaders, a two-year research project was initiated in Copenhagen in 2012, aimed at practice development for children's transition to school where the joint agency of researcher and professionals was to identify solutions for how these tensions could be resolved in supporting children's transition to school and, at the same time, retain the value that play is important for children's development in kindergarten.

The dilemma in early childhood education: Does it have value in itself for development of life competences or is it primarily a preparation for children's learning in school?

Part of the dilemma in Danish early childhood education is that the political discourse for preparing children for school has gradually changed from being valued in itself to being seen as a preparation for children's transition to school. Starting in 1962, the Ministry of Education initiated a kindergarten class (Andersen, 2004; Ellegaard & Stanek, 2004) with the idea of supporting a smooth transition to school. At this point kindergarten pedagogy was still valued in itself for children's social formation. With the introduction of the kindergarten class in school the aim is to prepare young children for the rhythm and demands of school. That is, children are introduced to time schedules, sitting at tables, listening to a teacher, waiting to talk until asked, using the bathroom at breaktimes, etc.

When we started the project in 2012, it was obvious that the demands that were previously part of the kindergarten class in school (now class zero) were brought into the kindergarten in the last half of the year before transition to class zero, and subject learning in the form of reading and mathematics were brought into class zero. Kindergarten pedagogues in Denmark have been relatively free to decide the content of the activities in kindergarten even though national learning goals for kindergarten were formulated in 2004. These learning goals were not implemented in the daily practice of most kindergartens (Gulløv, 2013). Consequently, in 2012 a task force initiated by the Ministry of Children and Youth (MBU, 2012a, b) formulated demands for how these learning goals should be implemented to prepare children for school. Here, the idea of starting subject teaching also crept into kindergarten. The political initiatives from the ministry's task force programme created a demand for the professionals in kindergarten to be more oriented to school practice than to children's care and social development. Now the demand for better scores in the PISA tests has also reached kindergarten practice, along with its demands for academic skills.[1] At the same time there was a contra movement to keep the values of the practice tradition in kindergarten focused on care and social development. The dilemma for the government in accepting these values can be seen in a note from a political meeting, also in 2012, where ideas for a New Nordic School were discussed. This explained that the aim of this New Nordic School approach should, in kindergarten, lead to the preparation of children for a new kind of school that would promote preschool children's life competences (*livsduelighed*).[2] This produced the idea for a project with the aim of explicating the custom in the Danish kindergarten and what day-care professionals thought mattered for their practice, at the same time as examining how this became reflected in the activities they promoted when preparing children for school life.

The researcher, with help of the Union of Pedagogues (BUPL), contacted the head of two kindergartens. These day-care professionals explained that they felt the demands of preparing children to go to school as a burden and they wanted to find a way forward without losing what they valued as important, i.e., children's play and creative activities.

Play and its relation to life course development

What characterizes play in kindergarten is that children's initiatives direct the theme of the play. In kindergarten the adults follow and support children in their exploration. Children's play is created within the conditions that the pedagogues give for activities through structuring the practice of the kindergarten, but pedagogues do not decide what children play: it is up to the children's initiatives to create the content of their play activities.

---

[1] The PISA tests are designed to assess to what extent students at the end of compulsory education can apply their knowledge to real-life situations and be equipped for full participation in society: http://www.oecd.org/pisa/aboutpisa/.

[2] The New Nordic School plans were silenced and instead whole-day schools were implemented to start August 2014.

To argue why play is an important activity in kindergarten and how it may contribute to both social development and competence in school I will draw on Vygotsky's theory (1967, 2016), that has been elaborated by Fleer (2013), Schousboe (2013), Hedegaard (2016) and many others.

In his theory of play, Vygotsky points out that through play young children become able to separate meaning from objects and actions (Vygotsky, 2016). That is the foundation for children to become literate. Through their play activity children start to develop collective imagination (Fleer 2013) and become able to move between the spheres of reality, imagination and planning (Schousboe, 2013). Furthermore, relations between events and feelings may become transformed through children's play so that emotions and feelings become released from events in the same way that meanings in play are released from objects and actions (Hedegaard, 2016). Play may be a way for imagination to *transform* emotions and feelings (Winnicott, 1977), so children in play can try out what makes them unsure or anxious (i.e., playing what it means to go to school).

Play and learning are processes that follow individuals throughout life, but the way people play and learn connects to institutional practices and their objectives, and play and learning therefore cannot be seen as uniform processes. With Leontiev (1981) and Elkonin (2005) one can say play is the leading activity in kindergarten and learning is the leading activity in school, but in other places where there is no school, work can be the dominant activity even for 7–8 year old children (Hundeide, 2005). However, these activities can be found across age periods in different ways and in different combinations depending on the institutional practices they are connected to. In Danish society, play is expected to be the dominating or at least leading activity in preschool and learning the leading activity in school, but these traditions for kindergarten were questioned in Denmark with the educational agenda of the task force programme from the Minstry of Children and Youth in 2012. Conflicts between values therefore influence the activities in kindergarten, as we will see in the following examples. For the kindergarten teachers in the project it was very difficult to create successful learning in kindergarten and for schoolteachers to create successful play activities in class zero in school.

The project

The question for the project that the researcher and the kindergarten professionals agreed on was to find a way forward in the dilemma of how one can best prepare children for transition to school and for life competences.

It was decided this would be done through observation and discussion of kindergarten practice.

The persons involved in the project were six kindergarten professionals (the head and two pedagogues from respectively The Oak Tree Garten and The Butterfly Garten), a researcher and a research assistant.

The design of the project was practice development that intertwined the method of participant observation with discussion meetings in the following ways:

- Observation of kindergarten practice with focus on the pedagogue's activities with the oldest group of children in the kindergarten (around 12–15 children in each kindergarten). There were twelve observations in each kindergarten (24 observations altogether).[3] Each observation resulted in approximately a twelve-page protocol (the observation and interpretation draws on the interaction-based observation method described in Hedegaard, 1995, 2008). This involved the pedagogues first accepting each protocol before it was sent out to the other participants in the project.

- Children were followed into two schools, by participant observers. Observations of school practice were carried out by the same research assistant as in the kindergarten, over two periods (May–August 2013 and 2014, with each observation lasting four hours and a total of 11 observations being made). The schoolteachers involved in the project accepted each observation protocol and understood that it was to be used in the kindergarten professionals' discussion sessions. Since the children were spread over several schools it has only been possible to follow four children's transitions in 2013 and again four children's transitions in 2014. From these analyses, a focus child's transition will be discussed.

- Discussion sessions between the researchers and kindergarten professionals were oriented to aligning new demands from kindergarten to school with the kindergarten professionals' values (16 meetings over the two-year period [see Table 1]). Each discussion session was tape recorded, lasted two hours and had three main parts:
  - Discussions of the observations from the professionals' perspective
  - Discussions of the observations from the children's perspective
  - Planning how to cooperate with school personnel

---

[3] The observation was made by the research assistant and alternated between morning (8 am–12 noon) and afternoon (12 noon–4pm).

- Added to this, in the spring of the second year of the project, were an internal conference for all participants working in the two kindergartens and two conferences in the municipality meeting with schoolteachers from grade zero and kindergarten teachers in the municipality to present our project and to discuss life competence and its relation to children's transition to school.

A detailed description of the progression of these three phases is presented in Hedegaard (2017).

The results will be presented in three sections:

I.   Focusing on misalignment of values between pedagogues and school.
II. Change in pedagogues' issues of concern (values) of preparing children for school related to discussion of school observations: play becomes the key for supporting children's acquisition of life competence.
III. A case analysis of how a focus on play supported a child's transition to school.

I. Focusing on *misalignment of values between* pedagogues *and school*

The pedagogues discussed in the 1st session what they thought was important in kindergarten practice: play was seen as a central activity and they formulated life competences and creativity as central for children's development. This led, at this first meeting, to a discussion of how life competences could be recognized in the activities initiated with children in kindergarten, and how this could be seen as a bridge to school practice. The head of The Oak Tree formulated it as follows: 'Life-competences can be found in children's imagination expressed in play, their ability to handle different contexts, to participate in a collective, relate critically to a situation, and to put oneself in another person's place.' (Discussion protocol, 1st meeting, 26–9–2012).

When we started the project, the kindergarten professionals found that the values they were concerned about were in conflict with the parents' expectations and the expectation formulated in the political task force programme for the kindergarten (MBU, 2012a, b). Although the kindergarten professionals held the view that they should create a smooth transition for children to school, instead of simply introducing learning activities in kindergarten they also wanted the schoolteachers to reach out to the kindergarten and be able to draw on its playful and creative activities, e.g., each child could bring a small suitcase with his or her creative contributions, which the teachers could relate to.

What we found in the project was that both kindergarten and school tried to orient to a smooth transition, and that both reached out towards each other though without much success. In the two kindergartens, even though they did not like it, the professionals tried to prepare children for school discipline. The schools also tried to take into consideration the individual child's experience and focus on their creative products. However, neither side was very successful in doing this. The following examples will illustrate the problems respectively of implementing the expectations of school activities in kindergarten and how school has difficulties in focusing on the individual child's creative production.

Problems connected to introducing learning activities in kindergarten

The example can be seen as prototypical for the form that activities take in kindergarten for preparing the oldest children for transition to school in the researched kindergartens.

4th observation Monday morning 14 January 2013 in The Oak Tree
Focus children: Else, Lise, Ibrahim, Bushra, Fredrik, Esme, Hasan
Pedagogue U

1. Pedagogue U places a card with a drawn facial expression on the table. He asks: 'How do you feel when you look like this?'
2. Several children climb onto the table.
3. U directs his question to Ibrahim, after some other children have shouted their proposals.
4. Ibrahim says: 'He is frightened.'
5. U confirms.
6. U places other cards on the table – they form a cohesive cartoon.
7. Several of the children comment on the drawings on the cards.
8. U again asks Ibrahim to explain and tell a story.
9. Ibrahim give a long answer and U goes into a dialogue with him.
10. Fredrik then turns around and moves some magnetic images around on the blackboard.
11. U: 'Huh, Fredrik, you have to help us here!'
12. Fredrik makes a disgruntled sound and then says: 'It is boring.' He comes back though and sits at the table.

13. Else and Lise both support Fredrik in his view that the activity is boring. Else: 'Can't we play another game?'
14. Now there is a rather high noise level (the children have started to talk to each other).
15. U says that they have to be quiet – 'It's something simply you must learn.'

The learning material used in this extract from the kindergarten learning session has relevant content for the children's acquisition of life competence, but the pedagogue's intention to create a school activity did not succeed in engaging all the children exploring this content. Instead, the primary goal becomes that children should learn to be quiet, and only talk when asked. In general, it was difficult to get the children to concentrate on the learning material that the pedagogues brought into the learning session and to involve the children in the learning activity, because in these activities in the kindergarten the *form* of schooling became the focus, rather than to create conditions for children's motive orientation to the *content* of the activity. This way of imitating school does not give children relevant competences for school activities, neither in the form of life competences, nor in the form of subject matter competences.

Problems connected to introducing kindergarten values in school

In schools it was difficult for teachers to be inspired by the activities in kindergarten and use creative material that fits with the objectives of school. From our protocols, we could only find one extract. This is presented below.
Example of a creative school activity from one of the involved schools
Class zero, Wednesday morning 20 August 2013
Focus: children from The Butterfly Garden that had entered this school
Teacher: J

1. The teacher J has planned a walk so the children can see where some of the children live. Before the walk, she will use posters that children had constructed the day before.
2. The children have each made a poster where they glued photos and wrote names of family members and drew pictures of their house.
3. Teacher J picks one of these posters. It is Wilfred's.
4. Wilfred comes up to the whiteboard and talks briefly about what is on his poster. J asks if there is anyone who has some questions for Wilfred.
5. A boy asks: 'I could not hear what your father's name was.' Wilfred repeats.

6. Eight children ask questions. The children have their hands up and Wilfred chooses one who may ask. They asked: 'What is your favourite food? What floor do you live on? Are your parents divorced? Does your brother also go to this school – in which class?'
7. The other children are silent. Only those who have questions speak.
8. J: 'So we say thanks to Wilfred and applaud.' Children and teacher clap.
9. Teacher picks Victoria's poster and she comes up and presents the poster she made.
10. The children look at the teacher and the poster, while Victoria is explaining.
11. Two children have raised their hands.
12. They have a number of questions for Victoria, including: Do you like your mother? What do you like to eat? Do you live in an apartment or house? What does your mother do?

In this extract, the teacher tries to take departure from the children's personal history (a wish that the pedagogues expressed for creating a smooth transition from kindergarten to school).

The activity in this extract is not related to any subject matter and has very little to do with learning in school. Again, the disciplinary aspect is in focus (i.e., that children can raise their hands, be quiet, and wait when it is not their turn). In both the context of kindergarten and school, when focusing on transition to school, the focus is on a single child's performance rather than the content of the activity.

This focus reflects an absent understanding of what competences should be the result when children play and when they participate in learning activities and how play and learning in different ways are needed as activities in both kindergarten and school to realize the expected competence goals.

Instead, the activities in the two different institutions – kindergarten and school – should be connected to the main objectives of each institution. In Denmark, in kindergarten, play, care and social competences are the main objectives. In school, subject matter competences, such as communicating through reading and writing, and mathematical operations such as calculation, are the main objectives for the activities initiated here.

To be able to realize these different objectives one needs to be clear about what play activity implies and how play may be related to school learning. The professional in kindergarten can then create play activities that may give children competences that are important conditions for learning subject matter in school; that is to act with meanings connected to symbols independent of concrete objects and actions, e.g., to act with meaning in one's mind. In school, the question should be how play can become part of a learning activity to promote exploration and engagement without school learning losing its focus on subject matter learning.

II. Change in pedagogues' issues of concern (values) of preparing children for school *related to discussion of school observations*: Play becomes the key for supporting children's acquisition of life competence

In the project, we could follow how change in the pedagogues' issues of concern changed. When we started the project the pedagogues focus was to promote preparation for school as a planned activity with special materials. But their concerns were also to promote both play and creativity as part of life competence. These were seen as conflicting activities and therefore were felt to be stressful and pedagogues did not see how to accomplish both (1st and 2nd meetings).

Being presented with observation protocols at the following meetings, pedagogues were confronted with the activities that were initiated by them and their colleagues in their daily practice and found that there was not much play in the daily practices, which the researcher pointed out.

The topic at the discussion sessions changed during the research period, from focusing on how difficult it was to live up to the expectation from the municipality and school to prepare children for school, to formulating forward directed values regarding what was important in kindergarten pedagogy for preparing children for school, as can be seen in Table 1.

When the pedagogues engaged in the analyses of their own practice using the observation protocols (3rd–6th meetings) they concluded that play was important but they did not have a clear understanding of what that involved for children's acquisition of competence and how they could support play activity. Instead, they focused on the importance of children bringing their creative products with them into school.

In the 7th session, in May, when two school consultants from the municipality were invited to participate in the meeting, they explained how difficult it was for teachers to take creative materials that children brought with them into consideration in their teaching, because children from kindergarten were distributed to different schools so they only had a few

Table 1 The themes that were discussed in the different discussion sessions between day-care professionals, the researcher and her assistant. 'Obs' indicates where the observation protocols were discussed

Discussion meeting	Themes in the discussions at the different meetings		
	School readiness	Life competences	Play
1. 26–9–2012	Discussion of goal formulation for school and kindergarten and new demands	Introduction of life competences	
2. 19–11–2012	Demands of preparing children for school	Life competence through play	
3. 3–1–2013	Support children's readiness for school and how to become ready for daily demands	Support children to find solutions when it is necessary	
4. 24–1–2013 Obs. Kindergarten	How to get into dialogue with school		
5. 19–2–2013 Obs. Kindergarten	How to prepare children for transition – what to bring to school		
6. 4–4–2013 Obs. Kindergarten	Contact the municipality for discussion of transition		
7. 13–5–2013 Obs. school-care	Discussion with school consultants brings into focus that children transcend to different schools: to be able to handle transition		
8. 4–9–2013 Obs. School		Discussion of how to evaluate children's life competency	How the adult should relate to children's play
9. 26–9–2013 Obs. School	Comparison of the goal for school and kindergarten Conference with school personnel takes form		

Table 1 *(Continued)*

Discussion meeting	School readiness	Life competences	Play
	Themes in the discussions at the different meetings		
10. 30–10–2013 Obs. Kindergarten	Reject formal plan for teaching in kindergarten	Children have to learn to be in a social arena	The pedagogues have to follow children's trail
11. 6–1–2014 Obs. Kindergarten	Communication between kindergarten and school is important		Pedagogues create conditions but do not structure play
12. 23–1–2014 Obs. Kindergarten			How do we give possibility for play
Muncipality conference 3–2–2014			
Internal conference 27–2–2014			
13. 26–3–2014 Obs. Kindergarten		Children show curiosity, they associate and immerse themselves, try out solutions, ask questions and provide solutions	The pedagogues dare to set the play free The pedagogues follow the children's trail and value children's contribution and ideas
Project conference 29–4–2014			
14. 27–5–2014 Obs. school-care			Children can plan and carry out play They work through experiences and relate to what happens in their life through play
15. 26–6–2014 Obs. school-care			The pedagogues do not feel that they need to control everything
16. 21–8–2014 Obs. School	Children will become oriented to start school	Children contribute to a distinct child culture that is recreated through children's interactions	Play and learning are ranked equally in transition from kindergarten to school Children contribute to a distinct child culture that is recreated through children's interactions

children from the same kindergarten in their class. The value of bringing children's creative production with them into school thereby disappeared from the discussions and instead play was discussed as the central activity. At this point the researcher pointed out that play involved a separation of meaning from actions and feelings.

A major change was connected to one insight into school practice that came after analysing the observations protocols from school at the 8th–10th meetings. A discussion started about what play meant and how it should be seen in relation to preparing children for school (see Table 1). In the 8th discussion meeting, the professionals came to give context to their understanding of the importance of play for how children acquire life competence.

From The Butterfly:

> Ped Sy: 'Life competences are to be able to take the lead in play.'
> Ped S: 'To be able to handle conflicts. Instead of starting a new play when there are conflicts, it is life competences to be able to continue the play. Here the adult could enter and support so that the play may continue.'

From The Oak Tree:

> Ped Dz: 'There is a tension between to enter into a play situation, when something happens and support and at the same time take care that the play is not destroyed.'
> Head: 'It is a dilemma between taking care of the whole group and the small group and to catch the small group's play ideas. In play, the children set the agenda and it is this agency we have to support.'
> 'It is to be stronger to read the context, and find out when you have to support a play and when you have to withdraw. Sometimes we act too fast. It is important to let the children build relations.' (Discussion protocol, 8th meeting, 4–9–2013)

After these analyses, children's play activity became delineated and the pedagogues formulated a wish to discuss the importance of the relation between play and learning with the professionals in school and the idea of a conference started to take form, and was realized in the spring of the following year. In preparing for the conference the pedagogues stopped arguing for a smooth transition between kindergarten and school. They concluded that it is important that children have engagement to enter activities in school but not that the activities in kindergarten and school need to be alike.

III. A case analysis of how the focus on play supported a child's transition to school

Play received a more central role in the everyday life in kindergarten, especially after the 3rd discussion meeting, where the researcher pointed out that there was not much play to be seen in the observation protocols from the first two observation periods. After this meeting, play took up more time in the daily schedules in the two kindergartens. How the discussion meetings influenced the activities of preparing children for school can only be indirectly seen following changes in the children's activities. We will present one of the children, Frida, whose relation to the other children changed over the period in the way she participated in different activities.

The first time we visited the kindergarten the pedagogues told us that they worried about Frida because she did not have a good relationship with the other children. The pedagogues wonder if they should advise the parents that Frida should stay for one more year in kindergarten because of her way of interacting with the other children and because they think she kept too close to the pedagogues, and did not show enough autonomy.

We can see how the interaction between Frida and the other children and the teachers changed in the research period and how Frida acquired competences to make contact with other persons without creating conflicts. It seems as though her experiences in finding strategies to enter into play with other children is the way in which she came to handle her problem of how to make contacts and be accepted as a participant in the other children's activities.

To illustrate her development we will draw on observations from when we first met her in November 2012 to her entrance into school in August 2013.

The 1st observation is a morning in November when Frida is sitting together with two other children to draw on cloth-bags, an activity that the pedagogues initiated the day before. Today Frida has started to draw on a bag and has a small conversation with Luna about her drawing and the colours. However, a pedagogue then enters the setting and discovers that the day before Frida had started to draw on another bag and she finds the bag for her. This made Frida stop her activity and she subsequently just sat quietly looking into space until lunch.

This pattern of Frida becoming passive when there is a problem was also found at the second observation in December, a day with snow, when the children are out in the playground.

Frida was sitting on a tricycle and focused on the sledge that Luna and another girl were pulling. Frida grabbed the sledge and tied it to the bike she was sitting on. Luna complained to the pedagogue that Frida took her sledge. Frida stayed although Luna and the other girl have left. Later she was hesitant to leave the bike when the children were called inside.

In the third observation, during an afternoon in January 2013, Frida starts to try more directly to get into contact with the other children, but does not succeed very well because her strategy for approaching them is to push the other children away, as can be seen from the observation extract:

The children are outside. Frida is sitting by the sandbox in a go-cart; she has been sitting there for 20 minutes. She has a book in hand. She then starts to speak with two children that build sand cakes on the edge of the sandbox.

One of the girls gives Frida a sand bucket filled with sand.

One of the schoolboys helps her to turn the sand bucket over to make a sand cake at the go-cart carrier. He then says: 'Your cake broke.'

One of the two girls that gave her the bucket says that you ruined it, so you do not get any more.

Frida: 'So I will build one myself.' She goes down to the other end of the playground but, soon after, she comes back to the sandbox. She then starts to push sand down from the edge of the sandbox a little distance from the two girls. Then she removes the sand cakes that the two girls have built at the edge of the sandbox. One of the girls objects.

Frida sits right next to the girls. Now she chops her shovel into what the two girls have built

They shout: 'Don't do this Frida.'

Frida moves away, but comes back and hits out a little after the girls with a stick (she does not really try to hit them – rather, she pretends that she will hit).

The girls again shout 'don't do this', and one of the girls says, 'you are not allowed to hit'.

The girls look around. Frida enters the go-cart and rolls slightly backwards from the two girls.

Ped K enters the playground. One of the two girls from the sandbox runs over and talks to her about Frida.

Ped K asks if the girls have asked Frida if she wanted to play with them in the sandbox. Afterwards Ped K goes over and talks to Frida who is still sitting in the go-cart.

Frida's way of interacting with the other children seems problematic. She has little sustained contact with the other children around her and this contact often culminates in a provocation. After the discussion of the importance of play at the 3rd discussion session in January, this initiated a change in the way the pedagogues made room for play. It seems that this also meant something for Frida's opportunity to play as she has a better chance of entering into the activity with the other children, even though it is still difficult for Frida to be accepted, as can be seen in the extract from the 5th observation in mid-April 2013.

> Frida walks to the carpet in the play corner, where Mikkel and Kaya each are laying under a blanket with a pillow under their heads.
>
> Frida: 'Can I be a baby.'
>
> Kaya: 'No.'
>
> Frida: 'May I be a cat?'
>
> Kaya: 'Cats only sleep in the morning.' Kaya: 'Cat, you may better go over to the table and draw. You may go to Tivoli [a fair in Copenhagen].'
>
> Frida crawls on all fours in the direction away from where Mikkel and Kaya are located.
>
> Kaya says after a short while: 'Now its morning!' (Frida is at the other end of the room.)
>
> Frida crawls, like a cat, towards them. She is now back with the others in the play corner on all fours.
>
> Kaya and Mikkel are still under the blanket with their eyes closed.
>
> Frida crawls towards the door of the wardrobe.
>
> Mikkel crawls over and retrieves a toy. He comes back and goes to Kaya who is still under the blanket. He then sings: 'Today is Kaya's birthday!'
>
> Kaya and Mikkel are on the carpet in the play corner. They throw pillows at each other.
>
> Frida is also sitting on the carpet. She throws a pillow once.
>
> Kaya moves to the book corner. She says: 'I am sitting over here and I am sad.'
>
> Frida moves over into the corner and places herself next to Kaya. Frida says she could protect her with a shield.
>
> Mikkel said immediately: 'But I have a samurai sword.'
>
> Frida whispers to Kaya.
>
> Mikkel, standing two metres from the girls with his back to them: 'There is a thief who has stolen a doughnut from me.'
>
> Mikkel goes over to Kaya and Frida. He pretends he unlocks handcuffs on Kaya. Kaya rises.
>
> Frida gets up too and shouts: 'Now we have to catch them.'

Mikkel goes away from the play corner.

Kaya and Frida say something to each other. Kaya asks if she can come home with Frida and eat.

Kaya says: 'Frida, now you are in jail.'

Frida sits down in the corner where Kaya was previously.

Mikkel comes back: 'Oh, you play Rammasjang-mystery [A children's TV series].'

Frida hesitates and nods. Mikkel: 'So I'm Christian. But who is going to be the spy?'

Frida says: 'I am a Cat mystery.'

Mikkel says four times in a row: 'Who must be Bruno?'

Kaya rises: 'Okay, I'm Bruno.'

Mikkel: 'Message from Christian to Cat.'

Kaya: 'Now I really keep an eye on your eyes.' She looks at Mikkel and Frida.

Frida: 'Try to see there is ketchup and jam on the plate – it must be him.'

Mikkel: 'Yes, it must be him.' He jumps up and throws a pillow and runs to the other end of the room.

The play gives a possibility for Frida to enter the activity of the two children playing family, even though her role is minor as the family's cat that is sent away. She is accepted in the play and then she socially engineers to make the cat role relevant by extending the play theme, and this is accepted by the other two children. This elaboration of the content of the play is seen when Frida is pretending that she is comforting Kaya by talking about protecting her with a shield, then being a magic cat from a children's TV series.

Frida developed her competence in contacting other people by entering the play and through extending her role in the play, and therefore she succeeds in not being excluded. Play gave her this possibility to get a new position by extending her play role, a possibility that building sand cakes in the sandbox did not open up for her. Therefore, role play is an important way to get children included in shared activity and to contact and care for other children, aspects that are central in life competences, in the way the pedagogues discussed earlier.

When we follow Frida into school we find an important change in her life competences. She makes contact with other children, starts a play activity in the playground and accepts the teacher's intervention without losing her initiative. This is very different from the passivity we saw when we first met her in kindergarten.

Walking to the playground, in the after-school care, a morning in early June 2013

After lunch children have to form a row to walk to the playground.

Frida: 'Who will hold my hand raise your finger?'

Frida stands between four girls and says to Villa: 'I have pockets so we can gather stones.' Villa is saying something.

The teacher comes over and tells Frida to hold hands with another girl (not Villa).

Frida walks a little bit away.

Teacher: 'You have to.'

Frida: 'I will not!' Though later she walks together with this girl.

Later at the playground the teacher tells three girls, of whom Frida is one: 'The three of you have to play together.'

Frida then says: 'Shall we play together the three of us?'

Frida goes down towards a ring which is approximately 2 metres in diameter. The ring is flat so you can sit on it. The ring can be rotated and is slightly tilted so it is easier to gain momentum.

Frida: 'Okay, everyone goes on, so I will push it around.' There are three up on the ring now. Then two of the girls leave.

Frida asks the girls sitting on the ring: 'Is it fun?'

The girl: 'I think so.' Villa and a boy come to the ring and ask if they can participate.

In class zero in the playground, it seems as though Frida can use the life competences she acquired through her earlier play to be able to make contact with other children and to handle rejection from the teacher. In school, we also found that teachers are much more direct in advising the children about what to do – also when they are at the playground outside class hours.

Discussion of how an alignment was realized through focusing on play activity in kindergarten as central for preparing children for school

In the study presented here, we followed how kindergarten professionals integrated new demands from society with what matters for them in preparing children for school. The study has to be seen as practice developing research with the researcher as the facilitator through being a discussion partner (see Hedegaard 2017).

The issues of what mattered to the pedagogues changed over the two years of discussions about their practice through analysing observation protocols. To follow this change, we had to use several perspectives that are interwoven: *a societal perspective* where societal conditions and values were stated, and an

Table 2 The relations between the structure, processes and dynamic seen through the process and its dynamics

Structure	Process	Dynamic
Society	Societal conditions and values	Societal needs
Institution	Practice tradition demands and values	Value-laden objectives/ motives
Activity setting	Demands in an actual setting create individual's social situation	Situated motivation/ engagement
Person	Reciprocal demands for concrete ways of participation	Motive-orientation/ intentions

institutional practice perspective with conflicting educational values for the different activity settings. In kindergarten, these settings can be the morning when children arrive, the play period, lunchtime etc. In school, this may be the different subject class, lunchtime and recess. Institutional objectives and values in the activity settings create *children's social situations* with the possibility for engagement that is reflected in the participating persons' motive-orientation.

A general conception of the relations between demands and motives that create the dynamics between societal conditions and individuals' social situations can be seen in Table 2.

The societal perspective

The analyses in the concrete case have focused on the incongruence between societal demands and professionals' practice and values.

Dilemmas of differences between values in different pedagogical practice are historically anchored. Values thereby become central when changes are introduced. Values behind pedagogical practices are often implicit and not so easily researched: the expectation may be that institutions for children are created from a humanistic perspective but, as Chaiklin shows, this may not be the only reason. Chaiklin's (2014) analyses anchored the origins of day care to a priest in the South of France who in 1776 initiated a day-care programme for young children, otherwise left alone, to secure the children's survival. Although the values concerning day-care practice have evolved since this first care arrangement, Chaiklin's analyses shows that material conditions and economic values have influenced the evolvement of day care as an institutional practice.

The key idea is that changes in societal conditions are usually preconditions for change in societal needs, which are likely to be seen in changes in the practice that addresses those needs. From this point of view practice are only seemingly static, and better understood as potentially in transition in relation to changes in societal conditions, where the changes are often occurring at a time scale of years or decades. (Chaiklin, 2014, p. 224)

Studies of the evolvement of schools by Green, (1990), Meyer, Ramírez & Soysal (1992) and Ramirez & Boli (1987) support this conclusion that new educational practice may evolve not from humanistic intentions but from material aims. In their analyses they argue that school as an institution has been created in several nations from aims that did not focus on creating a better life for children, but rather to secure the nation's interest (i.e., to secure loyalty to the state after lost wars (Ramirez & Boli, 1987)).

We found that even over a period of two years, societal conditions fluctuate in relation to political changes. The Ministry of Children and Youth had responsibility for both kindergarten and school when we started in 2012, but within the following year this was changed so that a separation of responsibilities for kindergartens and schools was created: the Social Ministry was given responsibility for kindergartens and the Ministry of Education was given responsibility for schools. The municipality was also a partner that influenced what was formulated as societal needs, by introducing a practice of transferring children to the school day care in May when they first have to start school in mid-August.

Value changes in society influence children's life course. In the kindergarten practice studied here, the time when children were transferred to school influenced what happened, and also shows how school demands entered into kindergarten practice. In this chapter we have taken a small analytical step towards analysing how societal conditions may influence kindergarten practice but also how resistance to changing demands fortunately delays practice change, otherwise there would be too many fluctuating values for educating young children in kindergarten.[4]

---

[4] When we started the project in 2012 kindergarten and school belonged to the Ministry of Children and Youth. One year later this responsibility was split up, the kindergarten now belonged to the Social Ministry and school to the Ministry of Education. In 2016 the Ministry of Education now also covered 0–6 years old children's day care by creating a task force to formulate pedagogical foundations for the earlier formulated learning goals. In this new approach play was emphasized much more than earlier (formulated by the leader of the task force in the newspaper *Politiken* (Rash-Christensen 22–1–2017)).

The transition between institutional practices

Children's transition to school is a complex event that can be viewed from different perspectives. In an earlier study (Hedegaard & Fleer, 2012) this problem has been analysed from children's and their families' perspectives in relation to what it means for children's development. Other studies in line with this are Brostrøm (2000, 2007), Einarsdottir et al. (2009), Griebel & Niesel (2002), Højholt (2001), Jensen et al. (2013), Stanek (2011) and Winther-Lindqvist (2009). These studies focus primarily on how children's relations to other children and adults change when entering school. Dockett & Perry (2007) and Chan (2012) studied the differences between children's, parents', preschool teachers' and schoolteachers' values regarding children's transition from preschool to school primarily using questionnaires: both studies reported that preschool teachers were oriented to social relations. Schoolteachers and parents were oriented to children's ability to master academic skills and self-discipline – both were ranked highest. Though these studies were done in New South Wales in Australia and in Hong Kong, they fit with the difference in orientation between preschool and schoolteachers in Danish society (Brostrøm, 2007; Højholt, 2001; MBU, 2012b). Boyle & Petrewskyj (2014) have researched how kindergarten professionals' values regarding children's transition to school changed after getting in contact with school professionals – a change we also could follow in our study. We also found, especially through following focus children from kindergarten to school and analysing the protocols as demonstrated in Frida's case, that the pedagogy in kindergarten and school are different from the very start, even though the aim was to make a smooth transition. In kindergarten, the professionals support children to become agentive and take the initiative not to interfere too much, and through this support children to acquire life competences. In class zero in school, the teachers direct children and are much more oriented towards discipline, not leaving too much room for children to make their own decisions.

Activity setting for play and how this promotes children's life competences

The analyses of Frida's case gave us the opportunity to see how play would promote the skills that the kindergarten teachers formulated in our first meeting – something we kept going back to.

Through following Frida, one could see how the play activity gave her the opportunity of developing skills in entering into new relations with other children. Her ability to be creative in the play context: moving between the spheres of reality, imagination and planning in the play gave her a new position with the two other children, who from the start tried to exclude her from their play.

In school, teachers may use play but it takes other forms than in kindergarten. A way of using play can be found in Aidarova's (1982) experimental teaching of six-year-old children. This teaching was inspired by Vygotsky's theory of language and play. In the teaching, children learn the grammatical form in language, through the teacher's creating of play settings. Play here takes the form of preparing roles connected to a theme, where the theme then may become explored through the play activity (Hedegaard 2002).

Changes in the way children play through their life course have to be seen as connected to the institutional conditions, with its traditions, as well as children's motive orientation (Hedegaard, 2016). When children enter into a new institution, such as school, with new traditions and activities, they do not lose earlier competences but new challenges lead to a restructuring of how meanings, emotions and feelings relate. These changes can be seen creating children's different social situations of development that characterize their different life periods – of being preschool and becoming a schoolchild.

Conclusion

The societal vision of a smooth transition from kindergarten to school aims at creating knowledgeable citizens, but it is a shortcut that creates difficulties for both professionals and children. The professionals' alignment of values is not a process of formulating ideas for how to realize societal demands for children starting school activities earlier, in order to make children do better in school tests. Children's development into being a schoolchild cannot be accomplished through drawing school activities into kindergarten. Instead, the professionals in kindergarten and school have to acknowledge what the differences between the two practices mean for children's development and, through taking a life perspective on children's development, to see that kindergarten gives children competences they cannot acquire through school practice, but are important for children's participation in school activities. In kindergarten children receive the preconditions for literacy through acquiring abilities to play with meanings. Play is an important way to develop concepts, but it is not the only way. Kindergartens give children a broad spectrum of experiences that are necessary for this development in different activity settings, such as trips out of the kindergarten, talks around the lunch table, shared round table discussions where children are asked to tell or describe events Looking at picture books and pedagogues reading, as well as creative activities such as drawing, modelling etc. are also important. But play has a special role, because through play children may create collective imagination (Fleer, 2013), which they can explore together, thereby developing both their agentive relation to each other as well as their daring to be explorative that may be seen as life competences.

In the play event where Frida had the role of being a cat, we saw how Frida and the two other children created a play where they both became able to communicate and explore and extend their ideas. Their acquisition of such competence can be seen as a way to prepare children's engagement in school for exploring content in different subject areas.

In the project, it became clear that the traditions in school were different with respect to teacher guidance and allowing children to take initiative from the very beginning in class zero, but since the objective of school is different, where learning is related to the logic of the subject, this has to be expected. In transition between practices, the alignment of values demands that the professionals have the possibility to get to know each other's practices and the different objectives for this practice. They are then able to formulate common knowledge (Edwards, 2012), which implies knowledge of what is important in each other's practices, so that one can see how they may relate to each other preparing children for transition to school without imitating each other's practice. Transition to school creates opportunities for the development of children's social situation. In school, children's social situation of development is different and children meet new demands that lead to new motives.

References

Aidarova, L. (1982), *Child development and education*. Moscow: Progress.

Andersen, P. Ø. (2004), 'Daginstitutionernes indhold og pædagogik i historisk belysning', in I. T. Ellegaard, & A. H. Stanek (eds), *Læreplaner i børnehaven*. Vejle: Kroghs forlag.

Boyle, T. & A. Petriwskyj (2014), 'Special Issue: Transitions in the early years: Policy, pedagogy and partnership', *Early Years: An International Research Journal*, 34 4.

Brostrøm, S. (2000), 'Transition to school'. Paper presented at the 10th European Conference on Quality in Early Childhood Education (EECERA), August 2000, London.

Brostrøm, S. (2007), 'Overgang fra dagtilbud til skole', in I. N. Egelund (ed.), *Skolestart: udfordringer for daginstitutioner, skole og fritidsordninger*. København: Krogs Forlag.

Chaiklin, S. (2014), 'A theoretical framework for analysing preschool teaching: A cultural-historical science perspective', *Learning, Culture and Social Interaction*, 3, 224–231. doi:http://dx.doi.org/10.1016/j.lcsi.2014.02.009

Chan, W. L. (2012), 'Expectations for the transition from kindergarten to primary school amongst teachers, parents and children', *Early Child Development and Care*, 182, 639–664.

Dockett, S. & B. Perry (2007), *Transitions to school: Perceptions, expectations and experiences*. Sydney: University of New South Wales Press.

Edwards, A. (2012), *Being an expert professional practitioner*. Dodrecht: Springer.

Einarsdottir, J., S. Dockett & B. Perry (2009), 'Making meaning: children's perspectives expressed through drawings', *Early Child Development and Care*, 179, 217–232.

Elkonin, D. B. (2005), 'The psychology of play', *Journal of Russian and East European Psychology*, 43, 11–21.

Ellegaard, I. T. & A. H. Stanek (2004), *Læreplaner i børnehaven*. Vejle: Kroghs forlag.

Fleer, M. (2013), 'Collective imagination in play', in I. Schousboe & D. Winther-Lindqvist (eds), *Children's play and development: Cultural-historical perspectives* (pp. 73–88). Dordrecht: Springer.

Green, A. (1990), *Education and state formation: The rise of education systems in England, France, and the USA* (Conclusion, pp. 308–316). London: Macmillan.

Griebel, W. & R. Niesel (2002), 'Co-constructing transition into kindergarten and school by children, parents and teachers', in A. W. Dunlop & H. Fabian (eds), *Transition in the early years: Debating continuity and progress for young children in the early years* (pp. 27–42). New York: Routledge & Falmer.

Gulløv, E. (2013), 'Den tidlige civilisering', in I. L. Gilliam & E. Gulløv (eds), *Civiliserende Institutioner: Om idealer og distinktioner i opdragelse*. Aarhus: Aarhus University Press.

Hedegaard, M. (1995), *Beskrivelse af småbørn*. Aarhus: Aarhus University Press.

Hedegaard, M. (2002), *Learning and child development*. Aarhus: Aarhus University Press.

Hedegaard, M. (2008), 'Principles for interpreting research protocols', in M. Hedegaard & M. Fleer (eds), *Studying children: A cultural-historical approach* (pp. 46–64). Maidenhead, England: Open University Press.

Hedegaard, M. (2012), 'Analyzing children's learning and development in everyday settings from a cultural-historical wholeness approach', *Mind Culture and Activity*, 19, 127–138.

Hedegaard, M. (2016), 'Imagination and emotion in children's play: A cultural-historical Approach', *International Research in Early Childhood Education*. www.education.monash.edu.au/irecejournal/, 7 2, 57–72.

Hedegaard, M. (2017), 'When daycare professional's values from transition to school do not align with educational demands from society and school: A practice developing research project for daycare professionals support for children's transition to school', in A. Edwards (ed.), *Working relationally in and across practices*. Cambridge: Cambridge University Press.

Hedegaard, M. & M. Fleer (2012), *Play, learning and children's development: Everyday life in families and transition to school*. Cambridge: Cambridge University Press.

Højholt, C. (2001), *Samarb,ejde om børns udvikling: Deltagere i social praksis*. København: Gyldendal-uddannelse.

Hundeide, K. (2005), 'Socio-cultural tracks of development, opportunity situations and access skills', *Culture & Psychology*, 11, 241–261.

Hviid, P. (2012), '"Remaining the same" and children's experience of development', in M. Hedegaard, K. Aronsson, C. Højholt & O. Skjær Ulvik (eds), *Children, childhood and everyday life*. Charlotte, NC: Information Age Publishing.

Jensen, A. S., O. H. Hansen & S. Broström (2013), 'Transition to school: Contemporary Danish perspectives', in I. K. Margetts & A. Kienig (eds), *International perspectives on transition to school*. Abingdon: Routledge.

Leontiev, A. N. (1981), *Problems of the development of the mind*. Moscow: Progress.

MBU (2012a), 'Fremtidens dagtilbud. Pejlemærker fra task force om fremtidens dagtilbud. Ministeriet for Børn og Undervisning for Task Force for Fremtidens Dagtilbud'. Hentet 27 maj 2014 fra http://www.uvm.dk/Uddannelser/Dagtilbudsomraadet/Fremtidens-dagtilbud-Udviklingsprogrammet.

MBU (2012b), 'Baggrundsrapport fra Task Force om Fremtidens Dagtilbud. Ministeriet for Børn og Undervisning for Task Force for Fremtidens Dagtilbud'. Hentet 27 maj 2014 fra http://www.uvm.dk/Uddannelser/Dagtilbudsomraadet/Fremtidens-dagtilbud-Udviklingsprogrammet.

Meyer, J. W., F. O. Ramirez & Y. N. Soysal (1992), 'World expansion of mass education, 1870–1980', *Sociology of Education*, 65(2), 128–149.

Ramirez, F. & J. Boli (1987), 'The political construction of mass schooling: European origins and worldwide institutionalization', *Sociology of Education*, 60, 2–11.

Rogoff, B. (2003), *The cultural nature of human development*. New York: Oxford University Press.

Schousboe, I. (2013), 'The structure of fantasy play and its implication for good and evil games', in I. Schousboe & D. Winther-Lindqvist (eds), *Children's play and development: Cultural-historical perspectives* (pp. 29–54), Dordrecht: Springer.

Stanek, A. H. (2011), *Børns fællesskaber og fællesskabernes betydning*. Roskilde Universitetsforlag.

Vygotsky, L. S. (1967), 'Play and its role in the mental development of the child', *Soviet Psychology*, 12, 62–76.

Vygotsky, L. S. (1998), *Child Psychology. The Collected Works of L.S. Vygotsky*, vol. 5, trans. M. J. Hall, R. W. Rieber. New York: Kluwer Academic and Plenum Publishers.

Vygotsky, L. (2016), 'Play and its role in the mental development of the child', (trans. M. Barrs and N. Veresov), *International Research in Early Childhood Education*, 7, 1–19.

White, G. & C. Sharp (2007), 'It is different ... because you are getting older and growing up': How children make sense of the transition to year 1', *European Early Childhood Education Research Journal*, 15, 87–102.

Winnicott, D. W. (2003, org.1977), Leg, en Teoretisk Fremstilling. København: Hans Reitzels Forlag.

Winther-Lindqvist, D. (2009), 'Children's development of social identity in transitions'. PhD diss. Denmark: Department of Psychology, Copenhagen University.

Winther-Lindqvist, D. (2012), 'Developing social identities and motives in school transitions', in M. Hedegaard, A. Edwards & M. Fleer (eds), *Motives in children's development*. Cambridge: Cambridge University Press.

3

Becoming a Schoolchild: A Positive Developmental Crisis

Ditte Winther-Lindqvist

Introduction

There is a consensual ambition to establish a *coherent* educational system in Denmark. The aim of cohesiveness is believed to create the best conditions for children and adolescents to positively manage the obligatory shifts in institutional affiliation during childhood and thereby increase the child's ability and desire to learn (Weirsøe, 2012). Achieving coherence in the Danish educational context is considered particularly problematic during transitions between institutions, and special care in the arrangement around institutional transitions is therefore politically and practically reinforced. The current way of trying to ensure coherence during transitions is by making the induction into the new setting as lengthy and gradual as possible. This political aim is best recognized and underscored through Danish legislation – where the transitional year of reception class was made compulsory from 2009. Part of the legislation on day care, which municipalities must adhere to, includes a paragraph on transitions: '§7, part 5: daycare is to cooperate with parents in order to ensure a positive transition to primary school by developing and supporting basic competencies and the desire to learn. Daycares must cooperate with schools in order to create a cohesive transition into school and leisure-time centre' (Retsinformation 2017, my translation).

In 65 out of 98 municipalities, children start leisure-time centre in spring. This takes place on school premises, in order for them to become accustomed to the school environment before they formally start reception class in August (Bureau, 2000 (2017), p. 5). The reasoning behind this practice at the institutional level is to ensure cohesion and prevent a rupture for the child. This practice is also clear in the after-school leisure centre, where I carried out my research: 'I think of starting school as something in stages, step by step, they first start here in the leisure centre – and then when reception class starts, it is not all new to them.'

The discourse around the transition from day care to primary school is one of worry and concern for the well-being of the children, as it is in the general international debate within the area (Fabian, 2007). This I find rather puzzling, since Danish day-care children and the educational system seem to manage the transition via reception class well, and this is not only the case presently, but has been the case for many years (Undervisningsministeriet, 2017). A large Danish research project established that less than 5 per cent of 5–7 year old school-starters experience psychological problems (Elberling et al., 2010). Around 3 per cent of the children attend reception class for two years in a row (Undervisningsministeriet, 2017). Even though the number of children who need to start reception class twice has grown, since it became obligatory to start school in the year the child turns six years old 97 per cent continue into first grade and this high number does not indicate the transition to be problematic. In a recent report conducted by the Danish Children's Council (Børnerådet, 2013) entitled: 'School seen from daycare' the results are also positive. The survey was designed in order to create a valid quantitative review of day-care children's expectations of school and consisted of responses from 966 children (49.9 per cent girls, and 50.1 per cent boys). Ninety-one day-care centres from various parts of the country participated in the survey. The results show that the children are concerned with and excited about both their future social and academic life in school, and that the opportunity to meet new friends is one of the most prominent concerns on their minds (Børnerådet, 2013, p. 8). Furthermore, the results show that 73 per cent were confident that they would in fact succeed in finding new friends in school, 30 per cent worried that they would be teased by other children, 89 per cent expected to become 'good in school' (skilled learners) and 87 per cent pictured that their future teachers would be nice to them. In conclusion, the report states: 'Far the majority of children in Denmark are brought up with a desire for and eagerness with regard to the change and new challenges, and with faith in their adults to arrange for them something which is fun, exciting and educational' (Børnerådet, 2013, p. 35).

The danger-rhetoric on the transition into school

It is almost exclusively cultural-historical and contextual understandings of development that inform and inspire the Danish practice tradition of gradual transitioning between day care and school (Sepstrup, 2017). This is hardly surprising, since especially the cultural-historical tradition (as well as Bronfenbrenner's ecological model) have theorized development mainly as an interplay between institutional practices and social life, through which the individual engages with demands and possibilities and develops motives and new skills through participation (Chaiklin, 2011, p. 345). Despite the general and substantial reference to cultural-historical ideas among researchers within this area, there seems to be an underlying basis for a more psychodynamic understanding of the school transition as a challenge, even a danger in the child's life. Even though only a very few direct references to psychodynamic theories are identified in the literature review carried out by Sepstrup (2017), the idea that transitions involve separation from important others echoes an attachment theory-informed thinking about development in young children. The idea is that the child, in order to develop in a healthy way, needs a secure base provided by attachment figures that are stable, reliable and caring (Bowlby, 2005): 'the road to school is not straightforward, safe and secure. One can say that the transition in many ways is a free fall for the children. Some children make it more or less on their own, whereas others lose their footing and "fall"' (Cecchin, 2003, p. 94).

In this quote, the dangers of losing footing and falling through in the process of starting school are emphasized. Nevertheless, without denying that some children are immensely challenged by starting school and also acknowledging that some children lose their footing, it is after all, only 3 per cent of Danish children who need to start over again in reception class. My point is therefore this: in general, I find the dangers associated with the school transition to be exaggerated. Consider the following: 'We overlook that the goodbye with the former environment often involves a process of separation on equal terms with other separation processes in life, like for instance divorce or loss of a loved one, and that it demands the same attention and psychological energy from the child' (Larsen, 2009, p. 20).

This quote argues that starting school is an endangering event, and that we need to pay extra attention to children during the school transition because they are vulnerable, as their secure base is unstable and going through change.[1] What seems to be missing in Larsen's account (2009, 2010) is that the school transition only involves major changes in *one* of the child's institutional life arenas; the home and family life arena, where children are expected to enjoy

---

[1] Larsen then recommends the tool called the 'suitcase', first introduced in Italy and now a widespread transition activity method in Denmark (i.e., one of six suggested activities recommended on the website for school induction made by the Ministry of Education).

their primary relationships with parents, which are normally not disturbed by a school transition. So even from an attachment-system perspective, the school transition does not represent a complete rupture in the child's secure base. My basic argument is that we highly exaggerate the dangers of the school transition in the Danish context and that this essentially reflects a lack of appreciation of institutional transitions as the beginning of a potentially spurring developmental process. It also reflects a current lack of theoretical differentiation between various different transitions and also a lack of theoretical basis for comparing different stressors caused by these and their developmental impact. No matter what theoretical persuasion, equating the loss of a loved one, or divorce, with starting school seems a genuinely bizarre comparison – children generally enjoy starting school and look forward to this life-changing event, which is far from the case when children experience divorce or bereavement.

Stig Broström, a prominent scholar in early years education in Denmark, represents a less exaggerated concern for the children in school-transition, yet one where starting school is still regarded as a potential threat to the child's well-being; among other things, he warns that too abrupt a school start can lead to unnecessary defeat and disintegration for the children (Broström, 2007, 2013). His position is given some attention here, because it is inspired by the cultural-historical, activity theory tradition, like my own approach, yet one that – in my opinion – overlooks the positive developmental potential of transitions in general. Also, Broström addresses the school-transition as a problematic and endangering challenge for children. For instance, he writes: 'Because too many children experience the transition to school as a culture shock, during the past decade daycare teachers have implemented so-called transition activities in order to bridge the gap between daycare and school' (Broström, 2005, p. 17). He underscores this understanding of the school-transition as a problem by pointing to several observations of children who in day care were well-functioning, yet during the first weeks in school these children changed attitudes and became less active, expressing a form of insecurity. Although these children had obtained the necessary level of school readiness, they did not feel well in school, which impacted on their well-being and was a hindrance to their being active learners in the new environment. Another concern is that this temporary loss of competence might pave the way for poor self-esteem and insecurity in the new setting (Broström, 2007, p. 2).

First of all, it seems fair to ask how many children are too many children who experience school-transition as a culture shock? Also, we may critically ask if the findings in Broström's case material are not to be expected, when an individual is a newcomer and is adjusting to a new cultural environment? That a transition brings about a temporary sense of insecurity and lack of self-confidence, and even gives rise to anxiety during the first weeks in the new setting – is this really a problem that we need to avoid? Is it a just cause for alarm? Or is it simply a consequence of transitioning and developing in general?

Secondly, I find the solution to the problem of 'transition to school' problematic since it currently means that differences between the two settings (day care and primary school) are minimized and harmonized in order to ensure a smooth and gradual transition – and this levelling out of differences seems to be at the cost of the particular and valuable play-based practice tradition of day care developed over the last seven decades. The practice tradition of day care is historically one reflecting a child-centred and holistic approach to the child as a being who develops through play with peers as well as through meaningful activities with caring, engaged and professionally trained day-care teachers (called pedagogues in Danish; see Winther-Lindqvist (2013) for an overview). Since 2004, new legislation with a strong focus on learning has been implemented into this practice tradition, challenging the play-based curriculum and the child-centred focus on personal and social development. The prior focus on play, peer-group life, friendships and the development of socio-emotional competences (like self-regulation, emotion regulation, cooperation and group participation, respect for others and for oneself) has been challenged, not only by financial cutbacks but also by public ridicule. The Danish prime minister, in a famous opening debate in parliament back in 2003, stated that the *round-table pedagogics* should be replaced by a focus on more learning: 'We have to make progress. We need to be even better. We must set higher academic standards everywhere in the educational system'. Since then, the day care arena has struggled for recognition, as the immensely important and difficult task of supporting 3–6 year old children from various socio-economic backgrounds in their personal development has been regarded as *unserious*, i.e., frivolous and silly (wrongly disregarded as 'round-table pedagogics') whereas working on their skills and learning competencies has been given higher status and has been requested politically. The consensual danger-rhetoric on transitioning, where change and crisis is regarded as dangerous, coupled with this increased focus on learning has resulted in both the step-by-step school induction practice and challenged the practice tradition of day care, making day care resemble primary school more and more. I believe this current state of affairs requires a critical examination from a developmental perspective. Firstly, I contest that an institutional transition with a clear end and beginning is necessarily bad and secondly, I question the levelling out of differences between day care and primary school as the best way of ensuring 'school-readiness' in children. Of course, we have to help *every* child to a successful start in school. But if we organize our general system to cater for the 3 per cent and ignore the success of the 97 per cent, I ask myself if our emphasis, priorities and policies vis-à-vis the institutional transition from day care to school are placed correctly.

When I warn against the danger-rhetoric of the school transition it is because this can lead to a 'schoolification' of both reception class, and day care as the system is calibrated much more narrowly towards testable learning outcomes than it used to be. When starting school is problematized it threatens the pedagogical practices that sustain and support socio-emotional and personality development in early years education. I conclude that the transition to school generally is a positive developmental crisis, and that the children (as well as the school system) mostly benefit by holding on to a play-based learning environment in day care, rather than mimicking the didactic tradition developed in primary school in order to teach specific academic subject matter.

Current day care and reception class practice in Denmark

Ninety-nine per cent of Danish children attend day care at age 2–5 and compulsory schooling starts the year the child turns six years old. The day care environment is mainly play-based and more informal than in many other countries, which Danes consider is necessary, as the children spend most of their everyday life in early care from a very early age. Reception class is compulsory, and starts the year the child turns six years of age. The school week is 30 hours in reception class, and it is regarded as a *preparatory year*, based on shared premises with the school and handled by a team of day-care teachers. Today, reception class works with common goals in six obligatory competence areas, which resemble the learning themes governing day care: language, mathematics, natural phenomena, creative/musical expressions, body and movement, engagement and community. Yet, the way these common goals are reached didactically aims at a playful learning environment. The Legislation Act says: 'as before (before the common goals for reception class) play must be a central element in teaching. Acknowledging the intrinsic value of playing, and learning through play and playful activities' (Act for reception class, my translation).

By law as well as in practice, the way children are engaged in learning tasks in reception class resembles, in many ways, how project-based learning themes are practiced in most day-care centres. In an interview with a reception class teacher, Klaus, he explains:

'Reception class is mainly project based learning. For instance, we start the year with working on a theme called "My family". The children produce drawings and artwork depicting their particular family and are encouraged to discuss and reflect on their own family, and on different forms of family life in Denmark. This is also a way for us to get to know the child and the children to get to know each other.'

> I ask: But this project of 'My Family' reminds me of project-based work I've seen in day care.
>
> Klaus: Yes, this could be a project in day care too. Only we probably work more hours on such a project, in a more structured way – and our adult resources are more scarce.
>
> I ask: Do you work with the children on separate subjects; like maths and language?
>
> Klaus: Mostly, we do so implicitly, as part of the project-based work. It is in 1st Grade they separate teaching into different subjects and work systematically with learning to read, to write etc.
>
> I ask: What competencies and skills are important that daycares aim at in order to ensure the children a good start in school?
>
> Klaus: What we really need from the children, in reception class, is that they are able to work on these projects, individually and together in smaller groups. We need them to respect and adhere to the themes we introduce and cooperate on the tasks, more on their own, or in smaller groups – because we are only one adult to assist them.

I wonder if the difference between these practices, in day care and reception class, really creates a cultural-shock in many children? I find it more likely that the children in fact are familiar with these ways of working from their time in day care – and that some of them are disappointed in their expectations to learn 'real' subjects, because their parents and day-care teachers support their imaginings about school in scenarios that resemble 1st Grade, rather than the actual practice of reception class.

Transitions: A differentiated theorizing

In the cultural-historical theoretical tradition, development is recognized as changes in the complex interplay between the child and the environment. When the child changes institutional affiliation, they also respond to new demands, opportunities and restrictions from the new relational and socio-cultural environment in ways that qualitatively changes the psychology of the child (Hedegaard & Fleer, 2013). Institutional transitions are times of change in the child's objective and subjective relations to the environment. These changes concern the very system of relations, involving a new place that the child occupies objectively in social relations and a new internal position in the child (Bozhovich, 2009). Institutional transitions therefore involve a crisis, as the child needs to adjust to new conditions in her/his life and way of being towards the world. However, there are *many* different developmental transitions and a general absence of a unified and coherent theorizing of different transitions and their subsequent developmental consequences (Vrinioti et al., 2010, p. 18). I argue that general models of development through transition, like for instance the rupture-transition model by Tania Zittoun (2006), may overlook the phenomenological subjective differences as well as the formal differences inbuilt in various different forms of transitions.

A differentiated view on transitions, I suggest, must reflect the various forms of transition, and theorize their respective differences accordingly. There are at least three different forms of transition, which involve profound changes in a person's social situation of development; all resulting in a temporary crisis likely to spur development and affect the psychological life-course of a person:

1. Institutional transitions: changes of institutional affiliation and accompanying recognized identity. These transitions are societally organized, often compulsory, and collectively, institutionally and personally anticipated and prepared for (e.g., starting school and becoming a schoolchild). Institutional transitions are organized mainly to meet societal needs and those transitions are most prominent in children/young people's lives.[2]

2. Unexpected transitions (e.g., losing a loved one, the onset of illness, winning the lottery). Unexpected transitions are existential events that happen to us – events we have to respond to – but we did not prepare for and often did not initiate/plan for. Unexpected transitions are prime examples of the 'thrown' character of human existence.

---

[2]   Institutional transitions are societally organized in ways that 'fit' children following an ordinary developmental path; for children with disabilities, the coherence in institutional transitions is less automatically organized and therefore presents much more challenging times for the parents and children (see Boettcher, this book for an elaboration).

3. Self-initiated and chosen transitions (changing job/career, becoming a parent, leaving a spouse etc.). Self-initiated transitions are mostly relevant in adolescent and adult life, and they are prime examples of the agency with which we can conduct our lives in ways we find desirable or necessary for our satisfactory continued existence.

Younger children are mostly exposed to institutional transitions, and unexpected transitions, whereas self-chosen transitions are a privilege for older children and adults, who are conducting their own everyday lives and are allowed to initiate major changes for themselves, to a much greater degree than smaller children. The situations and life-events that are meant to illustrate these different forms of transitions (examples in parentheses) change not only with age, but also with societal-historical changes. The transition into parenthood has predominantly been self-initiated (the result of sexual intercourse), but before the legislation on elective abortion in Denmark in 1973, pregnancy was self-initiated but far from always wanted and self-chosen. Today, becoming a parent is more a matter of choice (for those lucky enough to be fertile) and it is mostly self-initiated but need not involve sexual intercourse, due to modern technologies allowing for artificial insemination, at least for women. Also, the same event may not involve the same transitions for the involved parties. A divorce is a self-initiated and chosen transition for the one who chooses to leave and thus could be a sudden and unexpected transition for the one being left (and for any children involved). Changing job and career path may be self-initiated and chosen, but could equally be the result of being made redundant, most likely resulting in two very different experiences in a person's life. Also a self-initiated transition like changing job on the part of the parent can, in the child's experience, be more of an unexpected transition, maybe even involving an institutional transition if the job change requires that the family moves to another place. Finally, this brings us to the next and crucial differentiation with regards to theorizing transitions and their developmental impact: which is the particular event that brings about the transition? I suggest distinguishing between *empowering* or *disempowering* events. Some events are disempowering, also termed hostile, and characterized by the philosopher Thomas Schwarz Wentzer as: an event which arrests our ideas of a future and one in which instead of being subjects we find ourselves subjected to our situation (Wentzer, 2015, p. 84). Conversely, other events that lead to a transition can increase action potency, increase participation possibilities and provide opportunity situations that are necessary in order to achieve competences that are requested and demanded in order to become a valued and respected member of society – like becoming a schoolchild through attending primary school. Assessing what counts as an empowering or disempowering event is complex, since what in the first place is experienced as a dis-empowering event may prove in the long run to be a blessing (the fired person finds a new and less desired occupation, which actually proves more satisfactory than the former, or the depressed deserted spouse starts a new life and ends up grateful for the broken marriage). Even the most hostile events (like losing a loved one) can, with time, transform the existential outlook of the bereaved and deepen the appreciation for other relationships and for the beauty of life (Brewer & Sparkes, 2011). Likewise, sometimes what we have most desired only proves disappointing when realized. Having studied children and adolescents both as they live through institutional transitions (e.g., starting school) and as they live through unexpected transitions (the hostile event of serious parental illness and/or parental loss), it is clear that the unexpected situation of illness and death is a hostile event, whereas starting school is not (Winther-Lindqvist, 2016).

A cultural-historical view on crisis and development

In order to understand why starting school is usually an empowering event, and institutional transitions in general spur a positive developmental crisis, we will start with Vygotsky's developmental psychology. In fact, on this basis I will argue that the school transition is the opposite of Wentzer's definition of hostile events. The school transition is vested with ideas of a future – and when mastering the challenges of starting school one grows accordingly and becomes a subject (rather than subjectified) through becoming a schoolchild. According to Vygotsky, children's development occurs as a consequence of continuous interaction with the cultural environment; development is thus cultural and interactional rather than merely a natural unfolding or inner realization of potentials (Fleer, 2014). Vygotsky stresses the emergence of the new through socio-cultural interaction: 'development is a continuous process of self-propulsion characterized primarily by a continuous appearance and formation of the new which did not exist at previous stages' (Vygotsky, 1998, p. 190).

   This means that developmental periods are characterized by, in his words, 'a stormy, impetuous, and sometimes catastrophic character' (Vygotsky, 1998, p. 191). Vygotsky's point is that these stormy periods are structured differently, due to the child's cultural age, and are dependent on exterior conditions for the child's participation in cultural practices and social relationships. These critical periods of change are also characterized by neo-formations in the child's current understandings, needs, competences and motives. Prior to a critical period, the child experiences ruptures in their social relations, which – together with the neo-formations – compose the child's 'social situation of development' (Vygotsky, 1998, p. 199). Institutional transition as a developmental phenomenon, comes about as a response to the new demands for participation in the socio-cultural practice (like the new school environment) – demands that the child cannot yet honour from their current mental capacity developed in the former developmental period. The child is suddenly 'a different child whose social existence cannot but differ in a substantial way from the existence of the child of an earlier age' (Vygotsky, 1998). Transitional states thus causes conflict and interruption between old and new forms of social relations – and the child's place in them – and the child is confronted with tasks that challenge old patterns and probe for new ways of participation, new tasks and the development of new motives. Vygotsky states: 'From this point the essence of every crisis is a reconstruction of the internal experience, a reconstruction that is rooted in the change of the basic factor that determines the relation of the child to the environment, specially, in the change in needs and motives that control the behavior of the child' (Vygotsky, 1998, p. 296).

While in such crises, new psychological functions are undergoing development. The child is in a 'zone of proximal development', consisting of 'the area of immature, but maturing processes' (*Vygotsky, 1998*, p. 202). The child is approximating a new cultural repertoire and is in need of developing new understandings through new ways of participating in social interaction. Through imitation, understood as a 'sensible imitation based on understanding the imitative carrying out of some intellectual operation' (*Vygotsky, 1998*, p. 202), the child starts imitating the suggested new ways of participation, either by imitating adults or more skilled peers. Provided that the participation and imitation is connected to the child's actual level of development, the imitation process and social mediation leads to the child's adaptation of a new psychological strategy and state of being (Vygotsky, 1998, p. 201). Mariane Hedegaard (2003, 2012, 2014) further develops Vygotsky's and Leontiev's developmental psychology by theorizing how development takes place in concrete practices in different societal institutions, involving different activity settings that encourage the development of different motives for participation. Hedegaard argues that a cultural-historical view of development entails that starting school is a developmental crisis, which spurs development because the child acquires new skills, competencies and motives through participation in new activity-settings and new relations during the transition. There is a crisis involved in this process because the child experiences a temporary discrepancy between present skills, competences and self-understanding and the demands of the new environment in a way that motivates the child to acquire new skills, motives, relations and competencies: 'Crisis entails a conflict between old and new relations, where the new relations demand that some of the child's former understandings, competences and motives vanish' (Hedegaard, 2003, p. 39).

If cultural-historical developmental psychology is correct in its main assumption, that development is spurred due to changes in institutional affiliations and ways of participating and that this involves periods of crisis, I wonder if the current tendency to harmonize and minimize differences between institutional environments actually undermines the developmental potential in the school transition.

According to Bozhovich (2009), we need to pay attention to what school life means to the day-care child (objectively and for each child individually) in order to understand the transition into school life as either satisfying the child's developmental needs or not. The objective meaning of school is a valued and prioritized institution in our society, and thus it represents a necessary and positive opportunity for the child to engage with. Starting school is an empowering event in a child's life and is, therefore, a celebrated and supported transition valued as an important step for children by society at large. This applies to institutional practices generally as they have evolved during sociogenesis to fit societal needs. Children's development of motives, learning of skills and competences, internalization of commitments and values in ontogenesis is intrinsically interwoven with this sociogenesis of institutional practices and goals. Children in most cases internalize the values held by their parents and other adults in their society, so that school is also positively awaited from the child's own perspective. Hedegaard's point (2012) of integrating the child's perspective when researching developmental situations from a wholeness approach is a parallel theorizing to Bozhovich's recommendation to pay attention to what school life means to the child. Both scholars are inspired by Vygotsky's suggestion that the child's emotional experience is the central unit for studying the social situation of a child. In further elaboration of this affective relationship, Bozhovich suggests the concept of *place* to account for the position a child occupies within the environment as well as the internal position the child holds towards this place, which together structures 'their attitude toward reality, toward those around them and toward themselves' (Bozhovich, 2009, p. 81).

On outgrowing day care as a function of preparation

When a transition is expected – as institutional transitions usually are[3] – it is also prepared for. In the case of starting school, this is prepared for in various ways. Not only collectively through didactic transitional activities arranged for in day care, but also personally; as the child imagines him/herself in his/her future-self, as a result of knowing that s/he is going to become a schoolchild soon. This I recognize as the internal positioning and place in Bozhovich's terminology. This is an imaginary process that most children go through in the last months before starting school, and obviously one that can be supported by various social activities and conversations, and also one that can be obstructed, exhausted and drained of energy. In Kurt Lewin's pioneering work on environmental forces in child development he makes the observation that: 'to the psychological situation belong not only those facts that are actually perceptible and objectively present, but also a range of past and future events… an expected event may have psychological reality in advance of its occurrence' (Lewin, 1935, p. 87). Lewin's observations have importance for the theorizing of institutional transitions; as school life, and the activity of school learning clearly has a psychological reality in advance of its materialization in the school context. Lewin emphasizes that the lead up to changing places (just before) is a time of particularly tension. As the half-imaginary goal is approaching the boundary of the now-situation (in our case the continued day-care existence) creates a much stronger marked barrier, separating the individual from her/his almost attained goal (Lewin, 1935, pp. 87–88). This is a crucial point with consequences for how we ought to organize the school transition, and for how long we should encourage preparation. As the children imagine themselves as *already* almost schoolchildren – which shows in their play, in their attitude towards activities, and in a shift in their dominant motive[4] – they also need to be treated as such, and they at the same time *stop* being fully involved and engaged in their present environment in day care. One can say that during this preparation they outgrow day care psychologically. It is important that this process is not stretched out for too long, as outgrowing a place is marking time, both developmentally and experientially. To rephrase Bozhovich, the child in transit is, in a way, a child out of place: 'Starting school

---

[3] Only the transition into nursery for the infant is not prepared for by the infant, and thus this particular institutional transition follows a different pattern than in the suggested model.

[4] Hedegaard, 2009 has an illustrative example of a boy in day care, who is no longer satisfied with reading childish books and being caressed by his day-care teacher – only when she chooses a serious 'school-like' book does he identify with the activity and participate without a conflict p. 67).

inaugurates a breaking point in children's lives, characterized first and foremost by the fact that, by becoming school children, they receive new rights and responsibilities and for the first time enter into a serious, socially significant activity, their level of achievement in which will determine their place among and their relationships with those around them' (Bozhovich, 2009, p. 81).

As argued by Bozhovich, as well as Hedegaard & Fleer (2013), most children by the end of day care strive towards the new socially significant activity of learning. If a child has a potent learning motive and strives towards their new social position as a schoolchild, such a child will have his/her needs satisfied by starting school – and will be frustrated and bored in an environment that does not stimulate this curiosity and engagement. Obviously, a child still mostly or fully dominated by a play-motive will be overly challenged by starting school – unless the school succeeds in very quickly and skilfully enabling the neo-formation of the learning motive in the child. In the Danish context, I think that reception class is designed in order to achieve exactly that – ensuring that all children when approaching 1st Grade have developed a prominent learning motive and the competences for participation in school life. In any case, the child in order to positively integrate into the school environment needs to develop an inner position, entailing identification with the new tasks, responsibilities and rights that school life involves; only this does not have to happen far from the actual realization of starting school.

A model of institutional transitions

In agreement with the works of Bozhovich, Hedegaard and Fleer, theorizing the school transition phenomenon as a positive developmental crisis, I will try to depict a transitional model that pays proper attention to the fact that the transition into school is prepared for and anticipated both societally, collectively/ institutionally and subjectively. This is important, because it enables the neo-formation of especially the learning motive in children (Winther-Lindqvist, 2012). I argue that both the preparation and the realization play a central role in a successful school integration, but also that not all the potential challenges the child meets in school can be prepared for in advance by any educational effort or transitional activity in day care. This necessarily leaves a major responsibility for the positive integration of the child with the school, in the new environment. The model of institutional transitions suggested in this chapter is exemplified with reference to an empirical study I undertook some years ago, following children in their last four months of day care and into their first three months

INSTITUTIONAL TRANSITIONS

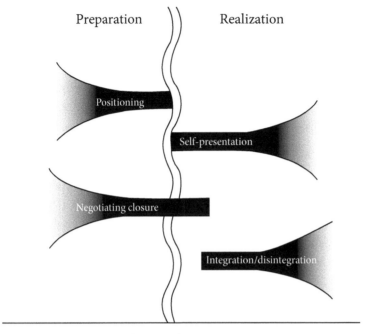

Figure 2 Model of institutional transitions

in reception class. The study involved intensive participatory observations, with paper and pen observations and audio-recordings, as well as interviews with the children. I was able to follow nine children from the daycare into the same reception class where they joined a classroom with 20 other children (from other daycares in the rural village area). This study provides the main background for the present suggested model for institutional transitions (Figure 2).

Preparation

The time of preparation has both an institutional and personal dimension. The institutional dimension is more than just the legislative obligation to ensure a positive transition in interventions such as transitional activities of various forms (visits to the local school, cooperation, particular activities arranged typically to be done on a weekly basis – the soon-to-be schoolchildren meet and do special activities). Also, more informally and spontaneously, the pedagogues in day care engage in more dialogues about school and start to refer to school expectations more often in daily life: *when in school, you know, there isn't anyone else to help you with your clothes* (implying you better learn now, fellow!) although it varies between children quite a lot how they prepare, and how much they imagine themselves ahead in time as a future schoolkid, they all are reminded by the collective efforts to engage with this idea. When the child imagines a future-self as a schoolkid, it is a process characterized by both anxious thrill and excitement, sometimes spurring anxiety and at other times impatience, especially when the time is drawing near. As part of this preparation, the children are positioning themselves and others in relation to the expected core activities and relationships and they evaluate their own position accordingly. This is central to the internal position, preparing them for what awaits. Alex, a boy in my observational material, was a child with a well-developed learning motive, probably supported by his identification with his older brother who had already started school. When I asked him if he looked forward to starting school, he replied: 'Yes! And my brother is in 2nd. I'll join him after the holiday.' Alex looks up to his older brother and often talks about how he has homework, an afternoon activity at home with the family to which Alex probably feels attracted, yet is incapable of taking part in from his current position as a day-care child. He looks forward to taking up the tasks and responsibilities that he imagines school life entails; a task that is also valued and encouraged in his home environment (homework with his older brother is a daily family activity setting). This shows in his activities and projects; he rehearses his parents' phone numbers, spells his name, pretends to read in books and seems impatient in the last months of day care. Rather than playing with the other children, he prefers to join in adult activities and also sets himself difficult tasks. One day he starts rearranging all the equipment in the shed at the playground; organizing it all into categories: bicycles, sandpit equipment etc. Often he just waits for his mother to pick him up in the afternoon. I recognize him as both unoccupied and under-stimulated, but also already almost a schoolchild. Sandra also prepares for school life and is happy to learn that she is to share a classroom with Alex and her best friend Clara. She often in her play explores the theme of school and enjoys enacting the role as the strict teacher.[5]

---

[5] Hedegaard & Fleer (2013) make similar observations in the child's home environment in their studies from a wholeness approach. So it is not only in day care that the child develops new motives in preparation for becoming a schoolchild; also at home, for instance, they start paying more attention to their siblings when they are doing homework, which is a valued practice and symbol of being a schoolchild.

Negotiating closure: this part of an institutional transition denotes a ritualized institutional practice, partly and mainly a collective and formalized celebration, organized by the adults and the educational management in the institutional culture – the preparation culminates in some sort of final ritual of the transition. During my observations there was a celebration, with a farewell party and a kind of ceremony for all the children enjoying their very last day in day care. They all walked on a red carpet and received a 'book' that the pedagogues had made about their time in day care. Sandra received a book with a collection of her many drawings of horses, reflecting her passion for horseriding and several photos of her as she participates in excursions and activities during her time in day care. Negotiating closure, symbolized in the farewell party, is also a more personal process, where most children realize (more or less reflected) that they are now indeed leaving day care behind. Alex, in my interpretation, used up day care for what it had to offer him and for some time he has been eagerly waiting for his new life in school to begin.

Realization

Self-presentation: actually becoming a schoolchild culminates in the first day of school. I call it realization because all the invested imaginary potential regarding school life is finally meeting reality for the child. All children are accustomed to the school environment as they have attended the after-school leisure centre on school premises in the months just before the holidays (and some children also during the summer). The children are holding hands with a parent as they arrive, suntanned after a long holiday. There is a blitz-show of enthusiastic parents taking photos of their children. They shake hands with the new teacher and only reluctantly leave the setting, after the class teacher announces that all reception class children are now going to their classrooms. They are seated in the classroom and expected to introduce themselves to everybody: saying their names and talk about themselves. The teacher asks about their family life, pets and hobbies and they are requested to participate. Shy children are aided and guided through by the teacher, but all children have to speak up and present themselves. Sandra is reluctant to speak up and is one of those who is aided by the teacher in introducing herself and she talks about the family horse and how she is learning to ride it. Then they are given briefcases for sheets of paper and assignments and asked to write their names on them. In the following days and weeks they are introduced to school life rituals and tasks: they learn to eat their lunch faster, they raise their hand before speaking, they learn what the bell ringing means, they learn new games at the blackboard and they play altogether on new premises – in the much bigger playground and in shorter time slots. Most children take great care and pride in adhering to all the new tasks and activities. The boldest ones also try out the teacher's patience by teasing and testing how disobedient they can be before she scolds; but mostly they are eagerly trying out and realizing what being a schoolchild is and how it is for them – and within a few weeks they seem accustomed to the new rules of school life. Most children are more timid, less confident and certainly more sensitive than they were in day care. Sandra is quiet in plenary situations but more confident in the playground where she and Clara are meeting new classmates and get to know the other girls through play. Alex is enthusiastic and prepared: he has chosen a table right in front of the teacher's desk and proudly shows me his enormous pencil house, full of equipment: he is particularly happy with his magnifying glass, enabling him to do drawings perfectly and in a very precise manner. There is a gradual build-up of new everyday routines, new games are played in the schoolyard and new friendships in the making – and also gradually less timid ways of participating as the new class gets established and the classroom as well as each child in it settles down.

(Dis)Integration: the temporary outcome of the transitional crisis is one of disintegration or positive integration. Integration describes the situation in which a child embraces his or her new role and place in the peer group and in the eyes of the teacher. All children are in a state of crisis at the beginning of the phase of realization. Their present social status, their relationships, prospects of fitting in, affiliation with shared values and commitments are unsettled, but already from the beginning the children try themselves out in self-presentations and the teacher encourages them and shows her approval. Alex integrates and throws himself eagerly into the different tasks. If they are asked to colour pictures, he makes sure to colour them perfectly. He also eagerly seeks the teacher's approval and she often rewards him with positive appraisal for his hard work. Disintegration denotes the situation when a child is negatively identified and finds him/herself in a marginalized social position in objection to or in direct conflict with the norms and values expressed by the teacher and peers. In cases of dis-integration the child only very reluctantly identifies with the new situation and his/her own place in it as a schoolkid. All children, except one in my observational study, integrated positively into the classroom (for an examination of that case see Winther-Lindqvist, 2009). The reason why this boy had trouble starting school had to do with his friendship status among the other

boys, who he used to play soccer with in day care. In school, they all stopped playing soccer and he therefore lost his popular status as the best soccer player. The other children all reported being happy with school during the systematic conversation round, carried out by the teacher ten weeks into the school year. The children were asked whether they enjoyed school life, the breaks, the lessons, their classmates, and most of them made only happy smileys. They also admitted to being exhausted at night and some even reported that they fell asleep during tea. Alex told his teacher that he was a little disappointed with lessons and explained that he thought that they were going to learn to write and read properly – but instead they were singing, drawing and playing a lot of the time. He also requested homework. With regards to breaks he said he enjoyed playing with his older brother and his friends. The teacher expressed concern about his social integration as he reported having no best friend. However, he was not used to having a best friend in day care and did not expect to find one in class. Sandra revealed that she was relieved upon starting school. She said in a small voice: 'I worried, because I thought that I was supposed to know how to read.' The teacher laughs heartedly: 'You thought so. No! that is what you'll learn here in school.' 'I know that now – that is nice', Sandra replied with a smile. In that way, the vast majority of children met the reality of school in ways that enabled them to engage with the new and although it is exhausting it is mainly exciting. The problems some of the children encountered with school were generated in the new environment, and their new relationships through the new activities; thus these are inherently unpredictable and unforeseeable from the perspective of day care. This ultimately places the main responsibility on the environment receiving the child, not on the environment that hands them over.

Cancelling the beginning: What's new in reception class?

Due to the stepwise transition practice in Denmark, the children are accustomed to the physical surroundings at school (they know their way around, and where to find toys and they know the different play areas), and most children also know most of their classmates on the first day at school; if not from day care, then from the leisure-time activity centre based at the school, where they have been for a few months before reception class. Obviously, there are new activities, rules and relationships in the new classroom and the reception class teacher is new. However, these new practices are soon, after the first 3–4 weeks, integrated as customary by the children and the content of most of the actual activities are in fact still preparatory. Tasks and demands involve more the working *form* of school rather than the actual working content or subject matter of learning specific skills. In this sense, both Alex and Sandra could have been corrected in their imaginings of what school would be like. Sandra thought and feared that she was expected to already know how to read and Alex thought he would be taught right away to read, write, do maths and have homework. Exploratory dialogues with each child during day care, investigating their expectations in a more detailed way, may have revealed some of these misguided imaginings. Yet, despite these misunderstandings, both Alex and Sandra settled well into school life, and integrated positively into their new social situations and identities as schoolchildren, although they both felt insecure and anxious about it at the beginning.

Concluding comments

Overall, it seems that the transition into school life is well managed in the Danish educational system. The compulsory reception class is designed to welcome day-care children into the school environment and hopefully challenges a boy like Alex, while at the same time avoiding stressing out those children with a less firmly developed learning motive. The danger-rhetoric of the school transition as a culture shock seems exaggerated and it also lacks empirical support. Regarding the school transition as an endangering event reflects a lack of appreciation of different forms of transition of which some are unexpected, others are prepared for; some result from disempowering events, and some are mainly empowering: the institutional transition of starting school is an empowering event vested with ideas of a future, of oneself as a schoolchild. That said, there remains room for improvement. It seems that the children imaginatively prepared for a school life (both individually and collectively) resembling the reality of primary school, rather than the much more play-oriented theme and project-based reception class environment that they meet in reality. This creates unnecessary disappointments and anxiety. Furthering the dialogue between day care and reception class, so that the children are encouraged to form realistic expectations of reception class could be a solution to this problem (see Broström, 2013 for further elaboration and solutions). However, this pedagogical preparation should take place *right before* starting school rather than as a lengthy process, which exhausts the engagement with day care and fosters impatience when actually realizing the change experientially.

The danger-rhetoric of the transition, which I challenge in this text, also has another and even more problematic implication, as it may serve to legitimize an overall tendency in the educational system towards focusing more and more narrowly on testable learning outcomes, and speeding up the academic performance of children. In this spirit, the 2nd and 3rd Grade curriculum of today will be tomorrow's reception class and 1st Grade curriculum, with the purpose of enhancing our chances in the global competition. If school induction is regarded as too much of a culture shock for children, why don't we start school earlier, or start teaching children subject matter already in early care? It is possible to teach children subject matter at a much earlier age than is the present case in Denmark – but according to cultural-historical developmental thinking, it violates the psychology of the preschool child, who mainly learns and develops through playing and who in that process also gain experience of how to navigate the difficult task of participating in social life and group activities with others (Hedegaard & Fleer, 2013). Playing together requires flexibility, initiative, negotiation, imagination, solidarity, seriousness, respect for others and compromising (Winther-Lindqvist, 2017). It is also an arena for making friends and sustaining friendships, solving differences and exploring themes together. These competences are much needed in reception class (and beyond), where adult resources are scarcer and children are expected to – and requested to – work in small groups on their own, solve conflicts between themselves and manage all together, with much less one-to-one assistance from adults.

So, rather than minimizing differences between day care and reception class, we should encourage even richer playing environments in day care and rebuild the professional pride in supporting children in their socio-emotional and personal development. If we succeed in this, the children are psychologically ready to profit from a clear experiential difference from the more project-theme-based teaching environment in reception class. If reception class does not involve anything substantially new it becomes merely a continuation of day care – and the children are being over-prepared. Over-preparation is preparing for another preparation, with exhausting engagement in the now as a result, as well as a sense of disappointment, when the transition is finally materialized. Perhaps a re-conceptualization of the transition to school as a positive developmental crisis, as suggested by scholars inspired by the cultural-historical developmental tradition, can create a more fruitful appreciation of what both day care and school have to offer the child in terms of development.

References

Boettcher, L. (in press), 'Children with disabilities growing up and becoming adults: Socio-cultural challenges around the transition to adulthood', in M. Hedegaard & A. Edwards (eds), *Support for children, young people and their carers in difficult transition: Working in the zone of social concern* (Ch 8). London: Bloomsbury Publishing.

Børnerådet (2013), *Skolen – set fra børnehaven: børns forventninger til og forestillinger om skolen*. Børnerådet.

Bowlby, J. (2005), *A secure base: Clinical applications of attachment theory*. Abingdon: Routledge.

Bozhovich, L. I. (2009), 'The social situation of child development', *Journal of Russian and East European Psychology*, 47(4), 59–86.

Brewer, J. & A. Sparkes (2011), 'Parentally bereaved children and post-traumatic growth: Insights from an ethnographic study of a UK childhood bereavement service', *Mortality*, 16(3), 204–222.

Broström, S. (2005), 'Transition problems and play as transitory activity', *Australian Journal of Early Childhood*, 30(3), 17–25.

Broström, S. (2007), 'Transitions in children's thinking', in H. Fabian & A. Dunlop (eds), *Informing transitions in the early years: Research, policy and practice*. Maidenhead: Open University Press.

Broström, S. (2013), 'Play as the main road in children's transition to school', in O. F. Lillemyr, S. Dockett, B. Perry (eds), *Varied perspectives on play and learning* (pp. 37–53). Charlotte, NC: Information Age Publishing.

Bureau 2000 (2017), *Udviklingstendenser på daginstitutionsområdet*. http://www.bureau2000.dk/images/udgivelser/Born_og_unge/Tendenser%20p%20dagtilbudsomrdet%202017.pdf.

Cecchin, D. (2003), Min vej til skolen er fuld af huller. I: *0–14. Årg. 13*, 2, (92–96).

Chaiklin, S. (2011), 'Kulturhistorisk psykologi. I', in B Karpatschof & B Katzenelson (eds), *Klassisk og moderne psykologisk teori* (pp. 319–348). København: Hans Reitzels Forlag.

Elberling, H., A. Linneberg, E. M. Olsen et al. (2010), 'The prevalence of SDQ-measured mental health problems at age 5-7 years and identification of predictors from birth to day care age in a Danish birth cohort: The Copenhagen Child Cohort 2000', *European Child & Adolescent Psychiatry*, 19 (9), 725–735.

Fabian, H. (2007), 'The challenges of starting school', in J. Moyles, *Early years foundations: Meeting the challenge* (pp. 159–172). Maidenhead: Open University Press.

Fleer, M. (2014), *Theorising play in the early years*. New York: Cambridge University Press.

Hedegaard, M. (2003), 'Børn og unges udvikling diskuteret ud fra et kultur-historisk perspektiv', *Nordiske Udkast, Årg. 31*, 1, 27–45.

Hedegaard, M. (2009), 'Children's development from a cultural-historical approach: Children's activity in everyday local settings as foundation for their development', *Mind, Culture & Activity*, 16(1), 64–82.

Hedegaard, M. (2012), 'Analyzing children's learning and development in everyday settings from a cultural-historical wholeness approach', *Mind, Culture & Activity*, 19(2), 127–138.

Hedegaard, M. (2014), 'The significance of demands and motives across practices in children's learning and development: An analysis of learning in home and school', *Learning, Culture and Social Interaction*, 3, 188–194.

Hedegaard, M. & M. Fleer (2013), *Play, learning, and children's development: Everyday life in families and transition to school*. New York: Cambridge University Press.

Larsen, I. S. (2009), 'Den gode overgang: om at komme godt af sted og sikkert frem. I', *0–14, Årg. 19*, 2, 12–17.

Larsen, I. S. (2010), 'Læring og udvikling i overgangen mellem børnehave og skole: børn har brug for voksnes støtte i overgangen. I', *Vera*, 52, 30–35.

Lewin, K. (1935), *A dynamic theory of personality: Selected papers*. New York: McGraw-Hill.

Retsinformation (2017), *Bekendtgørelse af lov om folkeskolen*. Lokaliseret d. 4. april 2017 på:https://www.retsinformation.dk/forms/r0710.aspx?id=182008

Sepstrup. A. (2017), Da første skoledag forsvandt. Unpublished Masters thesis, from Danish School of education.

Undervisningsministeriet (2017), *Statistik om alder for skolestartere*.http://www.uvm.dk/statistik/grundskolen/elever/alder-ved-skolestart

Vrinioti, K., H. Einarsdottir & S. Broström (2010), 'Transitions from preschool to primary school', in *Early years transition programme* (pp. 16–21). http://www.ease-eu.com/documents/compendium/compendium.pdf.

Vygotsky, L. (1998), 'Child psychology', in R. Rieber (ed.), *The collected works of L. S. Vygotsky. vol. 5*. New York: Plenum Press.

Weirsøe, M. (2012), 'Farvel til første skoledag: Goddag til én lang uddannelse. I', *Børn og unge.Forskning*, 15(4–8).

Wentzer, T. (2015), 'The eternal recurrence of the new', in S. Liisberg, E. Pedersen & A. Dalsgård (eds), *Anthropology & philosophy: Dialogues on trust and hope* (pp. 76–90). New York: Berghahn Books.

Winther-Lindqvist, D. (2009), Children's Development of social identity in transitions: A comparative study. Unpublished PhD dissertation. Department of Psychology. Copenhagen University.

Winther-Lindqvist, D. (2012), 'Developing social identities and motives in school transitions', in M. Hedegaard, A. Edwards & M. Fleer, *Motives in children's development: Cultural-historical approaches* (pp. 115–133). Cambridge: Cambridge University Press.

Winther-Lindqvist, D. (2013), *Early childhood education in Denmark*. Oxford: Oxford University Press. http://www.oxfordbibliographies.com/view/document/obo-

9780199756810/obo-97801997568100093.xml?rskey=pbJIxA&result=1&q=Early+C
hildhood+Education+in+Denmark#firstMatch

Winther-Lindqvist, D. (2016), 'Time together – time apart: Nothingness and hope in teenagers', in J. Bang & D. Winther-Lindqvist (eds), *Nothingness: Philosophical insights into psychology* (pp. 143–168). New York: Routledge.

Winther-Lindqvist, D. (2017), 'The role of play in Danish child care', in C. Ringsmose & G. Kragh-Müller (eds), *Nordic social pedagogical approach to early years*. Dordrecht: Springer Press.

Zittoun, T. (2006), *Transitions: Development through symbolic resources*. Charlotte, NC: Information Age Publishing.

Children from Expatriate Families Moving Countries and Entering School Mid-semester: New Entrants Transitioning into Established Practices

Megan Adams and Marilyn Fleer

Introduction

This chapter illustrates the unique developmental conditions of young children who regularly move countries as a result of their parents working for multinational companies. These families are termed expatriates. There are differences that distinguish the expatriate population from other transient populations. It is thought that expatriate families experience high mobility (Pollock & Van Reken, 2009), due to employment opportunities with multinational companies, staying for only a short time in one country prior to being transferred to the next country where the adults' specialized skill sets are required. Common to expatriate families is the belief that they will eventually repatriate (Pollock & Van Reken, 2009). This is different to families who transition to countries (immigrants, refugees) to gain citizenship and stay in the receiving country and return to their country of origin for short time periods only. Expatriate families experience a transient lifestyle, and it is argued in this chapter that this results in different developmental conditions for the children because they frequently experience multiple transitions during their early childhood years. How transitions are experienced and tensions resolved by children is the central problem of this chapter.

The aim of this chapter is to theorize the developmental conditions of expatriate children transitioning into the established practice traditions of classrooms in an international school. The concepts of demands and motives (Hedegaard, 2014) are used to discuss the unique conditions of expatriate children transitioning into a new country, transitioning into an international school and transitioning into a classroom midway through a school year: specifically, how children from expatriate families enter into an established classroom and experience free play time is explored.

A cultural-historical conception of transition informs the theoretical discussion in this chapter and is used to frame a holistic presentation of three focus children from expatriate families who moved countries and commenced their early education in an international school. The children's experiences are illustrative of new understandings of the complexity of transitions because the developmental conditions afforded through transitioning by expatriate families have not been fully discussed in the literature.

To achieve the aim of this chapter, the first part presents a general discussion of the central concept of transitions found in the literature. This is followed by a theoretical orientation to the cultural-historical conception of transitions (Hedegaard, 2014; Hedegaard & Edwards, 2014), followed by illustrations of the play activities of three focus children in transition. Like other chapters in this volume, our theorization elaborates on the existing understandings of the concept of transitions.

Different lenses on transition

To foreground the complexity of transitions in the context of the theoretical discussion in this chapter, the existing literature is considered and three key dimensions are discussed. In the first section transitions across countries are discussed. In the second section, transitions into schools are reviewed. Finally, a range of theoretical perspectives in relation to the specific studies are featured.

Children's transitions to a different country is the key focus of this chapter. In reviewing this body of work, there is a vast array of literature that comments on the phenomenon of large populations that transition across countries in the twenty-first century. This literature stems from diverse theoretical perspectives (see Srinivasan, 2014; Teras, 2012) and includes different populations such as immigrants and refugees (Walters & Auton-Cuff, 2009); the military who move family units within and between countries (Strobino & Salvaterra, 2000); missionaries moving countries (Cameron, 2003) and in some situations, only some members of the family move country for educational purposes. For example, Kim (2010) discusses South Korean mothers and their children who move countries so the children can be educated outside of the South Korean education system.

The father usually stays in Korea to continue working, to financially support the children's education. There is a growing body of literature that reports on families with young children where one or both parents work for multinational companies (Adams & Fleer, 2015; Useem & Downie, 1976). It appears that transitions across countries have been studied extensively over the past four decades, as populations move across countries (Märtsin & Mahmoud, 2012) and move between cultures (Hedegaard, 2005, 2011). However, the reasons for families with young children undertaking transitions across countries vary considerably.

The second key dimension noted when reviewing the literature on transitions is the large body of research that centres on children's initial transition into school. These studies primarily draw upon Bronfenbrenner's (1979) original ecological model of human development (e.g., Dockett, Petriwskyj & Perry, 2014) to frame their research. Some have also used Bronfenbrenner & Morris's (2006) bioecological principles for discussing transition, where the process-person-context-time (PPCT) frames the study design and findings (see Dunlop, 2014). Studies of transitions have also been framed through metaphors, such as 'bridges' (Garpelin, 2011) and 'borderlands' (Peters, 2014) as a way of better understanding transition into school. Transitions have been primarily defined as 'involving a range of interactions and processes over time, experienced in different ways by different people in different contexts' (Dockett et al., 2014, p. 3). However, these broad definitions say very little about the microgenetic movements that we might find as children transition between activity settings within institutions in a new country.

A third dimension evident in the transition literature is the relation between traditions and value practices across institutions and activity settings from a cultural-historical perspective. Teras (2012) argues that immigration and the mobility of large portions of a population provide challenges and tensions for societies due to the conditions created throughout the transition process at a societal, community and individual level. For instance, immigrants may experience challenging transitions due to 'rapid social and economic changes' (Teras, 2012, p. 504) in their life circumstances. De Haan & Elbers (2008) narrow this conception to concentrate on situations in schools and the way varying ethnic groups are placed together in collaborative learning situations. Some students experience stability, whereas others experience or challenge accepted traditions and values that are built from historical sameness. Collectively, a socio-cultural (Valsiner, 1998) or cultural-historical conception of transitions (Hedegaard, 2014; Hedegaard & Edwards, 2014) examines the demands made upon an individual throughout their everyday life experiences, and examines how the new demands are resolved and adjustments made to successfully support the transition experience. Hedegaard & Fleer (2013) argue that demands placed on children at home and school generate opportunities for learning and development. An integral part of learning that is often overlooked are the social motives and demands that children experience as they move across everyday life, but also within activity settings situated in the classroom (one notable exception being Hedegaard & Fleer, 2013). Lawrence, Benedikt & Valsiner (1992) found that during a transition into a new culture, participants may depart from a specific culture, which may cause discontinuity that requires some form of resolution. In contrast, Sánchez-Medina, Macías-Gómez-Stern & Martínez-Lozano (2014) examined school transition practices for children of immigrant families in Spain and found that the main goal of the school was to assimilate the students into the mainstream values of society. Interestingly, the parents' and schools' value positions were similar, as parents indicated that their children required learning and skills that would enable them to gain access and participate in Spanish society in the future.

Although there is a growing body of cultural-historical literature that examines transitions from one country to another, it appears that the majority of cultural-historical research is focused on practice traditions as children move between home and school (see for example, Hedegaard, 2014; Hedegaard & Fleer, 2013) or microgenetic movements within the classroom when working with digital technology (Fleer, 2014). In these studies, participants have shared histories, practice traditions, values and expectations of the activity settings (Winther-Lindqvist, 2013) and there is an understanding of the importance of children's assimilation into society for future possibilities (Hedegaard, 2005; Sánchez-Medina et al., 2014). However, in some instances, the child's history may be similar but not shared (de Haan & Elbers, 2008) with those in their classroom, resulting in multiple types of transitions that may be experienced by the children and their families. It appears that cultural-historical studies of young children's multilayered transitions is limited. Consequently, a cultural-historical exploration of young children moving between countries, attending new institutions, as well as transitioning within and between activity settings in a classroom midway through a school year, is urgently needed to understand this unique and complex set of conditions.

In this chapter, we argue that a broader analytical frame is needed for an examination of how children transition when moving countries, and how they simultaneously enter into established practice traditions in a school mid-semester. That is, a child's entrance into an institution part way through the year where practices, routines, values, learning schedules and friendship groups may be well established. As young children enter into an international school midway through the semester, a sequence of challenges and tensions may ensue, as children from expatriate families have other real-world experiences originating from home and previous countries resided in, which may be different to those within the current society and the established practice traditions in the classroom. It is in this transition between past experience and expectations and current practice traditions that complex demands are made on the transitioning child. This chapter seeks to theorize and better understand these new demands made on children from expatriate families by drawing upon Hedegaard's conception of transition.

Hedegaard's conception of transition

In Hedegaard's (2014) model, the laws and policies set by society are enacted at the institutional level and it is through participation in these institutions that demands are made upon the individual. In Hedegaard's (2005, 2011) original research, which is directly relevant to the case examples reported in this chapter, young people from migrant families residing in Denmark were interviewed regarding their transition into their new educational setting. The study showed how the Danish education system and immigrant family values varied and this put demands upon the youth. According to Hedegaard (2005), these demands were connected to the creation of societies that are imagined, originating from the immigrant's 'own lived community and family practice' (p. 188), which is different to living life in Denmark as a Dane and the immigrant's previous life in Turkey. In this example, young people imagine known traditions from lived experiences, which they bring with them as they transition into a new society. Adams (2014) in her previous research, points out that when moving countries with very young children, the absence of routine created tensions and challenges with highly charged emotional moments. Attending school was one of the first stable routines for the children, which supported emotional stability in the home. Different societies have different values, which are realized in the practice traditions of the institutions in their local communities. For young children entering into these new institutions, such as their new school, tension and challenges may be created or an easy transition may occur.

According to Hedegaard (2014), the institutional practices shape the activity settings. Resources may be made available to participants for learning or for play depending on the age of the participant and the practice traditions of the institution. When children enter into new practices they meet new demands, which in turn determine how successful or otherwise they are in the process of transitioning into their new school environment. The home and the school create different opportunities for learning as the traditions, aims and objectives vary, providing different possibilities within activity settings for play and learning (Hedegaard, 2014). In school, how youths or young children enter into new activity settings, is determined by their motive orientation and their expectations for play or for learning and the demands of others in the setting. In this chapter, we are concerned with better understanding the dynamic and complex forms of transition theorized by Hedegaard (2014) in relation to the experience of young expatriate children who move to Malaysia with their families. For example, one expatriate family with a three-year-old moved from New Zealand to Malaysia and the child entered full-time school for the first time. Therefore, we wanted to examine the demands that newly arrived children meet when transitioning from family practices into a new school midway through a school year. How do children enter into the classroom mid-semester, where practice traditions are in place, and how do children transition between the differing activity settings organized by teachers that have become routine for other children?

In the context of the international school studied, it is possible that children who begin school are likely to be oriented to play, even though schools create the conditions to orient children towards learning. Hedegaard (2002) has argued that teachers seek to orient children towards subject knowledge by using play activities that provide motivating conditions, and which in turn allow children to connect with the subject matter that teachers expect children to learn. This requires conditions that support play activities to develop over time. Therefore, when children transition into school midway through a school year established play activities and institutional routines are already set, placing new demands upon the children who seek to enter into these activity settings. How this is experienced and resolved by the children is the central problem theorized in this chapter.

Methodological considerations

In Hedegaard's research, the importance of gaining the child's perspective is seen as an analytical concept and is central to Hedegaard's (2012) wholeness approach. To understand the child's perspective, we need to analyse each participant's intentions in the social situation. This directs attention to the demands young children face within these activity settings and how this creates new conditions for children's development. In our exploration of transitions, video observations were used as the main approach for making observations of children as they entered into, and sought to participate in, the activities found within the new institutional setting after moving countries.

When making video observations the researcher is positioned to capture children's play, the dialogue with teachers and other children, to follow the demands children meet, to note the conditions for developing new motive orientations, and to document the valued institutional practices organized by the teachers (Hedegaard et al., 2008). The researchers are able to iteratively analyse the societal values, institutional practices and personal motives and demands of children participating in particular contexts, such as the international school. How children meet these demands forms the basis of the analysis. For example, if a child in transition is new to the institutional practices, play settings and players, they are less likely to know the expected social motives and demands, which include the roles and rules of play. The new children may be included/excluded or explicitly introduced to the rules. New practice settings create new demands upon the child, which in turn places demands upon the new setting and those children and adults working in the classroom. These moments potentially give insight into how the institutional practices are being experienced by the child as part of their everyday life in the institution. Collectively, an analysis of the demands and motives in the new activity setting provides insight into how the child is experiencing the transition into their new school midway through the school year.

Following three focus children

In this chapter, the illustrative examples originate from three children's experiences of starting school midway through the school year: Vissy (4 years and two months) Margie (4 years and seven months) and Zeb (3 years and nine months). Each child entered Malaysia with their respective family one month prior to entering school and had been residing in temporary accommodation until more permanent housing was available. The children were transitioning from home into an international school during the middle of the semester, having never attended preschool or an international school prior to their transition into Malaysia. The focus children were followed from halfway through the school year. These children were chosen because they were specifically from an expatriate family in transition into new practice traditions in their classrooms midway through the semester.

The broader study from which the illustrative examples originated

The larger study from which the focus children were drawn ran over a six-month period and included classrooms of focus children in three international schools and five family homes (Adams, 2014; Adams & Fleer, 2016). There was a total of 42 hours of video data collection sessions. There were 15 hours of interview data from parents, teachers and principals of the focus children. There were 90 hours of data collected.

Introducing Malaysian societal values, the institutional practices and the activity settings of an international school

Hedegaard (2005) argues that within society, the cultural and historical environment provides conditions that enable a person to learn and develop so as to create their future life. A country's history, constitution, laws, policies and regulations combine to determine the conditions for what it is to be a young child within a specific society. In addition, within a country there are both traditions, which influence the populace (history, economics) that lead to similarities in the way citizens are treated, and differences in relation to cultural and political ideals (Hedegaard, 2005). In order to understand how children enter midway through the semester into new practice traditions in an international school situated in Malaysia, it is important to examine the societal values, the established institutional practices and individual perspectives of the focus children. We briefly introduce the conditions in Malaysia and the international school as a backdrop for understanding the illustrative example of Vissy, Margie and Zeb presented later.

Malaysian societal context

Similar to other countries in today's highly mobile world, in Malaysian society there is 'a racial mix of people including indigenous tribes, the Malays (65 per cent), recent Chinese immigrants (26 per cent) Indians (8 per cent) and others (1 per cent)' (Zhao, 2011, p. ix). Malaysian society has a unique cultural identity, which is influenced by Persian, Arabic, Portuguese and British cultures (Zhao, 2011). Expatriates move to Malaysia mainly in professional roles with multinational companies. The Malaysian Department of Immigration (MDI, 2014) suggests there are over 90,000 visas issued for expatriates working in Malaysia. The number increases to 200,000 when other types of visas are included, such as those residing in Malaysia with dependent visas (MDI, 2014). This is a small percentage of the overall population. The main interest here is the positioning of the British international school situated within the constraints of the Malaysian society. The school provides a British education for expatriates and local national families who decide that an international education based on the British system would best suit their child's future opportunities.

Institutional perspective: The expatriate home practice traditions

As expatriate families transition into countries, the initial few weeks are usually spent in temporary accommodation while more permanent housing is sought. Children often attend school while residing in temporary accommodation such as a hotel (Adams, 2014). Families begin to frequent new institutions where new social interactions and contacts are established. It is in these new institutions that families may experience institutional practices that vary from routine family practices, resulting in contradictions 'between the child's known and the new social situation of development' (Adams, 2016, p. 93). For example, having a playdate in temporary accommodation may be a challenging experience as the family does not have the same resources (games, toys) as in the family home.

The children from the expatriate families that we followed all stayed in temporary accommodation for up to six weeks and the children began attending school from the hotels. Mothers commented that routines were challenging to establish and there were many emotional moments due to the lack of a normal everyday life (Adams, 2014). Initially, when the families arrived, the fathers travelled for work purposes. The mothers were left in Kuala Lumpur with the children to sort out everyday life, which involved locating permanent housing, finding schools, equipping children with school uniforms, locating transport, medical practitioners, and becoming organized socially. All of the mothers interviewed felt they had initially been deserted and tasked with sole care of the children in a foreign country (Adams, 2014). This included weekends as when the fathers returned and were present, they were exhausted due to their challenging travel schedules, working across differing time zones and settling in to a new position.

Institutional perspective: The international school practice traditions

The school that the three focus children attended is situated in Kuala Lumpur, Malaysia and caters for children ranging in age from 3 to 18 years old. International schools originated to cater for children of expatriate families with practice traditions similar to those in their country of origin (Hayden, 2006). However, more recently, international schools are open to all those who are able to pay the fees, with numbers limited by government directives.

The school implements the British curriculum across all age levels. Specifically, in the early years, the British Early Years Foundation Stage Statutory Framework (EYFS), is implemented and provides standards for learning and development for children ranging in age from birth to age five (Department for Education, 2014). The school has been assessed by the Office for Standards in Education (OFSTED), which is the accreditation body for all schools that follow the British Statutory Framework. Following the EYFS, the school advocates that for very young children the day should be divided equally between play and structured learning.

The international school is regulated by combining local Malaysian laws with British laws, for example, 'Agama', is a compulsory subject for local nationals only and is specifically targeted at the indigenous Malay populace. The subject has its foundation in local ideology, geography, history, language and religion and is taught alongside the British curriculum. Therefore, there is 'situated local practice' (Hedegaard, 2005, p. 190) as there are some institutional traditions of practice regulated by the Malaysian government as well as the British curriculum, catering for local and international students through everyday life in the school. Therefore, a space between and within cultures that refracts transitional processes as dynamic movements and dialectic relations (Teras, 2012) between the young children and cultural practices is present within the international school environment.

Specific to the focus children in this chapter (Vissy, Margie and Zeb) is their classroom and Ann, their teacher. Ann catered for families with very young children, by introducing a 'rolling drop off system' between 8.30–10.30 am and delaying attendance reporting until after 10.30. According to Ann, this was received positively by the parents with toddlers and babies as implementing this system recognized physical societal constraints (poor road system, large distances travelled by some families and an inner-city school with heavy traffic congestion) and the demands of very young children when leaving the house for an 8.30 am school drop off. The classroom organization was also fluid, with children moving in and out of free play and completing discipline-specific work either one-to-one with an adult or in small groups of up to five children. Ann acknowledged the main goal for early years' education was the social and emotional development of each child and the foundational skills of academic learning. Many of the activities provided children with the possibility of linking their life outside of school to their learning in school and acknowledged the culture of Malaysia (for example, providing playdough with a dim sum basket and rolling pins during Chinese New Year). Ann encouraged all of the adults in the room to support the children to help one another in learning and following routines: some examples include teachers stating, 'Tommy needs help remembering to put his hat on before play, I wonder if Mark would help him remember for the rest of today?' or 'Sue, could you invite Faye into your play?' or 'What do you need to do and say when you want a teacher's attention? … (put hand up and say excuse me)', 'We don't push in line'. During delivery of these instructions, the teacher would make sure that they were on the same level as the child, making eye contact and with their voice loud enough so that each person in the vicinity could hear. The children in the class were invited to participate in school learning activities such as addition and subtraction games or completing writing activities. As the activity was completed, the children were encouraged to participate in free play with their peers.

Ann is supported by two assistant teachers, Kiran and Nellie, who were in the classroom for the majority of the day. The classroom was a double room with windows on the north and south sides and had direct access to a self-contained lush tropical garden. The room was similar to a well-resourced class in Britain with a variety of objects, materials and large pieces of furniture. The room was divided into learning centres, consisting of a mat for whole class activities (story reading and at the beginning and end of the day); a reading corner with a large comfortable chair, settee and English language books; dress-up area with three rows of dress-up clothes hanging on a clothes rack at the children's height; games area with tables and chairs and four computers. The room was decorated with children's artefacts, such as paintings, art and craft, numerical and alphabetical work on the walls and hanging from the ceiling – as it was Chinese New Year many of the artefacts were red and of Chinese origin.

The majority of the children in the classroom were from expatriate families originating from British heritage and Commonwealth countries such as Australia and New Zealand. The other nationalities were Asian children originating from Sri Lanka, Korea and local Malay nationals. The language of instruction was English with two support staff (Nellie and Kiran), both of whom could speak

Malay, Hindi and Mandarin fluently. The first named researcher noted that the majority of children often played travel games, such as making passports and moving through scanners at the airport, pretending to travel to different countries on aeroplanes, or packing and unpacking suitcases.

Children's perspective: Vissy, Margie and Zeb

At an individual level, each person (children and adults) participates in everyday life with their own motives, competences and demands, contributing to their own development and understanding of the world (Hedegaard, 2014).

Vissy's family originated from Sri Lanka and had previously lived in London. Vissy's father had entered Malaysia two months prior to the family with the aim of establishing a life for his family in Kuala Lumpur. However, he travelled extensively and was unable to find the time to locate more permanent housing prior to the family arriving so they were living in temporary accommodation. Vissy did not participate in 'playdates' due to the mother being busy with organizing more permanent accommodation and transport. Vissy was new to the country and the British school was her first time in a formal classroom. In the classroom, Vissy spent time watching other children and attempting to enter the play. Ann (the teacher) had asked for a volunteer to help Vissy with routine tasks. The volunteer was keen to play with her friendship group and although occasionally she offered to help Vissy, her focus was not with Vissy.

Margie's family originated from the Netherlands and had resided in Texas and France. Margie's first language was Dutch and she was developing as an English speaker. Margie had a younger brother and an older sister. The family had recently moved from temporary accommodation into a housing compound close to the school. Margie and a class peer, Seon, enjoyed completing jigsaw puzzles and in free play they gravitated to the various puzzles in the classroom. The British international school was Margie's first experience of full-time school. Margie's mother commented that they had not invited other children from school to playdates as everyday life was too challenging when living in the hotel.

Zeb's mother originated from England and his father from New Zealand. As a family, they had resided in Singapore and New Zealand. Zeb had one younger sister. Zeb's home life was described as 'chaotic' by his mother as they were unpacking boxes and trying to sort out their belongings. The British international school was his first full-time school. Zeb had an intermittent start to the school as after starting there he went with his mother to Britain for a holiday and there were many Malaysian public holidays (Adams & Fleer, 2016).

Being an expatriate child in a British international school

We followed the three focus children Vissy, Margie and Zeb as they entered into the institutional practices of the school midway through the semester, and as they participated in the activity settings in the same classroom.

Vissy and the suitcase children

Two groups of children had completed their number game with the teacher and were released to play. The children divided themselves into two seemingly fluid groups. The first consisted of three children who chose a large jigsaw puzzle; they began to complete the puzzle on the carpet in front of the digital video camera. The second group consisted of four girls who walked to the dress-up area and on the way picked up a small plastic see-through suitcase. One of the girls using a playful voice suggested they pack for a holiday. Penny, the self-designated leader started to take clothes off the dress-up hangers, fold them and place them gently into the suitcase. This action initiated an imaginary situation where Penny shared that her father was going to his 'business shop' in another country and Mummy was packing his suitcase ('I am Mummy'). A discussion ensued regarding whose father travelled for work, which led to a negotiation of what to pack in the suitcase and what to take in carry-on luggage for Daddy's trip to another country.

Vissy was standing observing the four children participating in the imaginary suitcase play. Focused on the play, Penny indicated that pressed shirts and ties needed to go in the suitcase, neatly folded and then the case needed to be closed. The children could not close the suitcase and they began to negotiate which clothes were required and which ones could be discarded. Vissy was standing apart from the group and observed the play, she smiled and mentioned that the children forgot to put in clean socks and that her Daddy visited other countries for work too. Penny explicitly stated that Vissy's Daddy did not go to the same country as everyone else's and therefore Vissy could not join the play. Vissy showed visible signs of emotion (head down, pouting lips) and relocated herself to the other group of children nearby, who were completing a jigsaw puzzle on the carpet. Vissy stated in a high-pitched, wavering voice, 'They're not playing with me'. One of the children responded with, 'You can play' and another one stated, 'You can play with us Vissy' and provided Vissy with a jigsaw piece to position. Vissy sat near the puzzle holding the jigsaw piece, she did not move to place the piece in the puzzle and averted her eyes towards the children playing with the suitcase. Vissy had a sad face, shown by a slightly pouting lower lip and glassy eyes.

Analysis: Suitcase play

Vissy explicitly tried to enter the play by using socially acceptable actions, smiling, moving into close proximity with the collective and making a suggestion of what was missing from the suitcase. However, prior to the moment of interjection by Vissy, the intention of the children packing the suitcase was to discard some clothes so the suitcase could be closed. We can interpret Vissy trying to enter the play as making a demand on the children packing the suitcase that could not be met within the sphere of play (Schousboe, 2013) as putting more into the suitcase was opposite to the negotiations of the children discussing what to take out. Therefore, Vissy's demands were not in line with the motive of the collective.

In the suitcase example, we interpret varying motive orientations within the sphere of reality of play (Schousboe, 2013). Vissy's intention was to be included and play with the suitcase children. Through Vissy's interjection in the suitcase play, we infer she had experienced seeing her father's suitcase being packed for a business trip at home. Although holding similar knowledge and experience to the established children in the class, this experience was met with exclusion from the dominant sphere of imagination by the suitcase children. Once excluded, Vissy moved to sit close to a group of children completing a jigsaw puzzle. Vissy voiced her opinion about being excluded from play to the children working on the jigsaw puzzle, who welcomed her into their play. However, Vissy excluded herself and sat with her back to the jigsaw puzzle and watched the suitcase children.

From an institutional perspective, there were varying points of tension that occurred between the institutional traditions, which meant the meaning-making motives of the children did not align. The space between the inclusive cultural expectations of the adults and the actual play in the activity setting created tension for Vissy but not for the group of children packing the suitcase.

From a personal perspective, the play scenarios of packing the suitcase and completing the jigsaw puzzle, there were variations in demands and motive orientations between the collective and the individual. The suitcase example highlights two forms of exclusion: first Vissy was excluded from the play that was taking place within this activity setting; second, Vissy self-excluded (jigsaw puzzle play). The exclusion from the activity setting was instigated by the established children packing the suitcase and then by Vissy, whose second choice was to sit near the jigsaw puzzle. After listening to Vissy's explanation of what had occurred, the jigsaw children encouraged her to join in but Vissy showed obvious signs that her intention was to play with the children packing the suitcase and therefore excluded herself from participation in completion of the jigsaw puzzle, highlighting that the collective motive of the established children and Vissy's individual motive did not align – even though the theme of the play was similarly motivating. The new institutional setting placed demands upon Vissy that resulted in collective and self-exclusion. Researching how Vissy met the new demands is important for understanding the dynamic of the activity setting (Hedegaard, 2012) and how children can and do enter into but are excluded and also self-exclude from established play practices.

Margie in the puzzle activity setting

The suitcase and jigsaw puzzle play continued. Vissy moved away from the puzzle to another group. The children who invited Vissy to play continued to piece together the large jigsaw puzzle on the floor. The jigsaw was almost complete but the children could not locate the last piece. Margie, who was new to the classroom, located the last piece of the puzzle, pointed excitedly to the remaining space in the jigsaw and with a high pitched voice stated quickly, 'Here it goes, here it goes.' Margie walked quickly across the almost completed puzzle to obtain the missing piece. Seon saw the piece simultaneously, both children bent down quickly to fetch the jigsaw piece. Margie stood up with the piece in her hand and returned joyously to place the last piece in the puzzle. Margie looked at Seon with a big smile and said, 'DONE!' Seon returned the smile.

Penny (the leader of the suitcase group) who continued to play with the suitcase out of frame stated, 'You just snatched it. Sophie, Margie just snatched, this um, snatched that piece because Seon had it first.' The four children (one holding the suitcase) walked to where Margie was standing. Penny crouched down on the floor directing her gaze towards Margie stating, 'You must not snatch Margie you must not snatch, you must say please Margie, say please Margie. Say please, can I have it? Just don't go like' (repeats a snatching motion with hands).

Mel adds, 'Don't just grab it off somebody', to which Fiona responds, 'Don't just sweep it off somebody', moving her body from left to right in a sweeping motion and repeats the movement. Penny reinforces the earlier statements, 'You must say please Margie.' Margie turns to look at the researcher, eyes wide and turns back in the direction of the jigsaw puzzle with her head down. Margie does not contribute to the conversation. The suitcase girls move away.

Analysis: The jigsaw activity setting

It is interpreted that for Margie, her motive orientation was both social – to play with Seon – and to learn by matching shapes during completion of the jigsaw. Although not explicitly watching other children play, Penny noted that two children had tried to pick up the same piece of puzzle simultaneously and without questioning the intentions of either child stated that Margie had 'snatched' a piece of puzzle. The suitcase group was alerted to this potential violation of a social norm and this resulted in the four suitcase children moving quickly to the vicinity of the jigsaw puzzle, where they explained the expected rules and values to Margie.

Inclusion occurred between Margie and Seon, yet exclusion of Margie's practice occurred between the suitcase children and Margie. As the suitcase children were alerted to a situation where a piece of puzzle was allegedly snatched from another child, the suitcase children left their imaginary sphere and entered into another activity setting – the jigsaw puzzle. This was matched by physical movement of the suitcase children to the jigsaw group who were positioned on the floor looking at the completed puzzle. The suitcase children collectively reinforced the existing practice of explaining the rules of play. They surrounded Margie, moving to her level on the floor and in turn stated and reiterated the expected practice of not snatching and saying 'please'. This may be interpreted as occurring due to children imitating the practice traditions in the classroom initiated by their teachers. When a child displays some form of challenging behaviour the teacher moves to the vicinity and bends to the level of the child to explain expected practices and reiterate in explicit language expected values and rules. Similar to the first example of Vissy's exclusion, the small collective of four children supported each other in their practice of correcting Margie's actions. However, in this example the collective excluded Margie through alerting her to an expected practice tradition related to the rules and values of established classroom practice, which according to the suitcase children, Margie did not uphold.

The contradictions between the institutional traditions and practices of the British international school, where children are encouraged by teachers to include and play with each other, was not realized in the activity setting where practices, rules and values needed to be adhered to and explicitly pointed out to alleged 'offenders'. We interpret this as children following the practice traditions established by the teacher and developed through play in the activity setting. The teachers had explicitly and repeatedly stated to the children in general to include others in their play and specifically to single children to invite another child into the play. There was no mention from the adults that children should correct each other's actions. However, the teachers did practice this type of correction in a subtle way, therefore it was present in the children's everyday interactions in the activity setting. The suitcase children showed agency and corrected a situation that they interpreted as not being acceptable to the values and rules of the classroom. Therefore, we interpret this as children beginning to instruct others and creating processes for maintaining the expected rules and values of established classroom practice. This example further highlights the nature of inclusion/exclusion. Margie was included in the jigsaw play, her play practice (of allegedly snatching a jigsaw piece) resulted in exclusion by others and explicit instruction on how values and expected practices were required to be enacted in play in the classroom.

Zeb and flying high to London

Zeb was observing three children dressing up. They were discussing going on a picnic together, what to wear and what food to pack in the basket. Zeb asked if he could join the picnic but there was no response from the children. Zeb dressed himself in a purple cartoon character costume with wings. Zeb placed his arms out and started running from one end of the classroom to the other. One of the children remarked that Zeb was not allowed to run in the classroom. Zeb responded over his shoulder, 'I am not running! I am flying high to London and my plane needs the passengers to sit down, we are going too fast.' The other children looked at each other and watched Zeb do one more lap of the classroom. One of the children stood, smiled and moved towards Zeb, and it seemed possible that the child would become a passenger. At that moment, the teacher clapped her hands and stated it was time to pack up.

Analysis: Flying high observation

From a personal perspective, it can be interpreted that Zeb's motive was to join other children in their play. Zeb was explicitly excluded by the children who did not reply when asked if he could enter their play. Entrance into the play was not successful. However, Zeb changed his tactics from asking directly to constructing his own imaginary situation from a recent experience (flying return from Malaysia to London) and indirectly inviting others into the play. Initially the children rejected Zeb's running, which did not fit with expected or allowed institutional practices found in the classroom. However, Zeb explained through the imaginary situation of flying to London a different interpretation of his actions, which also appeared as an invitation to the other children to join the play by being passengers.

From an institutional perspective, there is a need for rules to keep children safe in classrooms. However, in this instance, the rules and routines of the classroom stopped Zeb from playing with another child. Once again, the children familiar to the classroom explained a valued rule (running was not acceptable). However, Zeb's answer seemed to placate one child who moved to join the flying high play. Changing the meaning of the rule from not running to a new sense of 'flying' in an 'imaginary situation' gave Zeb an opportunity to play with another child. The child appeared to accept the imaginary situation of a plane needing passengers, and this provided the possibility of a play partner for Zeb. However, in the next moment, Zeb's play was stopped by the classroom routine. Although the teacher indirectly ceased the play by calling on a routine practice (snack time), Zeb could in the future reintroduce the imaginary play. The ceasing of the play meant that Zeb's attempt to enter into and invite others to play was prevented at that moment, but this imaginary situation could be taken up again during the next free play period. In this instance, free play for skilful play partners did support a successful transition and suggests that using imaginary situations to engage with other children, gives positive developmental opportunities for expatriate children.

Discussion

It has been previously found that children of expatriate families experience multiple transitions (Adams, 2014). These movements mean that some children experience a variety of cultural and historical environments, ostensibly directed towards the development of their future life (Hedegaard, 2005). This chapter followed three focus children (Vissy, Margie and Zeb) who transitioned into Malaysian society as well as the British schooling system, experiencing new laws, regulations and values expressed through established institutional practice traditions.

An exploration of the children's transitions showed that the practice traditions created new developmental possibilities for the children as they entered into the established institutional practices of their new school. The societal practice traditions of the Malaysian and British cultures were found in everyday life in the classroom through the values, rules and regulations of the classroom. The valued practice traditions were in turn realized through the differing possibilities afforded to the three focus children during their free play time. It appeared that the teachers understood the importance of linking practice traditions of the children's everyday life outside school to the learning in the activity setting (Hedegaard, 2002) and this was shown through the provision of play spaces and relevant objects such as suitcases and clothes for the children to build imaginary play scenarios, and materials such as puzzles and books to orient children to the curriculum. The suitcase play and the flying high play both exemplify the importance of the content of children's play. Both play scenarios featured routine family practices, such as one parent packing to go on a business trip and another family going on a holiday, flying to another country.

The chapter also showed that children's play partners provide children new to the activity setting with insight into the established rules, roles and routines of the practice traditions found in the classroom. Specifically, the explicit teaching of established rules, values and expectations by the established group of children to the three new participants was noted. How children dealt with the established rules and expectations within an activity setting of free play influenced their transition experience and this gave different possibilities for their development. For instance, both the suitcase example and Margie's movement across activity settings during free play time, illustrate aspects of unsuccessful transitions. Vissy tried to enter into the play and did not follow the expected rules of play that the established group of children demanded. Even though Vissy sought to enter into the play by offering a storyline that was similar to their play, the transition into the play was unsuccessful. The flying high play demonstrated a potentially successful transition into the expected rules and roles of the established activity settings, by Zeb expanding the storyline and disrupting and reinterpreting established rules and play practices. These examples contribute to the literature by drawing attention to the role of play in understanding how expatriate preschool children enter into classrooms for the first time when moving midway through the semester where practices are already established.

Theoretically, it can be argued that there were varying degrees of inclusion and exclusion of children during their play, and this brought about tension and challenges for the focus children. Vissy understood the play plot, but the storyline she offered was not accepted. This appeared to cause Vissy to self-exclude when invited to participate in another activity setting. In the second example of Margie's transition, the rules of play were enacted but when violated by Margie, she was clearly told and instructed how to play and socially engage correctly by the established children in the classroom. Margie was included in the puzzle play, only to be surrounded by the suitcase children and told about valued play practices and expected cultural traditions of saying 'please' and not snatching. By contrast, in the third example of Zeb, a more successful transition was discussed. He verbally attempted to enter the picnic play. When excluded he changed his approach by initiating an imaginary situation stemming from the reality of his recent everyday life (returning from London). In so doing, he created new conditions for the other children to implicitly be invited to enter into the play. Similar to Margie and the jigsaw play, for the children in the flying high episode, upholding the institutional practices (not running) was high on the children's agenda. Yet the imaginary play situation was used to seemingly remove the need to uphold the rule of walking. This action gave the possibility of a different transition within the activity setting of playing with the other children, and being included in play changed the developmental conditions for Zeb.

Conclusion

Expatriate families with young children are part of an internationally mobile community where successive transitions across countries and institutions are part of the taken for granted practice of moving countries (Adams & Fleer, 2015). The expatriate families with young children illustrated in this chapter arrived in Malaysia and lived in temporary accommodation. This occurred concurrently with the children entering school for the first time, but midway through a school semester. In this chapter, we sought to better understand this unique and complex transition from the perspective of Vissy, Margie and Zeb.

By drawing on Hedegaard's (2005) model of child development and Hedegaard's (2014) cultural-historical conceptualization of transitions, we begin to better understand the complexity of expatriate children's transition as they enter into new countries and classrooms mid-semester. The conditions created at the individual level included tensions and challenges as the three transitioning children tried to enter into play. Tension was created between the collective motive of the established children to assert rules and expectations and the focus children's individual motive for being included in play. When successfully resolved, the tension appears to support the transition and positively contributes to child development.

It can be theorized through the illustrations of Vissy, Margie and Zeb, that the microgenetic transitions within children's play made visible important play themes and competences of children who frequently move countries. Free play time appears to provide a window into what matters for children who are in transition. Free play is an important activity setting because it appears to give the space and time for children to collectively make visible to each other the established rules and expectations. How children deal with the new demands that are placed upon them, and what competences they bring to the new practice traditions, appears to contribute to their success in transitioning. The place of play in supporting expatriate children's successful transition appears to be an under researched area, that we argue should receive more attention.

References

Adams, M. (2014), 'Emotions of expatriate children and families transitioning into Malaysia: A cultural-historical perspective', *Asia Pacific Journal of Research in Early Childhood Education*, 8(2), 129–151.

Adams, M. (2016), 'Young expatriate children forming friendships: A cultural-historical perspective', *International Research in Early Childhood Education*, 7(1).

Adams, M. & M. Fleer (2015), 'Moving countries: Belongings as central for realizing the affective relation between international shifts and localized micro transitions', *Learning, Culture and Social Interaction*, 6. DOI: 10.1016/j.lcsi.2015.03.003

Adams, M. & M. Fleer (2016), 'Social inclusion and exclusion: A cultural historical perspective on an international transition into Malaysia', *Australian Journal of Early Childhood*, 41(3), 86–94.

Bronfenbrenner, U. (1979), *The ecology of human development: Experiments in nature and design*. Cambridge, MA: Harvard University Press.

Bronfenbrenner, U. & P. Morris (2006), 'The bioecological model of human development', in W. Damon & R. Lerner (eds), *Handbook of child psychology, Vol 1: Theoretical models of human development* (6th edn, pp. 793–828). New York: Wiley.

Cameron, P. (2003), *The ecology of third culture kids: The experiences of Australasian adults*. Doctoral dissertation. Retrieved from http://researchrepository.murdoch.edu.au/498/. (EQSA number: PRV12163)

De Haan, M. & E. Elbers (2008), 'Diversity in the construction of modes of collaboration in multiethnic classrooms: Continuity and discontinuity of cultural scripts', in B. van Oers, W. Wardekkter, E. Elbers & R. Van Der Veer, *The transformation of learning*. Cambridge: Cambridge University Press.

Department for Education (2014), 'British Early Years Statutory Framework, [EYSF]', *Early Years Foundation Stage: Statutory framework for the early years foundation stage, Setting the standards for learning, development and care for children from birth to five*. Retrieved from http://www.foundationyears.org.uk/files/2014/07/EYFS_framework_from_1_September_2014__with_clarification_note.pdf

Dockett, S., A. Petriwskyj & B. Perry (2014), *Transitions to school: International research, policy and practice*. Dordrecht: Springer.

Dunlop, A. (2014), 'Thinking about transitions. One framework or many? Populating the theoretical model overtime', in B. Perry, S. Dockett & A. Petriwskyj (eds), *Transitions to school: International research, policy and practice* (pp. 31–46). Dordrecht: Springer.

Fleer, M. (2014), 'The demands and motives afforded through digital play in early childhood activity settings', *Learning, Culture and Social Interaction*, 3(3) (Special themed issue), 202–209. doi: 10.1016/j.lcsi.2014.02.012

Garpelin, A. (2011), 'Transitions to school: A rite of passage in life', in B. Perry, S. Dockett & A. Petriwskyj (eds), *Transitions to school: International research, policy and practice* (pp. 117–128). Dordrecht: Springer.

Hayden, M. (2006), *Introduction to international education: International schools and their communities*. London: Sage Publications.

Hedegaard, M. (2002), *Learning and child development: A cultural historical study*. Arhus: Arhus University.

Hedegaard, M. (2005), 'Strategies for dealing with conflicts in value positions between home and school: Influences on ethnic minority students' development of motives and identity', *Culture Psychology*, 11(2), 187–205. doi:10.1177/1354067X05052351

Hedegaard, M. (2011), 'A cultural-historical approach to children's development of multiple cultural identities', in M. Kontopodis, C. Wulf & B. Fichtner (eds), *Children, development and education: International perspectives on early childhood education and development 3* (pp. 117–134). Dordrecht, The Netherlands; Heidelberg, Germany; London, England and New York: Springer.

Hedegaard, M. (2012), 'Analyzing children's learning and development in everyday settings from a cultural-historical wholeness approach', *Mind, culture, and activity*, 19(2), 127–138. doi:10.1080/10749039.2012.665560

Hedegaard, M. (2014), 'The significance of demands and motives across practices in children's learning and development: An analysis of learning in home and school', *Learning, Culture and Social Interaction*, 3(3), 188–194. doi:http://dx.doi.org/10.1016/j.lcsi.2014.02.008

Hedegaard, M. & A. Edwards (2014), 'Transitions and children's learning. Editorial', *Learning Culture and Social Interaction*, 3, 185–187.

Hedegaard, M., M. Fleer, Y. Bang & P. Hviid (2008), *Studying children: A cultural-historical approach*. New York: Open University Press.

Hedegaard, M. & M. Fleer (2013), *Play, learning and children's development: Everyday life in families and transition to school*. New York: Cambridge University Press.

Kim, J. (2010), 'Downed and stuck in Singapore: Lower/middle class South Korean wild geese (kirogi)', in E. Hannum, H. Park & Y. Butler (eds), Globalization, changing demographics, and educational challenges in East Asia (*Research in the sociology of education, 17*) (pp. 271–311). Emerald Group Publishing Ltd.

Lawrence, J. A., Benedikt, R. & J. Valsiner (1992), 'Homeless in the mind: A case-history of personal life in and out of a close orthodox community', *Journal of Social Distress and the Homeless*, 1(2), 157–176. doi:10.1007/bf01071464

Malaysian Department of Immigration [MDI] (2014). Expatriate professional visas http://www.imi.gov.my/index.php/en/

Märtsin, M. & H. Mahmoud (2012), 'Never 'at-home'? Migrants between societies', in J. Valsiner (ed.), *The Oxford handbook of culture and psychology* (pp. 730–748). New York: Oxford University Press Inc.

Peters, S. (2014), 'Chasms, bridges and borderlands: A transition research "across the border" from early childhood education to school in New Zealand', in B. Perry, S. Dockett & A. Pertiwskyj (eds), *Transitions to school: International research, policy and practice* (pp. 105–116). Dordrecht: Springer.

Pollock, D. & R. Van Reken (2009), *Third culture kids: The experience of growing up among worlds*. Boston, MA: Nicholas Brealey.

Sánchez-Medina, J., B. Macías-Gómez-Stern & V. Martínez-Lozano (2014), 'The value positions of school staff and parents in immigrant families and their implications for children's transitions between home and school in multicultural schools in Andalusia', *Learning Culture and Social Interaction*, 3, 217–223 DOI: 10.1016/j.lcsi.2014.02.0132210-6561

Schousboe, A. (2013), 'The structure of fantasy play and its implications for good and evil', in I. Schousboe & D. Winther-Lindqvist (eds), *Children's play and development: Cultural-historical perspectives* (pp. 13–28). Dordrecht: Springer.

Srinivasan, P. (2014), *Early childhood in postcolonial Australia: Children's contested identities*. New York: Palgrave Macmillan. Retrieved from http://www.palgrave.com/page/detail/early-childhood-in-postcolonial-australia-prasanna-srinivasan/?K=9781137392176

Strobino, J. & M. Salvaterra (2000), 'School transitions among adolescent children of military personnel: A strengths perspective', *A Journal of the National Association of Social Workers*, 22(2), 95–107.

Teras, M. (2012), 'Intercultural space as transitional space: Movements, transformations and dialectical relations', *Research in Comparative and International Education*, 7(4). DOI org/10.2304/rcie.2012.7.4.503

Useem, R. & R. Downie (1976), 'Third culture kids', *Today's Education*, 65(3), 103–105.

Valsiner, J. (1998), *The guided mind: A sociogenetic approach to personality*. Cambridge, MA and London: Harvard University Press.

Walters, K. & F. Auton-Cuff (2009), 'A story to tell: The identity development of women growing up as third culture kids', *Psychological Functioning of International Missionaries*, 12(7), 755–722.

Winther-Lindqvist, D. (2013), 'Playing with social identities: Play in the everyday life of a peer group in day care', in I. Schousboe & D. Winther-Lindqvist (eds), *Children's play and development: Cultural-historical perspectives*, (pp. 29–54). London: Springer.

Zhao, Y. (2011), *Handbook of Asian education: A cultural perspective*. New York: Routledge.

5

Transitioning from Play to Learning: Playfulness as a Resource in Children's Transition

Paula Cavada-Hrepich

Introduction

Mostly based on economic rather than pedagogical reasons, industrialized educational systems around the world are aiming for universal access to kindergarten, even making it compulsory. Across countries, kindergarten class can be the last year of 'preschool education' or the initial year of primary school education.[1] However, kindergarten class often has a different curriculum, learning goals, conceptions of children's development and learning, teaching methodologies, structural dispositions and teachers' educational background to that of the primary school. Hence children of six or seven years old who are starting the first year of primary school, face a substantial change in their living conditions after a period of summer holidays, which calls for a new relation between the child and his or her new context. This experience has been conceptualized as a 'transition' between institutions, a concept that refers to the shifts punctuated in a person's trajectory in relation to educational settings (Hviid & Zittoun, 2008; Zittoun, 2008).

Over the last twenty years, research into learning has pointed out the continuity of development of different competences, which start before entering formal education in school. These findings have had a major political impact

---

[1]   In this chapter I will refer to the *kindergarten class* as the year that precedes the first year of primary school. This might not be part of the preschool educational level. Even if the *kindergarten class* is placed within the primary school (as is the case with 'reception class'), the emphasis is placed on the fact that in this year the institutional practice will be different to the rest of the primary school.

on the aims of preschool education and, as a result, school practices have been introduced in the preschool room at the expense of traditional early childhood activities based on play (Bodrova & Leon, 2006). However, the lack of knowledge of the process of transition between play and learning activities is reflected in structured school lessons introduced into the kindergarten class that go beyond the capacity and interest of children. Moreover, this intervention has created situations that do not contribute to children's development and also have undesirable outcomes for children, such as stress, feelings of guilt and doubtfulness (Bröstrom, 1992; Cassidy, 2005).

Drawing on a cultural-historical wholeness approach to children's development and learning (Hedegaard, 2012) enriched with concepts from cultural psychology (Rogoff, 2003; Valsiner, 2011a, b; Zittoun, 2006, 2009), this chapter explores how children's leading activities change during this transition by studying children's motive orientation when moving from the kindergarten class into the first year of primary school. In the following sections, the understanding of transition will be presented as well as development and learning and the perspective of children. The analysis of two case studies will be introduced – cases that are part of a research project that followed six children over a period of a year and a half in Santiago, Chile.

Developmental transitions

Transition is a concept that denotes the process of movement between two situations across time (Winther-Lindqvist, 2009), in which the daily routine is significantly shaken with the starting of a new 'becoming' (Valsiner, 2011b; Zittoun, 2006, 2008). Hviid and Zittoun (2008) propose that transition is an individual as well as a social process that demands or provokes some responsiveness from the environment, which feeds further transitional processes. In other words, transitions require transactions between the individuals and their social and material changing environment, which can be more or less clearly perceived or defined as such (Zittoun, Duveen, Gillespie, Ivinson & Psaltis, 2003). Hviid and Zittoun (2008) argue that this concept should be understood in terms of a shift, rupture or relocation punctuated in a person's trajectory or normal course of events that is 'partly created by, affected by, and responding to educational settings ... processes of catalysed change due to a rupture, and aiming at a new sustainable fit between person and her current environment' (p.123). Zittoun (2006, 2009) emphasizes that in a transition the person's social position, tools and personal orientations are in a state of rupture. This implies the reconfiguration of three interdependent processes: knowledge acquisition, identity and sense making (Zittoun, 2008). In relation to this last point, Valsiner (2011b) suggests that through processes of meaning making and the creation of signs, human beings 'construct the meanings that lead us to reconstruct the objective world, and the reconstructed world guides our further construction of meanings … constructed meanings are projected outward "to the society" and turned into social imperatives by which individuals organise their lives by their own "free will" or by socio-moral-legal forms of social coercion' (p.224).

Nevertheless, these ruptures are embedded in social configurations, where the institutions serve as social frames that can facilitate or constrain personal reconfigurations (Zittoun, 2008; Hedegaard, 2012). Likewise, van Oers (2009) states:

> Society and its institutions are not stable, unchanging structures. Emerging economic, political and cultural changes modify the ways people act and interact, and these changes also may have significant influences on human cultural development. However, the influence of changing societal structures on human activity and development is not a deterministic process. It depends on how these changes are perceived and how people cope with them (p. 213).

The aspects discussed above make even more sense when the concepts of developmental lines and crisis argued by Vygotsky (1998) are reviewed. He proposes that to understand children's development it is essential to take into consideration a child's social situation of development, which changes in relation to the different periods in the life course. According to Vygotsky (1998), development can move along in different ways in children's lives: from smooth little changes to abrupt and chaotic ones in relation to how a child thinks, acts and feels. In this sense, 'crises' are events or turning points that alternate with stable periods, conceived as spasmodic and revolutionary changes, and located in the child's experienced social situation and characterized by three phases: deconstruction, construction and mastering or neo-formation. This latter phase will become the stable part in the dominating activity at a newly developed stage. At the deconstruction and reconstruction phases of the social situation, children's competences and motives are allowed to proceed. Within the crisis the child's engagement and interests change deeply, and conflict can become more serious (Hedegaard, 2008a).

Vygotsky (1998) argues that a critical turning point is open at the school age, in which children evidently change. In fact, starting school gives children a new status, entering into a specific classroom together with other children, a situation that affects their own understanding and ways of participating in social life (Winther-Lindqvist, 2009). One could thus argue two ideas from this particular transition: first, that this change does not start on the first day of school, but is anchored in its anticipation in the previous years; and second, that this change is a process in which children will not be pre-schoolers anymore, but not yet school students.

Leading activities: Play and learning

As it has been pointed out, one of the main differences between preschool and school is the meaning and preponderance of play and the learning of content knowledge related to subject matter at each level. Vygotsky (1978) argues that in the process of guiding children within activities, it is fundamental to work from the child's own skills and interests, because development can only become meaningful if this is the result of an endorsement or transformation of what s/he can already do and wants to do. Taking this idea, Elkonin (1972) and later Leontiev (1981), introduced the notion of *leading activity*, which is when individuals display a preference for a certain type of activity that is related to reality in different ways at different moments in their development. This leading activity is aligned with the individual's interests and underpins significant changes in their psychic processes, enabling development. In other words, the development of the psyche depends on a child's leading activity and not on activities in general. Moreover, Elkonin (1972) identified periods of development that regularly alternate between being centred on the child's need-motivational sphere (subjects) to being focused on their learning operational and technical capabilities (objects).

   Without any doubt, learning as it occurs in the preschool years differs markedly from school learning. In this context, *play* has been recognized as the most important activity during childhood by the developmental psychology tradition. According to Elkonin (2005), play emerges from the social conditions of life, taking its internal content from the children's everyday life conditions and experiences. Motives for play arise through the child's relationships with others and the material world. Furthermore, Vygotsky (1998) suggests that play is not the predominant feature, but it is a leading factor in children's development. In this sense, he proposes that play has a mediating function and a potential for creating a zone of proximal development, because in play the child is above his or her usual everyday behaviour and tries 'as if' to accomplish above his or her ordinary behavioural level (Vygotsky, 1966). In this regard, van Oers (1999) specifies that play is an imaginary situation, voluntarily created and characterized by specific rules. Vygotsky (1966) points out that the rules in play are not formulated in advance, but are a result of the imaginary situation. In fact, only 'actions which fit these rules are acceptable to the play situation' (Vygotsky, 1966, p. 9). Play therefore relates to children's engagement in make-believe actions, as they play with others or alone. In this way, play is a child's activity that emerges and develops from themself and not from a defined institutional practice. Nevertheless, through play, children enact daily experiences and the rules of everyday life. In play, children also explore the rules that frame the social events in which they will participate in the future and that, in consequence, will direct what they are expected to do. Thus, children always have a certain understanding of the situation that they are imitating in their play (Vygotsky, 1966) that reflects what matters to them in their life (Fleer, 2010).

Another important aspect for understanding play as the leading activity in the preschool setting is related to the use of the objects within the imaginary situation. Vygotsky (1966) suggested that children's activity can be described as play when their motive is directed towards imagining activities where they give new meaning to objects. The child at play is in the imaginary situation, in which he or she sees one thing (within their optical field), and can give the object new meaning as when a child is imagining driving a car or being a mother taking care of a baby. Thus, the play materials in preschool for supporting children's play are not a trivial matter (Kravtsov & Kravtsova, 2010; Fleer, 2010).

Once children start the first year of school, they are exposed to new demands from the new school system. As Vygotsky (1987) says, school *learning* introduces completely new elements into children's life course development. Cognitive development will occur in the context of 'instruction'. As Elkonin (1972) suggests, when children start learning in school, then this becomes a particular activity in which learning to learn itself is the leading principle of activities. This is manifested in children's searching for right answers, procedures and problem-solving strategies. Children are consciously interested in finding how things function. Davydov (1999), following on from the work of Elkonin, developed the Learning Activity Theory in which he proposes that learning as an activity belongs properly to schoolchildren and has it owns demands, norms, conditions and new content to be acquired. Likewise, Hedegaard and Lompscher (1999) suggest that the learning activity is 'directed towards the acquisition of societal knowledge and skills through their individual re-production by means of special learning actions upon learning objects (subject matter methods and knowledge)' (p. 21).

In school the dominant institutional practice is school learning (Hedegaard, 2001, 2008a). However, learning does not merely occur on the basis of accidental situations, but is built on a system and logic of learning material guided by instruction, which is understood as a specific form of teaching and learning in the school setting (Vygotsky, 1998). In fact, social interactions, the development of motives and self-evaluation are core aspects of the learning activity, but the content (theoretical knowledge) and the characteristics of teaching will define how this kind of activity develops and how it influences psychic development (Davydov, 1999). In addition, Hedegaard (2002) states that 'the learning motive develops from the child's participation in teaching activity but the interest the children bring to this teaching has to be a starting point for their development of motivation' (p. 21). So, when the leading motive of children is in tune with a meaningful activity, academic learning arises as a result.

Transition of leading activities

At this point, it is clear that the development of a learning motive is different to the development of a play motive. Learning as a new leading activity does not mean that children will cease playing (Hedegaard & Fleer, 2013). Instead, Elkonin (1972) argues that this is a new stage in which the school situation creates another position for play in the motives hierarchy.

Elkonin (1972) points out that within the institutional demands, the transition to the first year of school entails crossing boundaries from the activity of play to the activity of school learning, calling for a development of higher mental functions and the development of children's learning motive. Likewise, he argues that play activity gradually evolves into a conscious (productive) learning activity, which gains the upper hand during the ages of 7 to 12. Nevertheless, Veresov (2006) points out that 'a new leading activity does not arise directly on the basis of the old leading activity ... [it] arises in the depths of the entire social situation of development of the preschooler' (p. 16). According to this author, play activity is not the exclusive preconditions and means for the emergence of the learning activity, yet learning is gradually created within the entire social situation of development. Veresov (2006) explains this transition as follows:

> Learning activity, having arisen in this social situation of development, rearranges the entire system of the child's activities and creates a new social situation of development within which play too has a place. Play passes the

"baton" to the learning activity, ceding it the position of leading activity but it does not do so directly. It leaves this baton, as it were, on the "field" of the social situation of development, on which the preconditions mature for the emergence of a learning activity that will be capable of picking up the baton (p. 16).

In line with this argument, van Oers (1999) proposes that it is an error to believe that children are exclusively engaged in play activity as a context for learning and development. The author argues that play activity dominates in the early years, but elements of learning activity and social interactive activity might be integrated because there is not a linear relation between play and learning activities. In fact, learning activities must be fostered as a new special form of play activity: 'when in play children consciously reflect upon the relationship between their pretend signs and real meaning they are engaged in a form of semiotic act that will provide valuable precursor to new learning activity' (van Oers, 1999, p. 278).

Children's social situation and the child's perspective

Bearing in mind that development and learning are conceived as culturally embedded and institutionally defined processes (Lave & Wegner, 1991; Rogoff, 2003), the study of children's social situation in everyday settings is acknowledged as an essential aspect in the comprehension of children's development (Bozhovich, 2009; Hedegaard & Fleer, 2008; Vygotsky, 1998). Specifically, these researchers emphasize the importance of the children's perspective in their participation in the activities of play and learning.

Hedegaard's wholeness model (2012) depicts children's social situation nested in different activity settings in different practices. Children have different social situations in the same activity setting, as the latter refers to the objectives for activities that are set by the teacher (Hedegaard, 2012). Using this term, the focus is directly on children's experience, taking their perspective to find out what is important for them. Children's social situations are of course related to children's social situation of development; that is a description of what their leading activity is since this influences their experience in an actual social situation. Taking the children's perspective leads to focusing on the activities in which they are participating and how they participate in these activities. How children participate can say something about their motivation, which is connected to what their leading activity and their motives in general are.

Studies that aim to address the perspective of children have explored what children think about when entering school, as well as their expectations and desires of the first year of school, showing both children's willingness to play but also to learn (Ebbeck, Saidon, Rajalachime & Teo, 2013; Mirkhil, 2010; Hedegaard & Fleer, 2013). Studies about the children's experiences of the first year of school show how children's expectations orient them to activities in the classroom in ways that do not align with the teacher's objectives (Fisher, 2012; Hedegaard & Fleer, 2013). As a consequence, these children start a learning path that leads to future difficulties if the teachers do not understand the child's intention and motive orientation (Hedegaard, 2012).

Nevertheless, there has been a lack of research into what happens to children in the classroom when the conditions of learning change from one year to another; and little is known about how they handle new demands and positions within this specific setting.

Studying developmental transitions: A microgenetic design in the classroom

In the context of the presented theoretical approach, the central question addressed in this chapter is: how does children's motive orientation change when the dominating activity changes from play to learning in the structured learning setting? Previous research on this transition takes the form of retrospective accounts of children in the first year of primary school and are focused on learning outcomes (Bröstrom, 1992; Cassidy, 2005; Einarsdóttir, Perry & Dockett, 2008). Nevertheless, exploring this transition, as a developmental moment, demands that one looks at the process of change, but also the underlying mechanisms as they occur (Siegler, 1991). This is what developmental psychologists have called *microgenesis* research designs, in which one carries out deep examinations of individuals by taking repeated measurements over a period of time in the course of transition in a particular domain (Siegler, 1991, 2006). As Wagoner (2009) says, microgenesis, as a process-oriented approach, can be seen as a way of analysing constructive processes, which are approached from the perspective of conceptualizing individuals as a whole person – studying their qualitative transformations over time. Microgenetic designs are individual-based and therefore highly related to the methodology of the case study. As Yin (1984) reports, this method is an empirical inquiry that investigates a phenomenon within its real-life situations, issues, problems, and context, in which multiple sources of evidence are used. Microgenetic designs enable the researcher to emphasize detailed contextual analysis of a limited number of events or conditions and their relationships. Nevertheless, the transition to the first year of primary school implies looking at two different educational levels over a time span of one year. This also requires the researcher to follow children in different moments, constituting a longitudinal design.

In connection to this, Hedegaard (2008b) argues that the methodology that attempts to study development should examine children in their everyday settings, focusing on their social situation. In other words, in order to understand children's development and learning, it is fundamental to examine the institutional practices, as well as the children's motives and competences. To study children's intentions or motives it is necessary to observe their actions during the activities in which they are involved. In this sense, observations of children's activities in the classroom enable the researcher to have a naturalistic approach to institutional practices and explore how children, through participation in shared activities within a setting, contribute to their own learning conditions.

Inspired by these methodological considerations, a research project[2] was initiated following six children[3] from the same kindergarten class to the first year of primary school in a municipal school in Chile.[4] To capture detailed real-time processes, video-recorded observations of the structured literacy or pre-literacy learning lessons offered by the teacher or pedagogue were taken in three periods: at the end of the kindergarten class, at the beginning of the first year of primary and at the end of the first year of primary. Each period took between four to six weeks, where twelve full lessons (between 30 to 45 minutes) were recorded with two cameras, each focused on one child, in order to gain their particular perspectives on the shared activity setting.

Also, to understand the institutional demands, the pedagogue and the teacher were interviewed following a semi-structured interview format regarding the aim of the literacy learning, the role of play and characteristics of the particular children.

---

[2] This is part of a larger research design of a PhD study from 2012 to 2013 that aimed to understand children's perspective in the transition to first year primary at literacy learning activities. In the larger project five case studies from Denmark are included.

[3] Three pairs of children were selected by the pedagogue considering her assessment on their 'literacy level' in relation to their class (competent, average and behind).

[4] The school had characteristics of the ones in which the majority of the child population attended by 2012. This means that the school was subsidized by the state enrolling children from middle or low-middle social-economic backgrounds, which represented the reality for 65 per cent of the schoolchildren population and had an average performance in national comparative assessments.

When exploring the processes of children's developmental change, it is important to consider analytical tools that capture the wholeness of a child's social situation. Hedegaard's (2012) wholeness model depicts children's social situation nested in different activity settings in different practices. In this study, the activity setting of pre-literacy and literacy learning lessons in the classroom was the setting in which children's social situation was studied. This provided the opportunity to analyse the dialectical relation between the child's social situation and the setting and its conditions for the child's activity, i.e., the social values and the institutional practice of each activity setting in relation to the children's motive orientation.

The analysis of the children's perspective was inspired by the work of Hedegaard and Fleer (2013) regarding the recognition of patterns of interactions, as well as Goodwin's (2000) work on embodiment and uses of semiotic resources. In concrete terms, the study focused on the moments of *engagement*[5] and *disengagements*, in relation to the learning situation proposed by the teacher. The following categories were used, paying attention to the use of the body (gestures) and language tone:[6]

- The intentional orientation of the researched persons
- The ways interactions occur between the participants (interaction patterns)
- The conflicts between different persons' intentions and projects in the activity
- The competence and motives that the researched persons demonstrate during their interactions.

In the following section an interpretation of classroom video-recorded observations of two case studies, Alejandro and Maria, sharing the same activity setting is presented. The video recordings were taken at the end of kindergarten class and at the beginning of the first year of primary (six months apart). Drawing on excerpts from the perspectives of each child in the same pre-literacy (kindergarten class) and literacy (first year primary)

---

[5] Engagement hereby is understood through the formulation of Hviid (2008) in terms of the child's involved participation that is created by the child in an experienced situation. This situation simultaneously invokes such engagement. Moreover, in 'the child is "more" than herself- she is herself and the situation (or object) of her engagement' (p. 184).

[6] This has been found to be a fundamental aspect when analysing children's actions as they widely use their body for communicating. It can be speculated that as higher psychological functions are developed and communicative tools (language) are learned throughout the life course, children's gestures, body postures and tones of voice are highly communicative on what matters to them.

structured learning activity settings, it will be illustrated how playfulness arises as a resource in this transition in relation to their competences and position.

One case study is Alejandro, a boy who was five years old when the data were collected in the kindergarten class. The pedagogue pointed out that he has an average performance in literacy learning compared with his peers. She says that Alejandro performs better than expected because he receives support for learning from home, and has had a language development delay for which he received professional support. He is also identified as a child who constantly gets distracted by his peers.

The other case study is a girl, Maria, who was also five years old. From the pedagogue's perspective, Maria is an underachiever in relation to her peers and has difficulties in learning. Maria is seen as barely being able to focus on tasks and is constantly wanting to play.

Analysing children's social situation when entering school: Maria and Alejandro

End of kindergarten class

General description of the institutional practice

In Chile the kindergarten class is for children aged between four and five years old. In this classroom, there are thirty children. Two adults are working every day with the children. One is an experienced pedagogue who has completed her university studies and is the pedagogical leader. Meanwhile, the other is a technical assistant who mostly takes care of preparing the material, organizing meals and attending to the needs of the children. Children go to school from 8.30 to 13.00, having breakfast and lunch at school. There is a daily routine that includes meals, as well as hygiene procedures (washing hands, brushing teeth, going to the toilet). There is time allotted for free playing, where the pedagogue supervises the children so they do not get hurt, or helps to resolve conflicts.

On an almost daily basis, there are programmed lessons related to early literacy and numeracy learning. For these lessons, the pedagogue follows a specific programme for promoting children's early literacy created by the Ministry of Education. This is organized into twelve units, which has an annual plan that the pedagogue should follow. At the end of each unit, the pedagogue has to send every student workbook back to the Ministry. Tasks are most often individually based.

Four children sit together at square tables. The furniture fits their height. The classroom is divided into corners: literacy (with books, carpets and pillows), numeracy (with different materials for counting, classifying etc.) and role play (different toys are available to the children). There are a lot of colourful decorations, words and signs hanging on the walls.

Description of an activity setting of a pre-literacy lesson (Friday 28th October, 2011. 8.30 am)

Children are using the workbooks given to them by the ministerial programme. The lesson is in relation to a previous story that the pedagogue had read aloud: 'Miss Cockroach Martínez'. In this individual task, children have to read from their workbooks, which include incomplete sentences, then select the missing keyword from a list written on one side of the page, link it to the blank space in the incomplete sentence, write it down and then colour the selected word. The lesson starts with the pedagogue reading each sentence aloud and writing the sentences on the whiteboard, as well as the missing word that has been found by asking all the children to answer together as a chorus. Then, children copy what the pedagogue has written on the whiteboard. Alejandro and Maria are sitting at the same square table with another child (Ricardo). They have a direct view of the whiteboard. The classroom is noisy, and children are moving around.

The following transcription lasts for 1 minute and 40 seconds.

Maria's perspective

	Content	Interpretation
1	Maria is looking attentively at the pedagogue who is reading aloud the sentence that is written on the whiteboard (the same sentence that is in the workbook).	Maria is oriented towards what the pedagogue is demanding.
2	She looks at the bunch of pencils that she is holding in her right hand and then looks back at the pedagogue.	She remains engaged in the task, although holding the colour pencils reflects that she is still learning how to use the writing tools (they are not needed).

	Content	Interpretation
3	She turns and looks at her workbook moving her face close to the book, searching for the sentence that the pedagogue reads aloud.	She is trying to engage in the learning situation.
4	After saying the missing word 'SU' (yours), the pedagogue spells it aloud reproducing the sound of the S and the U and putting them together SU: 'S and U is SU', this is exercised by the pedagogue presenting and making the repetitions with the different vowels 'sa, se, si, so, su'. Maria looks back at the pedagogue with her neck bent to one side and repeats along with her and the class. She reproduces each word, over-modulating them while gently hitting the pencils in one hand onto the other hand's palm at each word, still looking at the pedagogue.	She is still engaged in the task, while following the instruction with exaggerated movements and vocalizations.
5	Then she exaggeratedly stretches, holding the pencils in both her hands, and she yawns while looking at the workbook trying to find the sentence.	She briefly disconnects and reconnects with the learning situation.
6	She cannot find it. Then she touches her braid and tries to look at what Alejandro has done in his workbook.	She is oriented to support Alejandro in his task.
7	Alejandro complains aloud about a pencil while looking at her. She doesn't reply and instead selects a pencil, putting it closer to her while looking at Alejandro and smiling.	She starts a playful situation with Alejandro.
8	Miguel lifts her workbook, trying to find a pencil, but she does not react, just stares.	She is interested in what her classmate is doing.
9	She looks at Alejandro because he is waving the pencil that he has just picked up from the floor while looking at her with a surprised gesture. She nods.	She is attentive to Alejandro's actions, willing to engage with him.

	Content	Interpretation
10	Then she stares at how he starts writing the missing word while chewing a pen. She looks at both, what he does and at his face.	She keeps being attentive to Alejandro and his actions.
11	She starts writing the missing word, copying it from the whiteboard. She looks closely at her workbook trying to read the words while licking her pencil.	She re-engages in the learning task, using the pencil in an alternative way.
12	Alejandro points with his fingers at two words in her workbook and she looks at them and then looks at his workbook. As she cannot see, she bends her whole body over her workbook to get a closer look, while putting her tongue at one side.	She is interested in the suggestion of Alejandro for the learning task. She uses her body as she would do in a play situation to get closer to what interests her.

During most of the lesson, as well as in other lessons, Maria is attentive towards what the pedagogue says and demands, showing interest in the learning task, but this is not her main priority. Maria aims to engage in the situation using her body and the tools in a playful manner. For example, quite often she cannot figure out how to resolve the task but she remains seated and tries to pay attention while holding all the pencils in her hand, moving several times in her chair, touching her braids, stretching and bending her body to the side. As the examples show, she is interested in seeing what her classmates are doing and how they are solving the task, thus showing prevalent social orientation. Even when she tries, she does not necessarily write down the required words or finish the task.

Alejandro's perspective

	Content	Interpretation
1	Alejandro is looking at his workbook and licking his ruler while the pedagogue is reading aloud the sentence that is written on the whiteboard (the same sentence that is in the workbook).	He wants to fulfil the task despite having problems with the material resources.

	Content	Interpretation
2	Alejandro puts back the ruler in his pencil case while trying to find a pencil from inside it. He closes his pencil case and places it beside him covering Maria's workbook partly without noticing. He feels in his pockets, but he finds a pencil on the table. While he is repeating 'SA' along with the pedagogue, he tries to write, but the tip is broken. He looks at Miguel while moving his broken pencil to a red one that is in the middle of the table. Miguel does not look back, and Alejandro tries to put the tip back into the pencil. He doesn't succeed and looks back at Miguel again, leaving the pencil near the red one in the middle of the table, smiling.	He aims to resolve the problem with the pencil and tries to keep doing the task, which shows an interest in the learning situation. However, in this process, he engages with his classmate in a playful manner while trying to solve the problem with the pencil.
3	He tries to write the missing word with the tip of the pencil, copying from the one that is written in the workbook.	He remains engaged in solving the problem with the pencil.
4	He stops writing and looks for a pencil on the table, then looks at Maria's handful of pencils. He asks for a pencil, frowning, but Maria picks up the one that she has in her hand, bringing it closer to herself smiling.	He does not engage in the playful situation with Maria as he needs to resolve the problem.
5	It seems that Alejandro feels with his feet, and finding a pencil on the floor, he picks it up. He realizes that it has a tip, and he grabs the pencil from there with his fingers waving it to Maria, putting on an excited face. He reviews the pencil, like searching for a name, gets back in position to work and starts to copy the word from the whiteboard.	He resolves the problem, showing a visible playful satisfaction and returns to the learning situation.
6	He stops writing and puckers his lips, touches his face with the back of his hands and looks at Maria's workbook. He says 'these two!' while pointing at them in her workbook with his fingers.	He uses his whole body when he cannot continue and orients himself towards his classmate, using his body and gestures playfully.
7	He looks at his workbook and grabs his face exaggeratedly, and looks at the whiteboard again.	He uses his body to get back into the task.
8	He starts saying aloud 'S and U SUUUUU' in an exaggerated way, moving his head at each sound while looking at me (the researcher). He repeats this while looking at Miguel.	He turns the learning situation into a playful one. However, he stills remains engaged with the content.

Alejandro is also highly attentive to what the pedagogue says, repeats all of the words from the group exercises, and is focused on solving the task, showing that he has an orientation towards the learning situation. When he cannot keep doing the task or he is trying to figure out what to do, he will exaggerate an expression with a body movement, i.e., licking his ruler, puckering his lips and rubbing his eyes, or scratching his head. He will also actively seek support, by asking or just looking at his partners' workbooks.

Beginning of the first year of primary school

General description of the institutional practice

There are forty-two children in the classroom, who are between 5 and 6 years old. Two teachers are also in the classroom every day. Both are teachers that obtained a university degree in teaching. Nevertheless, both are new teachers teaching for the first time in the first year of primary school. One of them is the pedagogical leader, and the other one assists with technical aspects, which creates problems for both of them. Like the kindergarten class pedagogue, the teacher must work with the programme from the Ministry of Education, but also with a specific programme set by the local municipality to enhance children's performance in literacy.

In the first year of primary school, children start being assessed in their learning through tests and they receive marks. The teachers are assessing them at least five times during a semester in every subject, and a calendar of these tests hangs on the wall. Besides this internal testing practice, the municipality tests children once every semester in literacy and numeracy. There are no toys in the classroom, play is relegated to breaks and the children share the playground with the whole school (until 8th grade). Tasks are usually individually based.

The children are in a new classroom, they sit in pairs and the furniture is big in relation to their size (children's feet hang). The classroom has a few letters and numbers hanging on the wall.

Description of an activity setting of a literacy lesson (Tuesday 27th March, 2012. 10.30 am)

The children work with an individual worksheet that has different drawings. They have to recognize the initial phoneme and write down the initial letter of each drawing. The drawings have no connection between them (an apple, a butterfly, a wing, etc.). Once they have written the correct letter, they paint the drawings. Maria and Alejandro are sharing tables with other classmates (Ricardo and Claudia). Alejandro is sitting behind Maria. At each board, there are two alphabet charts, which each child has coloured and glued as personal reminders. The class is noisy, and the teacher is constantly reminding the children of the rules of the class (work alone, be quiet, finish your work, etc.) but is also threatening them: 'you will not have a break if you do not finish your work'.

The following transcription lasts for 1 minute and 40 seconds.

Maria's perspective

	Content	Interpretation
1	Maria is copying the date from the whiteboard in her worksheet. She is properly sitting in her chair and focusing on the task. She stops writing and picks up an eraser that is in the middle of the table to place it in her pencil case, dropping her pen on her arm.	She seems to be engaged in the learning situation, following the conduct expected in school.
2	Ricardo, the boy sitting beside her, says 'lend me your pencil' and he takes the pencil laid on Maria's arm. She lets him and scrubs the worksheet with her hand. She turns to look at Alejandro, who is sitting behind her and is calling out to Ricardo.	She disengages from what she was doing, not confronting the interruption of her classmate. She is momentarily absent.
3	Ricardo throws the pencil back over onto Maria's workspace and turns to Alejandro. She picks up the pencil and returns to her writing. She keeps copying from the whiteboard. When she finishes copying the current date, she starts copying a new letter at the bottom of the worksheet. She is copying letter by letter. (The teacher says 'closed mouth and keep working' [might equal the English expression 'keep your mouth shut']).	It seems that she returns to the task, mechanically.
4	When she finishes writing the letter she scrubs her hand over the sheet, looks at the whiteboard and then starts to move her fingers back and forward scrubbing the table. She gets focused on trying to get something out from the table. She takes a closer look at a little thing glued to the table.	She is no longer engaged in the learning situation.
5	Ricardo takes the pencil from Maria's hand. She doesn't seem bothered at all and keeps focused on scratching something out from the table.	Again, she does not respond to the actions of her classmate, getting absorbed in another action.

This year Maria is wearing glasses, which could partly explain her difficulties in the previous year. During most of the lesson, she puts a lot of effort into acting as a student and meeting the requirements of the position of a schoolchild: she sits with her back straight, holds the pencil appropriately, takes care of her pencil case and her school utensils, remains quiet and does not get up from her seat. She writes carefully, copying letter by letter and erasing many times to complete it as best she can; this probably shows that she is not yet reading. Frequently, she does not finish the tasks, completing just those sections that she has to copy from the whiteboard. She disengages and instead of seeking help, imitates or copies from her classmates; she tends to be absent, scratching the table, not even confronting Ricardo when he takes the pencil from her. She does not use the alphabet chart glued on her desk. Maria has not developed the learning competences for understanding the content requirements of the task, hence limiting her participation in the classroom. It seems that her efforts and engagement are focused on pleasing the teacher by fulfilling the role more than actually learning how to read and write. However, on another occasion she approached me, took a look at my notes and said 'That is not good, you have not finished and you have a misspelt word, and I will have to call your parents', while pointing her finger in an accusatory way, afterwards laughing out loud. This denotes a playful attitude and act towards me in which she is taking the position of the teacher, rehearsing those aspects that are remarkable for her in such a position. She uses this playfulness approach as a way to engage with something that both matters to me and to her.

Alejandro's perspective

	Content	Interpretation
1	Alejandro is looking at the whiteboard.	He seems attentive to the learning situation.
2	He calls to Ricardo (who sits in front of him). He composes himself to write, but he calls out to Ricardo once again. Ricardo doesn't turn, and Alejandro tries to take a look at Ricardo's work from the side and calls to him again.	He is interested in resolving the task, asking for support from his classmate.
3	Ricardo turns and shows Alejandro his worksheet. Alejandro smiles, looks at the worksheet and erases something from his own worksheet.	He seems to enjoy completing the task with his classmate.

	Content	Interpretation
4	Ricardo explains to Alejandro which letter they are using and searches for it in the alphabetical letter overview that Alejandro has on his desk. Meanwhile, Alejandro looks at the letter overview that hangs on the wall and then at Ricardo's worksheet held in front of him until Ricardo says 'this one' pointing to the letter M.	He is focused on resolving the task.
5	Alejandro responds, 'this one?' showing Ricardo a letter. Ricardo points again to the letter and Alejandro replies 'ah, ok'. He looks at the letter on the board and at his worksheet. He prepares to write but instead asks Ricardo to give him his worksheet, reaching for the worksheet bending his whole body over the table.	He keeps being focused and engaged in the learning task.
6	Ricardo says wait, and he paints the butterfly (mariposa in Spanish). Alejandro waits with all his whole body bent over his desk trying to see what Ricardo is doing. Alejandro asks, 'what about eight (ocho in Spanish)?' and Ricardo turns and says 'starts with O'. Alejandro returns to his sitting position and Ricardo points to the drawing of eight on Carlo's worksheet. Alejandro writes the letter O down. Then Ricardo says 'and one (uno in Spanish) starts with U'. Alejandro nods while writing.	He keeps being focused and engaged in the learning task.
7	When he is done, he asks 'What about cage (jaula in Spanish)?' while bending his body over the table trying to see Ricardo's worksheet. Ricardo says, 'jaula starts with that letter', pointing at J that is also written on the whiteboard. Alejandro smiles and is back in his seat about to write, but then he says 'when I write my name I put this', pointing at the J letter in his alphabet while Ricardo looks. Both are smiling and pointing at the letter. Ricardo points to another letter of the alphabet and Alejandro starts to copy it. They both stare at the whiteboard.	He goes beyond the task and expands the knowledge into what is familiar and meaningful to him, sharing the joy of his discovery with his classmate.

	Content	Interpretation
8	Alejandro suddenly turns to Claudia, the girl sitting beside him who has been looking at his work for a while, and says 'do not look', while putting his arm over his worksheet in an exaggerated way. He writes and then looks at her again as if waiting for her reaction with an exaggerated stare.	He is engaged in the learning situation, and he engages playfully with Claudia in relation to the performative aspects of the student position (i.e., work by yourself).

During the lessons, Alejandro is engaged in successfully resolving the learning task. He actively seeks assistance from Ricardo, who is sitting in front of him and they jointly resolve and expand the task. In this sense, learning is shaping the way in which Alejandro is relating to others, organizing his participation in the classroom. However, while doing so, they are also challenging the norms of working individually, remaining silent and sitting properly looking at the front. The boys are engaged and enjoy each other's joint learning task while both seriously and playfully talking, teasing and touching each other. Playful attitudes and actions also appear when other aspects of the position of being a student are demanded, such as not copying each other's work. In this way, he remains engaged in the task while removing the seriousness of the situation.

Discussion

Learning as leading activity: the institutional demand

In line with Elkonin (1972), this study shows that when starting school in the classroom setting children relate to the world through a new principal activity: learning. The change of leading activity for children is both required and promoted by the shift in the demands of school practice. As previously described, the learning lessons are similar in their content and structure in the kindergarten class and in the first year of primary school, though framed in institutional practices that differ in their goals, concrete material conditions, social positions and social others. In other words, the learning lessons in the kindergarten class are inserted into a practice that has a goal to promote children's social, emotional, physical and cognitive abilities; while, in the first year primary, these activities are inserted in an educational level that aims primarily to develop knowledge and cognitive competencies.

One of the major changes of this transition is related to the demands for participation and the *new positions* associated with it. The 'student position' is not expected in the kindergarten class, yet is signified as 'learning how to become a student', although this latter practice is limited to the 'literacy lesson' or 'maths lesson' during the day. Meanwhile, from the perspective of the first year primary, children have to fulfil the student position in all the activities that take place in the school. It can be formulated that children are offered a position in the kindergarten class 'as-if students'; a new position ('student') that is highly defined under a restricted set of cultural signs that frame their new becoming, i.e., in relation to their academic performance based on outcomes (children are constantly being assessed with tests and given marks) and not necessarily to other aspects, such as fellowship, effort, disposition, emotional regulation, subjective experience, and so on.

Playfulness as a transitional resource: The child's perspective

The question that arises from the analysis of these activity settings is: how do children navigate this change? As has been shown in Ebbeck et al. (2013), Fisher's (2012) and Fleer's (2010) work, children in both years do want to fulfil the 'student position' and finish the tasks, but they also want to play. In fact, children actively try to make personal sense of the demands of the learning activities, resolve them and fulfil the position offered. As we have seen, children's playfulness and social interactions become their resources for participation within proposed structured activities created by the teachers during the literacy lessons in both years.

Playfulness is understood as brief moments, in which children through attitudes and actions might create imaginary scenarios for exploring and performing without having direct consequences for the curriculum activities. To some extent, this relates to Podd'iakov's (2012) formulation: 'playfulness manifests itself in the preschooler performing some actions in addition to those actions necessary to accomplish some required serious activity … give it a certain coloration or hue suggestive of rather happy and buoyant overtones' (p. 24). However, the author does not elaborate about the specific changes that children face when starting school and how playfulness is developed in relation to the specific institutional conditions, i.e., the new positions that they experience. In that respect, this study has found that in the kindergarten class, children's motive orientations are directed towards play during the literacy learning lessons, creating playfulness situations most of the time *with other* peers (turning individual tasks into social interactions), yet also with themselves. In the first year of primary school, playfulness moves from being mostly socially based into a more individual task, in which self-dialogues appear in relation to their performance. Social interactions are still important for making sense of the activities, intertwining academic assistance from their peers or teacher with playfulness situations, in order to resolve the learning tasks.

These findings lead to two different reflections that are linked. First, as it has been pointed out by Elkonin (1972), Veresov (2006) and van Oers (1999), the change in leading activity does not imply that one of them disappears, or that one leads to the other. Both activities certainly coexist, and one of them takes the leadership in orienting children in their participation. This occurs when children understand the institutional demands, have the minimum competence for resolving the task and have the will to participate. Second, through playfulness children develop functions that facilitate the new required fit with the new activity in the new institutional practice. Anticipation and exploratory positioning through as-if situations, allows them to understand the new situation.

These two considerations can be formulated as an argument for proposing that the overlooked playfulness of children represents a resource for them to make sense of the new situation, thus remaining engaged and participating in it. In fact, Hviid and Zittoun (2008) pointed out that playfulness mediates the process in transitions of leaving behind things, relations or aspects of oneself (as conducts, ways of thinking or of defining oneself) and moving towards new forms. They argue that this situation rarely occurs all at once and, instead, it seems that it is developed through an exploratory process (as-if modes) that enables experience and performance of 'possible' new positions, not yet fully settled: 'the playfulness bridges the actual present and anticipated new future. In other words, every transition requires a space or time for play – through as-if actions, try-and-fail, by trying actions and performances that do not yet have stability and density of the "for-good" and "real-life" consequences' (Hviid & Zittoun, 2008, p. 126). This argument is in line with what Valsiner (2011a) proposes: development occurs at the intersection of negotiations of conditions of as-is, as-if, as-could-be and as-I-want-it-to-be in which the sign construction takes place. Moreover, 'dominance of the imaginary over the real is crucial for understanding cognitive functions and their development–cognition is needed for creating meaningful thought basis for the construction of the future rather than merely serve as a factual commentary about the reality of the world' (Valsiner, 2011a, p. 147). Extending the ideas of these authors to the transitions explored in this study, it can be argued that playfulness brings the functions of play such as 'as-if', no consequences for real life and happiness. Playfulness is then a psychological resource used by children during the neo-formation of learning as a leading activity where the as-if position is supported and projected into the future, thus remaining engaged in the new situation.

In this study, playfulness is indeed revealing the active role that children have in creating their conditions of participation. This is in line with Hedegaard and Fleer's (2013) study in which they found that children's playful orientation has an important role in framing their interaction with adults through both teasing and opposing their caregivers' demands.

Consequently, for this particular transition, playfulness also presents a meaning-making resource in the learning tasks. Playfulness is an attempt by children to make the learning situation more meaningful in its content and in its new required position and its bounded rules. But does this mean that if the learning activities were meaningful in school, more related to what matters to children and making them part of their creation, that playfulness will disappear? No. This is a resource to make sense of new situations and to remain engaged. Moreover, considering the work of Zittoun (2008), Hedegaard and Fleer (2013), Hasse (2008) and Podd'iakov (2012) among others, it is possible to propose that this is a resource that continues along the life course, but that changes in its content and form, although not in its functions: as-if, no direct consequences for real life and happiness.

Quality of the developmental and learning transitional environment

So far the specificities of the Chilean sociocultural context have not been considered in this discussion, as it is not the central objective of this chapter, yet it becomes unavoidable to reflect and discuss the developmental and learning features of this particular educational environment. As it was presented, the children of this study are under highly restricted learning conditions that are established top-down by the Ministry of Education and the municipality, and are reinforced by a surveillance system of assessment implemented at different levels and to different actors. At a more specific level, we could note that the learning literacy lessons are mandatory activities defined by the Ministry of Education, the municipality and the external learning assistance programmes. This affects both levels, but it becomes more accentuated in the first year of primary school, as the overall value of the school programme is centred on promoting learning skills and competences. This latter is not a problem in itself, until in practice it becomes reduced to marks and scores as outcomes that drive the whole public education agenda, specifically funding decisions. Unfortunately, this reductionism left no space for the teacher to design learning activities appropriate to the needs of the students. The activities tended to be decontextualized in relation to children's everyday life experiences, uninteresting for them, going beyond or below their achievement and knowledge levels. In this way, 'learning' became a *performative activity* directed by compliance to the norms as the object of learning instead of being an activity in which the appropriation and expansion of subject matter methods and content is the main object. This performative aspect has been pointed out by Fisher (2012) in her study of six-year-old children learning to read and write, in which she found that children in school have to be students but also learners of writing and reading (or any other subject content), where individual performance is a central feature. However, the cases presented in this chapter show that when the performative normative aspect of school life takes over the learning as the object of the activity, the risk is that children like Maria are not learning to read and write but are performing as 'good students', are out of the teachers' sight and, thus, invisible.

Nevertheless, as has also been shown here, children find their ways of making sense of these adverse conditions in which playfulness emerges as a resource. Still, for promoting development, as Zittoun (2008) and Hedegaard and Fleer (2013) point out, it is fundamental that the institutions care about fostering a transitional process that leads to developmental change. Looking at the evidence presented here about playfulness and learning, it is impossible not to encourage the teaching practice of subject matter to be more sensitive to children's interests and abilities, which also implies promoting broader spaces for free exploration. Addressing Zittoun and Hviid's (2008) words, by giving spaces for try-and-fail, by protecting, tolerating and even promoting uncertainty, fuzziness and disorder, I believe that meaningful learning could be accomplished.

References

Bodrova, E. & D. Leong (2006), 'Vygotskian perspectives on teaching and learning early literacy skills', in D. Dickinson & S. Neuman (eds), *Handbook of early literacy research* (pp. 243–256). New York: The Guilford Press.

Bozhovich, L. I. (2009), 'The social situation of child development', *Journal of Russian and East European Psychology*, 47(1), 59–71.

Bröstrom, S. (1992), *A Cross-cultural, ethnographical and comparative study of one Danish and one American kindergarten plus the psychological development of these Danish and American 6 years old children*. Copenhagen: EDRS price. Retrieved from http://eric.ed.gov/?id=ED369478

Cassidy, M. (2005), "'They do it anyway": a study of Primary 1 teachers' perceptions of children's transition into primary education', *Early Years*, 25(2), 143–153.

Davydov, V. (1999), 'What is really Learning Activity?', in M. Hedegaard & J. Lompscher (eds), *Learning activity and development* (pp. 123–138). Aarhus: Aarhus University Press.

Ebbeck, M., S. B. Saidon, G. Rajalachime & L. Y. Teo (2013), 'Children's voices: Providing continuity in transition experiences in Singapore', *Early Childhood Education Journal*, 41(4), 291–298.

Einarsdóttir, J., B. Perry & S. Dockett (2008), 'Transition to school practices: Comparisons from Iceland and Australia', *Early Years*, 28(1), 47–60.

Elkonin, D. B. (1972), 'Toward the problem of stages in the mental development of the child', *Soviet Psychology*, 10, 225–251.

Elkonin, D. B. (2005), 'The psychology of play', *Journal of Russian & East European Psychology*, 43(1), 11–21.

Fisher, R. (2012), 'Teaching writing: a situated dynamic', *British Educational Research Journal*, 38 (2), 299–317.

Fleer, M. (2010), *Early learning and development: Cultural-historical concepts in play*. Cambridge: Cambridge University Press.

Goodwin, C. (2000), 'Action and embodiment within situated human interaction', *Journal of Pragmatics*, 32(10), 1489–1522.

Hasse, C. (2008), 'Learning and transition in a culture of playful physicists', *European Journal of Psychology of Education*, 23(2), 149–164.

Hedegaard, M. (ed.) (2001), *Learning in classrooms*. Aarhus: Aarhus University Press.

Hedegaard, M. (2002), *Learning and child development: A cultural-historical study*. Aarhus: Aarhus University Press.

Hedegaard, M. (2008a), 'A cultural-historical theory of children's development', in M. Hedegaard & M. Fleer (eds), *Studying children: A cultural-historical approach* (pp. 10–29). Maidenhead/New York: Open University Press.

Hedegaard, M. (2008b), 'Developing a dialectic approach to researching children's development', in M. Hedegaard & M. Fleer (eds), *Studying children: A cultural-historical approach* (pp. 30–45). Maidenhead/New York: Open University Press.

Hedegaard, M. (2012), 'Analyzing children's learning and development in everyday settings from a cultural-historical wholeness approach', *Mind Culture and Activity*, 19, 127–138.

Hedegaard, M. & M. Fleer (eds) (2008), *Studying children: A cultural-historical approach*. Maidenhead, New York: Open University Press.

Hedegaard, M. & M. Fleer (2013), *Play, learning and children's development: Everyday life in families and transition to school*. New York: Cambridge University Press.

Hedegaard, M. & J. Lompscher (eds) (1999), *Learning activity and development*. Aarhus, Headington: Aarhus University Press.

Hviid, P, (2008), '"Next year we are small, right?" Different times in children's development', *European Journal of Psychology of Education*, 23(2), 183–198.

Hviid, P. & T. Zittoun (2008), 'Editorial introduction: Transitions in the process of education', *European Journal of Psychology of Education*, 23(2), 121–130.

Kravtsov, G. & E. Kravtsova (2010), 'Play in Vygotsky's non-classical psychology', *Journal of Russian and East European Psychology*, 48(4), 25–41.

Lave, J. & E. Wenger (1991), *Situated learning: Legitimate peripheral participation*. Cambridge: Cambridge University Press.

Leontiev, A. N. (1981), *Problems in the development of the mind*. Moscow: Progress.

Mirkhil, M. (2010), '"I want to play when I go to school": Children's views on the transition to school from kindergarten', *Australasian Journal of Early Childhood*, 35 (3), 134.

Podd'iakov, N. (2012), 'A play-like position, or a play-like attitude toward life, is the most important quality of the preschool child's personality', *Journal of Russian and East European Psychology*, 50(2), 23–30.

Rogoff, B. (2003), *The cultural nature of human development*. Oxford, New York: Oxford University Press.

Siegler, R. S. (1991), *Children's thinking* (2nd ed.). Englewood Cliffs: Prentice-Hall.

Siegler, R. S. (2006), 'Microgenetic analyses of learning', in W. Damon & R. M. Lerner (Series eds) & D. Kuhn & R. S. Siegler (Vol. eds), *Handbook of child psychology: Volume 2: Cognition, perception, and language* (6th ed., pp. 464–510). Hoboken, NJ: Wiley.

Valsiner, J. (2011a), 'Constructing the vanishing present between the future and the past', *Infancia y Aprendizaje*, 34(2), 141–150.

Valsiner, J. (2011b), 'The development of individual purposes: Creating actuality through novelty', in L. A. Jensen (ed.), *Bridging cultural and developmental approaches in psychology* (pp. 212–234). New York: Oxford University Press.

van Oers, B. (1999), 'Teaching opportunities in play', in M. Hedegaard & J. Lompscher (eds), *Learning activity and development* (pp. 268–289). Aarhus: Aarhus University Press.

van Oers, B. (2009), 'Developmental education: Improving participation in cultural practices', in M. Fleer, M. Hedegaard & J. Tudge (eds), *Childhood studies and the impact of globalization: Policies and practices at the global and local levels* (pp. 213–229). New York: Routledge.

Veresov, N. (2006), 'Leading activity in developmental psychology', *Journal of Russian and East European Psychology*, 44(5), 7–25.

Vygotsky, L. S. (1966). 'Play and its role in the mental development of the child', *Voprosy psikhologii*, 12(6), 62–76.

Vygotsky, L. S. (1978), *Mind in society: The development of higher psychological processes*. Cambridge, MA: Harvard University Press.

Vygotsky, L. S. (1987), *Collected works 1896–1934* (Vol. I & V). New York: Plenum Press.

Vygotsky, L. S. (1998), *The collected works of L.S. Vygotsky. Vol. 5, Child psychology*. New York, London: Plenum Press.

Wagoner, B. (2009), 'The experimental methodology of constructive microgenesis', in J. Valsiner, P. C. M. Molenaar, M. C. D. P. Lyra & N. Chaudhary (eds), *Dynamic process methodology in social and developmental sciences* (pp. 99–121). New York: Springer.

Winther-Lindqvist, D, (2009), Children's development of social identity in transitions: A comparative study. Ph.D. thesis, Copenhagen: University of Copenhagen.

Yin, R. K., (1984), *Case study research: Design and methods*. Beverly Hills, CA: Sage Publications.

Zittoun, T. (2006), *Transition-development through symbolic resources*. Greenwich, CT: Information Age Publishing Inc.

Zittoun, T. (2008), 'Learning in transitions: The role of institutions', *Journal of Psychology of Education*, 23(2), 165–181.

Zittoun, T. (2009), 'Dynamics of life-course transitions: a methodological reflection', in J. Valsiner, P. C. M. Molenaar, M. C. D. P. Lyra & N. Chaudhary (eds), *Dynamic process methodology in social and developmental sciences* (pp. 405–430). New York: Springer.

Zittoun, T., G. Duveen, A. Gillespie, G. M. Ivinson & C. Psaltis (2003), 'The use of symbolic resources in developmental transitions', *Culture & Psychology*, 9(4), 415–448.

6

Negotiating the Demands and Motives in Primary School Transitions

Judith MacCallum and Veronica Morcom

Introduction

Children make many transitions, from home to school, from one year level to the next and from activity to activity at school, and between school and home. How do children negotiate the demands made on them as they make these transitions and in what ways does the process contribute to children's development of motivation and learning? We use Hedegaard's (2012) cultural-historical concepts of motives and demands as children transition across and within institutions to examine the demands different classroom practices make on children and how the children are oriented to these demands as they transition from one classroom to another and between different activities within a collaborative primary classroom. Our conceptualization of transition also draws on Zittoun's (2014) notion of transition as a catalysed process of change, in which an event is experienced as a rupture, 'a disruption of a previous state of acting, feeling and being' (p. 234). The aim of this research was to examine how children's motives change as they experience transitions and are oriented to different demands in new activities. These entailed practice motives (Hedegaard, 2014) of learning together, expressing emotions, respecting each other and making new friends, with the experiences creating new demands and the possibility of a rupture. In this chapter the analysis focuses on how two target children in year 3, Trent and Tina, made sense of the ongoing activities of the collaborative classroom, as well as past activities and possible future activities, and how they negotiated the demands in each new setting.

Theoretical perspectives

From a cultural-historical perspective, children's learning and development are the consequences of meaningful interaction in the social practices of school, home and the neighbourhood (Hedegaard, 2014). Like many researchers trying to unravel the complexities of child development, Hedegaard has drawn on the work of Lev Vygotsky and his colleagues to develop ways to think about and examine children's learning in the school and the home. Vygotsky's cultural historical theory encapsulates the 'system of relations' between the child and their social reality in the concept of the social situation of development (Vygotsky, 1998, p. 199), which enables a focus on the child's perspectives, their motives and competences as they learn and develop across different contexts that include the institution of school.

Hedegaard and Chaiklin (2005) argue that children develop motives through participation in institutional practices. Their conceptualization of motivation and motives as 'the dynamic relation between person and practice' (p. 64) is a development of Leontiev's position of motive development as originating in the environment. Hedegaard (2014) takes this further by adding the child's perspective, and what interest the child brings to teaching, as the starting point for their development of motivation. This allows analysis of situations in different ways. In classroom research, studies have often overlooked 'the socially, situated components of learning' which has potential to capture 'the complexities and messiness of school' (p. 232).

To support exploration of the dynamic relation between child and practice, Hedegaard (2012) has identified different perspectives of analysis, each with a specific dynamic. The perspectives are interrelated with actions in activities nested within institutional practices that are influenced by broader cultural expectations and traditions. It is in the actual social practice in activity settings where children meet demands that support and challenge their motivation. Thus the activity setting of the classroom, while framed by the traditions of schooling of a particular country or culture, can be quite different in different schools and classrooms where the practices are created by the teacher and children as they participate in them. Hedegaard argues,

> From the child's social situation of development, it is how the child experiences the activity emotionally and acts in the situation, whereas from the institution's perspective, it is how the activity takes place in recurrent activity settings. This dialectic is the key to understanding the dynamic of a specific child's learning and development through participation in a specific practice. Motive development

can then be seen as a movement initiated by the child's emotional experience related to the activity setting. (2012, p. 21)

This framework has been used to understand and research children's motives as they create a homework setting with their mother (Hedegaard, 2012), the development of motives in children's play (Fleer, 2012), and how practice traditions in school influence the motives adopted by children (Fleer, 2011).

Transitions create the possibility of change. There may be different motives within different social practices and between the same social practices in different settings, creating a rupture for children as they move between these social practices and settings. The dynamic created by tensions and crises in transitions generates the possibility for disruptions in subsequent learning and development (Zittoun, 2008). In this research, tensions were created as the children transitioned to a classroom with collaborative social practices.

Collaborative approaches

Collaborative approaches to teaching and learning (e.g., Bennett & Rolheiser, 2001; Gibbs, 2001) have gained some traction in primary schools and highlight the importance of the peer group in children's learning, development and understanding of societal expectations of participation (Ladd, Kochenderfer & Coleman, 1996; Rubin, Bukowski & Parker, 2006; Wentzel, 2005). The Australian curriculum details the importance of personal and social capability as critical to learning (Australian Curriculum and Reporting Authority [ACARA], 2014), and the benefits of explicitly teaching values and social and emotional skills for academic learning are well documented (Bodrova & Leong, 2007; Elias, 2006; Ladd & Burgess, 1999; Lovat, Dally, Clement & Toomey, 2011; Morcom, 2012, 2014, 2015, 2016; Zins & Elias, 2007). In the current research, sociograms were used as one way to create group cohesion and support social and emotional development, which is fundamental to creating a collaborative classroom (Ashman & Gillies, 2003; Bennett & Rolheiser, 2001; Bennett, Rolheiser & Stevahn, 1991; Gibbs, 2001). The focus of the social practices was to develop the prerequisite communication, social and emotional competencies to work together (Hart, 1992) and clarify the 'norms, values, rules, roles and social relations' (Kovalainen & Kumpulainen, 2007, p. 141). In the research, classroom values were negotiated at the beginning of the year with children setting the parameters for participation during activities.

The role of the teacher is to provide guidance, as children negotiate participation in activities, by making the demands more explicit and providing timely support for children. Valsiner (1997) refers to this process as canalization by the social world, and more broadly as the ways in which social institutions and other people, consistent with their values and goals and those of the culture at large, channel a child's activities in certain ways so that development is organized in some, rather than another, future direction. In the next section the research context, the school and the classroom social practices are elaborated.

The research context

The research study was situated at Bushlands state primary school in metropolitan Perth, Western Australia. The broader cultural expectations and traditions in Western Australia are that children attend kindergarten (part-time at age 4), then transition to full-time schooling, so that by year 3 the children are 8 years old and have been attending school for 3–4 years. At Bushlands, staff promoted high achievement and performance and achieved above average results, as demonstrated in NAPLAN (National Assessment Program – Literacy and Numeracy) (NAP, 2017). Generally, family incomes tended towards the higher socio-economic bands and traditional teaching methods were widely employed, highly valued and actively supported by parents. Most primary classes were organized with interactions revolving around the teacher, and some teacher collaboration across classes for special activities.

The research classroom was organized differently with children sitting in specially arranged groups that changed about every eight weeks. Compared with most other classrooms in the school, there were more opportunities for children to interact and participate in decision making.

Collaborative social practices in year 3

Five specific social practices were developed for the year 3 classroom to create opportunities for increasing children's participation, interaction and problem solving related to everyday matters, such as learning to work in groups, supporting others and making friends. These practices created new demands and the potential for a rupture in the children's way of acting, feeling and being.

The Daily Social Circle was conducted at the beginning of each school day before children transitioned into their learning programme. The teacher/ researcher modelled the process and passed the 'talking stick' around the circle so the children could state their name, how they felt, and give a brief explanation. This routine assisted children to: develop vocabulary to express emotions; learn to listen attentively to each other and act on the social knowledge generated from the explanations to learn how to support their peers. The children were also enacting the values embedded in the five Classroom Agreements: attentive listening; mutual respect; appreciating others and no put-downs; participation and right to pass (Gibbs, 2001) and personal best (Bernard, 1996). These were negotiated with the children at the beginning of the year, and the charts were displayed in the classroom for future reference.

At the end of each week there were opportunities for children to raise issues, discuss and reflect during the Weekly Classroom Meeting. The agenda items were created and prioritized by the children and teacher/researcher. The person/s who wrote the item ran the discussion and the teacher/researcher was a 'guide on the side' to model to children how to share the talk, build on the ideas generated and make decisions (MacCallum & Morcom, 2008). The main purpose of this social practice was to learn how to solve problems by taking different views into account. After each class meeting the children individually reflected in their Reflection Logs on the class discussion and set personal goals.

Sociograms were used as a tool every eight weeks in year 3 to establish socially cohesive groups where children's aspirations for friendship or leadership could be realized. The children nominated up to four peers, using the criteria of making a new friend or the opportunity to experience a leadership role. Children's social and emotional needs were prioritized by the teacher/researcher so each child had at least one nomination in their new group. In addition to the collaborative practices, there were also opportunities for children to work in pairs and individually.

The research project design

The main research project was conducted over a school year from February to December, and all twenty-four children in the year 3 class and their parents participated. The study involved ethnographic observation over year 3, children and teacher reflections and regular formal interviews with children and their parents (in year 3 and year 4). Specifically, observations were made by the classroom teacher (teacher/researcher and second author) on a daily basis and discussed with the co-researcher (university-based researcher and first author) who conducted the formal interviews and made digital recordings of the weekly classroom meetings, and a range of group activities. Additionally, the project followed twelve children as they transitioned into their year 4 classes in the following year.

The different social practices made particular demands on the children. The children needed to learn, for example, what it meant to be respectful of each other, how to discuss alternative views and make decisions. We analysed the interactions and reflections of two target children, Trent and Tina, as they made sense of the ongoing activities of the collaborative classroom, as well as past activities and possible future activities and how they negotiated the demands of each new activity. Trent and Tina were two of the twelve children followed through to year 4, and were chosen for this analysis because of their differing goals for participation in class activities, and differing experiences. To examine change and development it is important to focus on the process of change (MacCallum & Pressick-Kilborn, 2011; Valsiner, 1997; Zittoun, 2014). Although transitions within year 3 are the main focus, our analysis takes account of the transition from year 2 to year 3, and the transition from year 3 to 4.

Transitions to year 3 and within year 3

In transitioning from year 2 to year 3, both Trent and Tina had the challenge of learning to work in new ways in the year 3 classroom and negotiating the demands these activities made on them and their peers, as well as the demands of their peers.

Coming into year 3, Trent's motive orientation was to do well at school and be better than other children. This was evident from his actions, written reflections and interviews early in year 3. Another motive he expressed was to make friends. Trent had joined the year 2 class mid-year when friendships had already been formed and that class structure did not support new friendship groupings.

Tina's motive orientation at the beginning of year 3 was social, to interact with peers and make new friends, which was consistent with parent expectations and practices at home for sharing ideas and making decisions. From the start of year 3, Tina was oriented to participate in the collaborative activities of the classroom. She differed from Trent in her early valuing of the social circle and class meetings. For Tina they fitted with her interest in sharing ideas. She put up an agenda item for class discussion in the first class meeting, and continued to offer more items than anyone else over the year. She couldn't think of any aspects that weren't good about the class meeting and they supported her motivation towards learning how to participate in class and to be a good friend. Tina described the class meeting as,

> when we discuss things that are good and bad. Mostly bad, things we need to sort out ... actually sort things out, things that ahh need to work at the moment. Learning what we have to do to be a good friend and be good in class. (Tina, Interview, Term 1)

Tina recognized that the year 3 class was not the same as other classes in terms of organization but still learned the same with respect to academic knowledge. Tina said, 'they don't have groups, they learn stuff but not in groups, not exactly the same. They would learn the same maths and writing' (Tina, Interview, Term 1).

In contrast to Tina, the new social practices created tensions for Trent and disrupted his familiar ways of acting, feeling and being in a classroom. Trent didn't see these activities as connected to learning. Although he participated in them, early in year 3 these activities challenged his motive orientation towards learning at school. From Trent's explanations, it was clear that he thought 'work' for learning was what you did in class. In the social circle 'everyone gets to tell about how they feel and a little bit of news', and he didn't 'have to do work' (Trent, Interview, Term 1). Consequently, he didn't think he learned anything. Similarly, he didn't think he learned anything from the class meetings where 'people in class want to talk about an incident'. Although he thought it was good that people could discuss things, he didn't like it because his back got 'sore sitting down that long'.

To guide the children's participation in the different class activities, the teacher/researcher regularly modelled how to participate and gave specific lessons at the point of need. In Term 1 these discussions were about how to choose a group leader and the actual process of reaching a decision. For example, to support children in this process, one focus was on how to hold a discussion when there were differing viewpoints and maintain respectful dialogue. In this way, the teacher/researcher promoted and supported particular ways of acting, feeling and being in the context of the social practices of the classroom.

In the first round of groups Trent and Tina were selected by their peers as vice leaders in their respective groups, so each had to meet the demands of being a leader in a new activity. To prepare the children for this activity, the teacher/researcher led the class in discussion about what a leader 'looks like', 'sounds like' and 'feels like'. This resulted in a chart of the characteristics of leaders to which the children referred when they chose peer leaders for each new group.

Trent's group used a lottery system to vote for their leader, which resulted in a shy girl, Ella, becoming the leader and Trent vice leader. The teacher/researcher observed that during the discussion Trent sat back in his chair, and did not contribute. She noted that 'Ella wanted to try out the leadership role to develop her confidence' (Teacher/researcher, Reflection log, Term 1). In response to the demands made by the children on the teacher and to promote particular forms of participation, the teacher/researcher facilitated follow-up discussions about the role of peers in supporting their leaders. Leadership issues were also discussed at class meetings and children set goals each week, which were reflected upon during the following week.

This first group experience was a disruptive event for Trent. He expressed his disappointment with his experience of Group 1 in his reflections and interview in Term 1. Trent thought his team members didn't care who was leader and he wasn't impressed with the group leader who didn't 'talk loud, have all the stuff that we should have' but added that 'it's not that I don't like her'. He thought the leader should be helping team members learn, not the other way around. Trent didn't think he learned but the group 'helped other people learn'. His comments about his dislike of groups further reveal his anxiety about the demands of working with others, and conflict with his competitive goals.

> I like learning with one other person because with a whole lot of people, everyone gets the same, no one is going to get it wrong. Not going to learn from that. They might not know and never know if just copying. With one other person, not so many people get the same answers. (Trent, Interview, Term 1)

Tina's initial experience in Group 1 was similar to Trent's in that her group found it difficult to reach a consensus about who would be leaders, and held a 'raffle'. Derek was elected leader and Tina became vice leader. Like Trent, Tina found the demands of actually interacting with peers in the group to be challenging and evoked negative emotions. After a few days Tina wanted to resign and stated 'I don't want to be vice leader with Derek. He doesn't listen. Nobody in our group listens' (Tina, Reflection log, February 19). However, Tina was still oriented to work collaboratively so she persevered, as 'first time in the group when we were just settling in, some people were fighting and it was a little bit hard to sort out fights, but now we are settling in'.

You do learn that you need to be responsible and self-controlled, like being a boss, like my dad, but not exactly. Can't just be silly all the time. Can have fun, can't be silly, as that is annoying for other people. (Tina, Interview, Term 1)

Although the leadership experience created a rupture for Tina, it enabled her to start acting, feeling and being in ways that supported her motivation towards learning how to work with her peers, which was supported at home. Tina's parents wrote that their goals for their daughter were 'to develop good relationships and decision-making skills' (Parent survey, Term 1). Tina's experience supported her social motive orientation at school and, thus, she thought working in a group was good most of the time. It is 'good, learn like, how to work together, what a team is all about, voting thing, work in a group, pair or alone'. She thought it helped her be motivated 'sort of because when we are working in a group, everyone does the same work ... does make us learn more things' (Tina, Interview, Term 1).

Trent and Tina were in the same group in the second round and this group followed the decision-making process modelled by the teacher/researcher. After a discussion about leaders they voted. Trent was voted leader, and when Alex and Derek drew for vice leader they agreed to go around the group again and Derek became upset when he 'did not win'. The initial disruption created opportunities for group members to participate in particular ways. The leaders, Trent and Alex, took control of the situation, Tina made useful suggestions, Derek persisted with uncooperative actions but it did not escalate to stop the group achieving its goal. This group achieved a completed design with each member participating and contributing to the final product as shown in the following dialogue.

> Tina:Put a little bit of everyone's symbol on the logo.
> Trent:We've got it covered (Trent started to sketch the symbol).
> Derek: It's my base so I want to do it.
> Alex: Let him do it (Derek finished off Trent's sketch).
> Alex:(turning to Tina and Sandra) You guys can colour.
> Tina: Guys use my pencil. It has a better grip.
> Derek: (nodded refusal to use Tina's pencil). (Group discussion, June 11)

One interpretation is that they had all met the demands of the task and the demands each other had made on them, and they were developing a motive of learning together. Tina had also been in Group 1 with Derek and was conversant with his ways of acting and had developed a level of self-control where she did not become upset with him. Tina was very aware of this issue and in relation to sharing ideas and helping each other said, 'we need to participate' (Tina, June 10). During this round of groups, the teacher focused class discussion on the qualities individual group members bring to their group such as being a supportive friend and showing mutual respect. Tina saw her role as 'being caring and helping others to have confidence in themselves' (Tina, Reflection on Group 2).

In the third round, Trent, Alex and Derek were together again, and Trent and Alex both nominated Sean and Jared as leaders as they thought these boys might benefit from leadership responsibility. The demands of working with these peers disrupted the way that Trent and Alex had worked in the previous group and challenged Trent's motive orientation to excel. Trent revealed his frustrations to the teacher/researcher and hoped his next group would be better.

> I felt annoyed and embarrassed because they were making my group look bad. It's the way they don't have self-control and do good for the group. They do their own thing. It is ok having a naughty child in your group but having Derek, Jared and Sean! It would have been a lot harder without Alex. Alex supported me by telling them to be quiet ... When Jared was vice leader he wasn't supporting the leader Derek but Derek wasn't as bad as the rest. (Trent, Informal interview, September 13)

Trent was beginning to understand how groups worked, so by the fourth group, and consistent with his competitive goals he appeared to be intentionally working out the best combination of children in a group so that he and his group would look good and he would get his work done. In the sociogram for Group 4, Trent nominated three girls and one boy to work with and ended up with two of his female nominations. Trent's nominations reflect his new goal to make new friends with girls (which these girls reciprocated) after his previous experience of being in an all boy group where it was difficult to reach a consensus with the boys often being argumentative. It was evident that Trent's motive towards making friends was developing.

During the weekly class meeting the teacher raised for discussion criteria for selecting leaders and the importance of providing reasons for your opinions. The following strategy was agreed by all the children and written on the board:

> Go around the group once and listen for the reasons given. Then the second time say, 'I agree with ___ because ____ or I disagree with ___ because ___'. Look at the reasons given not the person who gave them. (Weekly class meeting, September 13)

When Trent was reminded of this class decision, which disrupted his intended actions to become group leader, he decided to do what the other group members had agreed upon. One interpretation is that he wanted the group to work, so changed his motive orientation in response to demands the group made on him.

Trent demonstrated a growing understanding of how he could learn from others and what made him feel successful. This further suggests a change towards a motive of learning together.

> In decisions listen, you might trigger an idea. Appreciate what others do for you. Let people settle into the class and let them feel welcome. I try hard in all forms of work. When I understand and do something for the first time I feel successful. (Trent, Survey, September 21)

For the fourth round of groups Tina was in a large group with one other girl and six boys including Derek, whom she nominated as leader, which the rest of the group opposed. The size of this group made particular demands on its members to reach a consensus. The demand of this experience dashed her confidence (as she revealed in a later interview) and clearly disrupted her intended actions. In the reflection surveys for this group's decision making she wrote 'Don't be shy when there's a discussion. Do your best in the little things and the big things will take care of themselves' (Tina, Survey, September 21). She remained optimistic and in this group tried to care for others, showing her leading motive orientation was to make friends. Tina wrote 'I feel successful when I make friends' (September 21), but she was still working out how to best achieve this goal.

In the sociogram for Group 5, Tina received one reciprocated nomination from Jared who was on the sideline with peers, due to inappropriate behaviour. The demands the different groups had made on Tina had oriented her to helping others in the group. She had worked hard to develop self-control herself and, in the second half of the year, she began using her skills to support others such as Derek and Jared who had very similar dispositions.

Trent had experienced the demands that working in different groups made on him, but despite the benefits of feeling 'good and excited when people piggyback on my idea', he didn't like sharing his ideas, unless he was working with an able child.

> I don't feel entirely comfortable giving all my ideas because people don't give their ideas and may pass your level. Well to tell the truth I don't like sharing any of my ideas. I don't know it's just something telling me not to tell my ideas. Well it all depends on how your partner and friend is prepared to work. Well I have definitely learnt how to discuss but I have discovered my identity for working in pairs. I have self-confidence from having a chance to succeed. (Trent, Reflection, November 26)

Despite learning how to discuss and work with new friends in year 3 and work collaboratively, Trent's leading motive of learning was focused on being better than others, which was reinforced at home. 'Mum and Dad want me to be [best in class] but at the moment I'm 4th or 5th (Trent, Interview, Term 4). Trent struggled to excel in leadership all year and said that it was the 'hardest' thing he had to do (Trent, Reflection, December 3). Similarly, Trent was feeling overwhelmed by the parental demands of additional mathematics homework. This demand wasn't revealed until late in the year. Trent wrote,

> My mum and dad thinks it's no problem. My problem is about computer maths. My mum and dad think it is easy but it is my biggest challenge of my life for I only have one second to type my answer and I don't have enough time to type. (Trent, Reflection, November 26)

Although he resisted his parents' desire for more schoolwork at home, Trent was using his classroom learned cooperative skills and problem solving to help with fights he had with his older brother at home.

> I have big fights with my brother …. He's very tough, good for his age. [In groups] having group discussions and solving problems, same as with my brother and sister – we solve problems … sometimes it doesn't do much good in groups. (Trent, Interview, Term 4)

Like Trent, Tina had thought being a leader was important, but the reality of experiences had created a rupture for her. Tina perceived that she had the required leadership qualities of being caring and not 'bossy' yet the group didn't vote for her. She realized that 'I hate making decisions, and leaders have to' and she found it hard to cope with disagreements. By the end of the year she decided that being a leader 'was awful'.

> I wouldn't like to be a leader as they have to do all the work … Other people in the group expect you to have most ideas, use names, be honest. I can be, but I don't think I'd be very good with coping with people. In the first group I wanted to be leader, but after I thought about it, I didn't. (Tina, Interview, Term 4)

Yet, in group work, Tina saw herself as an 'encourager, talker, helper, ideas person, and organizer', which she stated were easy roles for her to play rather than being a leader. Over the year, despite the demands the group work and group processes made on her, Tina found that encouraging others, being supportive, focusing on the positives and not being bossy helped her make friends. In response to the question about making more friends she wrote, 'Yes. Definitely!' (Tina, Reflection, December 3). She maintained her dominant motive to make friends and learn together.

Tina's mother explained her observations of Tina's actions and emotions around the group activities in year 3. Being a vice leader and the time taken to make decisions was very tiring for Tina, and initially was quite stressful with tears in the car going home from school on a few occasions. However, this was temporary and the parent explained that over the year the tears disappeared, and Tina learned skills in cooperating with others. She had noticed that Tina had the right words to calm a situation at home, had developed some good friendships and appeared more resilient. This demonstrates how the skills learned in the school setting were being used in the home setting.

> We have noticed that in social life, with adults and children, she has learned which words to use to calm the incident, even when friends are over, she'll use the right phrase to determine what to do, compromising not confronting. (Parent interview, Term 4)

Transition to year 4: A time to reflect on year 3

Trent and Tina went into two different year 4 classes and both their teachers were mentored by the teacher/researcher in the social practices used in year 3. Transitioning to a classroom with similar and different social practices from year 3 allowed Trent and Tina to reflect on year 3, what they had learned about working together, friendships, sharing ideas, and about themselves and how they learn.

Trent saw that in year 3 and year 4 some demands were the same in that he was 'expected to be a good learner in both' (Trent, Interview, Term 1 year 4). In year 4, the teacher set the boundaries for the children and Trent was better able to do what he thought the teacher wanted. Trent appeared to find the transition to a more traditionally structured classroom suited his dominant motive orientation towards excelling, but noticed that in not having a social circle in year 4 he didn't have the social cues to know how others were feeling. Trent had been developing a motive to learn together in year 3, but with the different demands of year 4, his parents observed Trent to be 'a little more selfish in year 4'. However, he continued the motive to develop friends, and his parents commented that he was trying to be a good friend to a boy who had recently arrived at the school (Parent, Interview, Term 1 year 4).

In year 3 Trent had resisted computer maths at home, but in year 4 he was able to better manage this activity. Trent found year 4 school work 'easy' and said that 'year 3 was more taxing' (Trent, Interview, Term 1 year 4). Trent's explanation was that there was very little new work in year 4 as his family introduced him to schoolwork at home before it was introduced at school, and may explain why he responded more positively to schoolwork at home in year 4. For Trent in year 4, the demands and motives of school and home were not in conflict. He continued to make new friends as some of his year 3 friends had moved to other schools.

One of the key things that Tina learned in year 3 was how to make and maintain friendships. Year 4 was 'good' because she had 'made lots of new friends' (Tina, Interview, Term 1 year 4). She realized that she had been bossy and that 'if you are popular you don't know if someone is a real friend or not'. She had developed self-control in 'not saying bad things or telling secrets … [it is better] telling people good things and to focus on the positive'. Tina said that in year 3 she had also learned 'how to work together, how to take turns and how to agree and disagree'. She realized that she enjoyed talking, and 'talker' was a role she liked to play in group discussions especially if it was about funny things (Tina, Interview, Term 1 year 4).

Tina expressed that in year 4 she felt constrained by the lack of opportunity to say what she thought in class. She realized when talking was restricted in year 4, that not only did she like talking but that 'I learn with talking' (Tina, Interview, Term 1 year 4). She understood that 'different teachers teach differently, they have different ideas'. Although she accepted this as how it was in year 4, she found that she had begun to see herself 'as naughty' because the teacher told her off for talking. She added 'the teacher expects naughtiness and I think I am naughty but I don't really like it'. This difference in how children's views were perceived by teachers disrupted the way Tina felt about herself and the way she acted in class.

Discussion

The teacher/researcher explicitly promoted and supported particular ways of participating (Valsiner, 1997) in the year 3 classroom. These social practices were based on the values underpinning the national curriculum (ACARA, 2014) and by the broader research traditions of collaborative learning and teaching. However, the activities located in these social practices differed from the way other teachers in the school interpreted the values and objectives of schooling, thus creating ruptures in transitions within the institution of the primary school. These transitions were catalysed processes of change (Zittoun, 2014) and offered different types of participation, with different demands and practice motives (Hedegaard, 2014).

Many of the transitions described here reveal disruptions to the ways Trent and Tina were acting, feeling and being. When the children moved from year 2 to year 3, and from year 3 to year 4 new demands and motives arose. Both Trent and Tina understood that school was about learning, but in transitioning from year 2 to year 3 they each found social practices with different demands and different practice motives, presenting challenges for each of them. The motives within practices in the collaborative classroom were to express feelings, to learn to work together, to respect each other and develop and maintain friendships, which differed from the motives within many school practices. In analysing the dynamic between the environment and the child as the relation between institutional demands and values and the child's activity in their social situation of development as a member of a collaborative classroom (Hedegaard, 2012, 2014), we see the changes as they occurred. The children's observations and reflections provide insights into the child's perspective, highlighting how they each experienced the activity setting emotionally and acted in the situation. We also see how each was oriented to the demands made on them, which demands and motives created a rupture, their motive orientation, and what and how each learned in the process.

Children's motive orientation and the demands they recognize change when the practices they enter differ (Hedegaard, 2014). Trent's leading motive was to excel at school and be better than others. He initially found that the collaborative activities disrupted his ways of working and learning. The demands and motives of working in groups conflicted with his personal motive. At times he felt frustrated and disappointed with members of his group because they made him look bad, but Trent persisted because he was motivated to do what was expected of him in the collaborative classroom, and he wanted to excel at being a leader even though it was hard. He found that participating in the collaborative social practices provided him with opportunities to develop leadership skills and new ways of working, as well as make new friends. Trent's social situation changed when he entered a new classroom for year 4, and a motive related to being ahead of other children in the class was possible due to extra learning he engaged in at home with his family. For Trent the transition to year 4 also highlighted how some of the collaborative social practices motivated him and supported his learning.

In the process, his motive of learning developed to encompass not only excelling but also working together with both girls and boys, and with a respected peer.

Tina had a number of ruptures in year 3 and another entering year 4. In year 3, not being elected as a leader in Group 2, aspects related to being a leader and the Group 4 members not supporting her ideas were key ruptures for Tina. Motivated to make and maintain friendships, she realized through the collaborative activities that other children didn't perceive her in the same way that she saw herself. While she was vice leader with Derek in Group 1 they had many disagreements, and then in Group 2 she was not nominated as a leader. These events appear to have disrupted Tina's views and feelings about being a leader, and her confidence declined for a time. She recognized demands to act differently, to develop self-control and not be bossy in order to work better with others and make friends. Later in year 3, she used her renewed confidence and caring approach to support other children who could be disruptive and were still developing self-control. In year 4, entering different social practices with different demands and motives challenged her motive of learning by talking, and disrupted the ways of acting, feeling and being that she had developed in year 3.

The opportunities to participate in collaborative activities allowed Trent and Tina to understand what supported their learning and motivation, and how they could contribute to their own learning and development. By influencing the activity setting the child contributes to the conditions for his or her own learning and development. In this classroom, the children influenced the activity setting through their contributions in the social circle and the class meetings, and their nominations in the sociograms. The demands they made on each other in groups also made demands on the teacher/researcher to make the practices more explicit and support children's ways of participating in their groups and other class activities.

Both children saw relevance in what they learned in the year 3 classroom for life at home and in the world of work. Both Trent and Tina transferred motive orientations from home to the activity setting of the school. Tina brought her motive of sharing ideas from home and Trent brought his motive to be better than others from home, and this motive had been supported in the year 2 classroom. During year 3 Trent resisted activities at home related to learning. It appears that as year 3 progressed and into year 4 with a broader understanding of what constitutes learning and how they learned, the children were able to transfer learning from school to home. This was noted by the children and their parents and acknowledged as positive.

Conclusion

When children move between institutions, such as between classrooms with different practices, they meet challenges when practice motives differ in these different settings. As we see with Trent and Tina, their engagement in the activities in the collaborative classroom were influenced by demands and motives from previous practices (at school or home). While the key motive orientation towards learning at school (Hedegaard, 2012) was evident in the illustrations of Trent and Tina's experiences of collaborative social practices, the children experienced ruptures in what they understood as learning and over time developed diverse understandings of what learning is and can be, and their own role in learning. For example, learning not only concerned new subject knowledge, but also how to express emotions, how to be a leader and support the learning of others, how to solve problems taking different views into account, and how to make and maintain friendships.

The guidance of the teacher (Valsiner, 1997) is critical for children to negotiate the demands of different social practices in ways that contribute to their learning and motivation. Institutional practices don't just make demands on children, these practices embedded in societal traditions make demands on teachers and parents too. If children are to be fully supported in the development of learning motives that enable them to make decisions about their own learning and work with others to solve problems, schools need to be open to the development of social practices like the ones created in the research project reported here.

Zittoun's (2008, 2014) notion of transition as a catalysed process of change involving a rupture assisted our analysis of the development of a new state of children's acting, feeling and being. This allowed examination of Trent and Tina's experiences in the collaborative classroom from both the child's perspective and the institution's perspective.

References

Australian Curriculum, Assessment and Reporting Authority [ACARA] (2014), Foundation to Year 10 Curriculum. Retrieved from https://www.australiancurriculum.edu.au/f-10-curriculum/general-capabilities/personal-and-social-capability/

Ashman, A. F. & R. M. Gillies (2003), 'Peer support networks in school and community settings', in R. M. Gillies & A. F. Ashman (eds), *Co-operative learning: The social and intellectual outcomes of learning in groups* (pp. 198–209). London: Routledge Falmer.

Bennett, B. & C. Rolheiser (2001), *Beyond Monet: The artful science of instructional integration*. Toronto: Bookation Inc.

Bennett, B., C. Rolheiser & L. Stevahn (1991), *Cooperative learning where heart meets mind*. Toronto: Educational Connections.

Bernard, M. (1996), *You can do it! Teachers guide to boosting student motivation, self esteem and school achievement* (2nd ed.). Victoria: Australian Scholarships Group.

Bodrova, E., & D. J. Leong (2007), *Tools of the mind: The Vygotskian approach to early childhood education* (2nd ed.). Columbus, OH: Merrill/Prentice Hall.

Elias, M. J. (2006), 'The connection between academic and social-emotional learning' in M. J. Elias & H. Arnold (eds), *The educator's guide to emotional intelligence and academic achievement* (pp. 4–14). Thousand Oaks, CA: Corwin Press.

Fleer, M. (2011), 'Motives as a central concept in learning', in D. McInerney, R. Walker & A. Liem (eds), *Sociocultural theories of learning and motivation: Looking back, looking forward* (pp. 65–85). Charlotte, NC: Information Age.

Fleer, M. (2012), 'The development of motives in children's play', in M. Hedegaard, A. Edwards & M. Fleer (eds), *Motives in children's development: Cultural-historical approaches* (pp. 79–96). New York: Cambridge University Press.

Gibbs, J. (2001), *Tribes: A new way of learning together*. Windsor, CA: Centre Source systems.

Hart, S. (1992), 'Collaborative classrooms', in T. Booth, W. Swann, M. Masterton & P. Potts (eds), *Learning for all: Curricula for diversity in education* (pp. 9–22). London: Routledge.

Hedegaard, M. (2012), 'The dynamic aspect in children's learning and development', in M. Hedegaard, A. Edwards & M. Fleer (eds), *Motives in children's development: Cultural-historical approaches* (pp. 9–27). New York: Cambridge University Press.

Hedegaard, M. (2014), 'The significance of demands and motives across practices in children's learning and development: An analysis of learning in home and school', *Learning, Culture and Social Interaction*, 3, 188–194.

Hedegaard, M. & S. Chaiklin (2005), *Radical-local teaching and learning: A cultural-historical approach*. Aarhus: Aarhus University Press.

Kovalainen, M. & K. Kumpulainen (2007) 'The social construction of participation in an elementary classroom community', *International Journal of Educational Research*, 46, 141–158.

Ladd, G. W. & K. B. Burgess (1999), 'Charting the relationship trajectories of aggressive, withdrawn and aggressive/withdrawn children during early grade school', *Child Development*, 70(40), 910–929.

Ladd, G. W., B. J. Kochenderfer & C. C. Coleman (1996), 'Friendship quality as a predictor of young children's early school adjustment', *Child Development*, 67, 1103–1118.

Lovat, T., K. Dally, N. Clement & R. Toomey (2011), 'Values pedagogy and teacher education: Re-conceiving the foundations', *Australian Journal of Teacher Education*, 36(7), 31–44.

MacCallum, J. & V. Morcom (2008), 'Making classroom social practices explicit: Developing motivation through participation in collaborative leadership opportunities', in D. M. McInerney, S. Van Etten & M. Dowson (eds.), *Sociocultural influences on motivation and learning* (Vol. 8, pp. 191–221). Charlotte, NC: Information Age Publishing.

MacCallum, J. & K. Pressick-Kilborn (2011), 'Examining change in motivation: The potential of sociocultural theory', in D. McInerney, R. Walker & A. Liem (eds), *Sociocultural theories of learning and motivation: Looking back, looking forward* (pp. 163–187). Charlotte, NC: Information Age.

Morcom, V. E. (2012), *Motivation as negotiated participation in a collaborative classroom: A sociocultural perspective.* Murdoch University, Western Australia (Doctoral dissertation). Retrieved from http://researchrepository.murdoch.edu. au/14780/

Morcom, V. (2014), 'Scaffolding social and emotional learning in an elementary classroom community: A sociocultural perspective', *International Journal of Educational Research*, 67, 18–29.

Morcom, V. (2015), 'Scaffolding social and emotional learning within "shared affective spaces" to reduce bullying: A sociocultural perspective', *Learning, Culture and Social Interaction*, 6, 77–86.

Morcom, V. E. (2016), 'Scaffolding peer collaboration through values education: Social and reflective practices from a primary classroom', *Australian Journal of Teacher Education*, 41(1), 81–99.

National Assessment Program (2017), NAPLAN: National assessment program – Literacy and Numeracy. Retrieved from https://www.nap.edu.au/naplan

Rubin, K. H., W. M. Bukowski & J. G. Parker (2006), 'Peer interactions, relationships and groups', in N. Eisenberg (ed.), *The handbook of child psychology* (6th ed., pp. 571–645). New York: Wiley.

Valsiner, J. (1997), *Culture and the development of children's action: A theory of human development* (2nd ed.). New York: John Wiley.

Vygotsky, L. S. (1998), *Child psychology. The collected works of L.S. Vygotsky: Vol.5.* New York: Plenum Press.

Wentzel, K. R. (2005), 'Peer relationships, motivation and academic performance at school', in A. J. Elliot & C. S. Dweck (eds), *Handbook of competence and motivation* (pp. 279–296). New York: Guilford Press.

Zins, J. E. & M. J. Elias (2007), 'Social and emotional learning: Promoting the development of all students', *Journal of Educational and Psychological Consultation*, 17 (2–3), 233–255.

Zittoun, T. (2008), 'Learning through transitions: The role of institutions', *European Journal of Psychology of Education*, 23(2), 165–178.

Zittoun, T. (2014), 'Transitions as dynamic processes: A commentary', *Learning, Culture and Social Interaction*, 3, 232–236.

Part 2

Transition Between Daily Practices and Everyday Activity Settings

7

Children's Everyday Transitions: Children's Engagements across Life Contexts

Dorte Kousholt

Introduction

This chapter deals with everyday transitions in the early years of childhood. The aim is to provide knowledge about how children actively engage in transitions between different activities and communities and how they connect their different life contexts. In Denmark, almost all (in 2014, 98 per cent[1]) children between three and six years of age attend some form of public day care. This coincides with the fact that most women with preschool children go to work. The high participation rate in public day care in itself indicates that a significant characteristic of early childhood in Denmark is transition between the home and institutional arrangements, challenging us to conceptualize children's development as anchored in an everyday life across different contexts and different social practices. Furthermore, this situation must influence approaches to care and developmental support, since taking care of children involves gathering information about and relating to the child's everyday life in other contexts and cooperating with other adults to support the child's well-being and development. Analysing transitions from the vantage point of the children can provide knowledge about how children actively deal with and arrange their conditions as they move between different communities and practices, as well as the struggles and possibilities involved, which are not always visible to adult caregivers. This knowledge can be valuable in strengthening collaboration between parents and professionals regarding children's development.

---

[1] Statistical yearbook (see also Juhl, 2018; Winther-Lindqvist & Svinth, 2017 for an outline of the Danish early childcare system).

This chapter focuses on everyday transitions between the home and an institutional setting, which can be termed 'horizontal transitions' (Vogler, Crivello & Woodhead, 2008). As noted by Vogler, Crivello and Woodhead in a review of transition research, horizontal transitions have received less attention from researchers than vertical transitions, possibly because they are often less distinctive. Vertical transitions are often marked by a particular day or event (e.g., the first day of school). However, as a growing body of transition research has pointed out, vertical transitions are best understood as a social process over time (e.g., preparation for, actualization of and adaptation to the new context, as demonstrated in Winther-Lindqvist's transition model in this book) (see also, e.g., Lam & Pollard, 2006; Vogler et al., 2008). To explore transitions as social processes across time and contexts emphasizes that vertical transitions are necessarily embedded in horizontal transitions that take place on a daily basis. In this way, vertical transitions and horizontal transitions are interlinked. When children move through the chain of educational institutions, for example from day care to primary school, the everyday transitions between home and institution also change.

My focus on everyday transitions highlights the shifts between different activities and communities within institutional settings, as well as those transitions involving a change of context (periods of leaving and arriving). The detailed ethnographic account presented in this chapter can help in understanding children's active contribution to the various communities they take part in and their efforts and struggles when moving between them. In terms of a conceptualization of children's transitions, I employ the notion of conduct of everyday life to analyse the anticipatory, creative and coordinating processes involved in living a complex everyday life (Holzkamp, 2013). This entails paying attention to how children create and modify connections between their different life contexts as part of developing a personal conduct of life. I regard the different conditions for transition as related to children's participation in communities at the day-care institution and zoom in on *conditions* for and *variations* in how children can link their different contexts (Kousholt, 2011b).

Transition as part of children's developmental conditions and parental care

Within sociocultural theory and the cultural-historical tradition, children's development is studied in relation to their everyday activities in different settings, which serves as a fruitful foundation for my approach to everyday transitions. Building on this cultural-historical approach, development is conceptualized as a dialectical relation between children's changing participation and changes in the practices they take part in (Chaiklin et al., 1999; Hedegaard, 2012; Hedegaard, Aronsson, Højholt & Ulvik, 2012). Fleer and Hedegaard emphasize that, in this dialectical view of development, it is the '*child's relations* to the environment that changes' (Fleer & Hedegaard, 2010, p. 150). In continuation of this approach, the chapter investigates children's active participation in and changing relations to activities and practices across their different life contexts. Fleer and Hedegaard further state that 'transformation through participation means that not only do individuals change, but they change the communities in which they live' (Fleer & Hedegaard, 2010, p. 151). Rogoff makes a similar argument; that transitions 'can fruitfully be examined from a sociocultural perspective that asks how children's involvements in the activities of their community change, rather than focusing on change as a property of isolated individuals' (Rogoff, 1996, p. 273). This requires that we pay greater attention to children's involvement and engagement in various activities, as well as to different ways of taking part, as connected to what is going on in the communities in which the child participates.

Rooted in sociocultural theory, Lam and Pollard propose a framework for understanding children as agents in the vertical transition from home to kindergarten (Lam & Pollard, 2006). They stress the importance of understanding the context for transition; that is, of situating children's transitions in concrete social contexts. Lam and Pollard discuss transitions in relation to the notions of continuity and discontinuity, referring to children's experiences as they move from one setting to another (p. 126). They highlight that 'transition is not only a change of context, but also a process of change, and a shift of identity' (p. 129). While I also emphasize transition as a process of change, I find that their notion of a shift of identity underplays the processes of making connections across life contexts. The challenge, I contend, is to analyse different configurations of continuity and discontinuity that can exist for different children in connection with the child's active effort of moving between different practices and contexts. In order to further elaborate and clarify my analytical approach, I will now explore the concept of conduct of everyday life.

Employing the concept of conduct of life in analysing everyday transitions

I suggest that employing the concept of conduct of everyday life can contribute to transition research by specifically addressing the cross-contextual nature of everyday life. The concept has gained currency in psychological research in recent years, where it has been used to strengthen the focus on the practice of everyday living from a subject perspective (e.g., Dreier, 2008; Schraube & Højholt, 2016). With origins within subject-oriented sociology, the concept was developed to address people's active efforts to deal with the various (and often contradictory) demands from different spheres of everyday life (Holzkamp, 2013; Jurczyk, Voß & Weihrich, 2016). As formulated by Højholt and Schraube, the conduct of everyday life 'represents a mediating category between the individual subjects and societal structures, articulating in particular the subjects' experiences and the scope of action as they grapple with these structures through collective and structuring actions' (Højholt & Schraube, 2016, p. 4). This highlights societal structures as *conditions for participation* in and across different social practices (Højholt & Kousholt, 2018). Furthermore, it emphasizes that conduct of everyday life is something we do together; it is fundamentally a social endeavour. The conduct of life implies continuous social coordination with others (Dreier, 2011). Hence, it is important to emphasize the *collective* and mutual processes of developing the conduct of everyday life (Højholt, Juhl & Kousholt, 2018; Kousholt, 2016).

In relation to a focus on everyday transition, the concept of conduct of everyday life directs attention to the embodied practices of moving between different activities and contexts (with different forms of social organization, different demands and different social possibilities) on an everyday basis and to the *concerns and engagements people pursue across time and space.* Different activities are not discrete incidents, but are part of a whole (such as a maths lesson, comprising group work, individual problem-solving and teacher instruction, or a day, comprising a wide range of activities in a number of different contexts). Likewise, different contexts are not isolated settings, but a particular part of a whole life. How we experience the relationship between activities and between contexts, whether as fragmented, detached or coherent, influences our experience of the whole. Hence, investigating conduct of life means to pay attention to individuals' situated participation and social interplay in different contexts in connection with how possibilities for participation are created across different contexts. The process of conducting one's life across different contexts does not lead to some kind of harmonious coherence; pursuing engagements and concerns in our lives often entails leaving certain commitments and engagements behind in the process of moving from one context to another. This frequently involves changing how you participate, sometimes even hiding or supressing certain aspects of your engagement. In this way, conduct of everyday life is also about orientating oneself and experiencing what is possible in different places and with different people, using new potentialities in transitions in relation to personal engagements and concerns (2018). Conduct of everyday life is thereby closely linked to self-understanding; a person's self-understanding both emerges from and guides his or her conduct of everyday life (Dreier, 2011, p. 12).

In analysing transitions, the concept of conduct of everyday life emphasizes how the personal task of making life hang together across varied activities and contexts is a conflictual process that is deeply embedded in social coordination and influences social self-understanding.

Exploring children's everyday lives: Introducing Matthias

The following analysis of children's everyday transitions builds on empirical material drawn from ethnographically inspired participant observations across children's different life contexts and from interviews with children and their parents (Kousholt, 2008, 2011a, 2011b, 2012, 2016). Ethnographic methods are especially well-suited to exploring transitions as they, in Barrie Thorne's words, can 'fruitfully open insight into complex variation and into the processes and relationships that link varied institutional contexts' (Thorne, 2001, p. 360; see also Corsaro, Molinary & Brown Rosier, 2002).

In this chapter, I primarily draw on examples from a study that investigated the everyday lives of six children through participant observation in their day-care institution and at home and through interviews with their parents. The research was designed in such a way that I gradually got to know the children and their families. I started as a participant observer in the day-care institution over a six-month period, observing and engaging with the children. I then selected three girls and three boys for closer observation and interviewed their parents in their family homes. Later, I conducted '24-hour participant observation'; that is, I followed each of the six children for 24 hours, comprising an ordinary day at the day-care institution and at home, in order to deepen my knowledge of the child's social situation and get a sense of the transitions they make and the day in its entirety from the child's perspective (Kousholt, 2011a, 2011b).

The six families all live in the same small provincial Danish town. The town consists primarily of single-family houses, along with a few blocks of flats, organized around a main street. Most of the parents work in one of the larger neighbouring cities. In this chapter, I particularly focus on an excerpt from one of these '24-hour participant observations', where I spent a day with a boy I call

Matthias. Matthias is five years old. He lives with his mother and father in a single-family house. Both his parents have full-time (skilled labour) jobs in a nearby town. Matthias has a younger brother (aged two and a half), as well as a half-sister (aged eleven) who lives with him for five days every second week. Matthias's day-care institution is located approximately one kilometre from his home. It is a rather small institution with forty-five children aged between three and six (with an additional twenty younger children in a nursery in the adjacent building).

My analysis addresses questions of how to understand children's participation in day-care settings as both situated as part of particular communities in the day-care institution and as part of an everyday life across different contexts. I analyse Matthias's activities and engagements in his day-care institution as part of social interplay in the children's communities and in relation to institutional practices. In addition, I will draw on some examples from the everyday life of another boy, Jason, since this allows me to explore the different ways in which they participate and the different conditions they have for connecting their life contexts.

Excerpt from a day with Matthias

On a December day around noon, Matthias, Christoffer and Jason sit together at a table at the day-care institution and eat their lunch. They fool around and make jokes about who has a girlfriend. Jason and Matthias start to shout while holding their hands over their ears. Jonas, who works at the day-care institution, asks the boys to stop shouting and moves Jason to another table, saying that he is too noisy. Matthias asks if I want to play football after lunch. He explains that he and Christoffer will play as a team against me.

After lunch, we play football and several other boys join the match. Matthias decides who can join in and directs the players to the position they should play. 'The girls cannot play', Matthias tells me. Later, Matthias wants to show me how high he can climb the trees in the playground. Some other boys gather around the trees and start climbing. Matthias can climb the highest. He tells us about a tree he climbs in his garden at home. 'We will be picked up at three', Matthias tells me. 'That's late', he continues.

Later, Matthias wants me to tip over the football goal so they can climb on it. I am reluctant to do so and tell Matthias that I am not sure that is allowed. 'Can't you decide?' he asks me. 'Charlotte and Karen [the head and vice-head of the institution] decide at the kindergarten', Matthias explains, 'they have the secret keys'.

At 3.50 pm, Matthias's mother arrives to pick us up. Matthias runs towards her and gives her a big hug. We go to pick up Matthias's younger brother (he is in the nursery in the adjacent building). Matthias asks his mother whether he and I can walk home and she says yes. Matthias assures me that he knows the way and that it is not far. When we arrive at around 4.15 pm, his father is also home. 'We are going to play in my room', Matthias tells his parents. Matthias shows me his new colouring book and points to the pictures his older sister has coloured and we admire how skilled she is at colouring 'inside the lines'. Matthias tells me that he also likes to play with Lego. While we are playing in Matthias's room, his mother is doing some laundry and taking care of his younger brother. Matthias's father is preparing dinner in the kitchen. About an hour later, we eat dinner together in the dining room. After dinner, Matthias and I play some board games and borrow his older sister's computer for a while. At 8.30 pm, Matthias is put to bed. He does not want to sleep and protests loudly, throwing himself to the floor. He cries and calls from his room. His mother and father take turns trying to calm him. It takes a while before he falls asleep.

The next morning, Matthias's father wakes him up at 6.00 am. Matthias walks drowsily to the living room and turns on the television. His father helps him get dressed, while he watches cartoons. It is time to leave the house and Matthias puts on his yellow boots. His mother wants him to wear warmer boots. Matthias becomes agitated and shouts, 'you don't decide that'. Matthias's mother scolds him and insists that he change his boots. Matthias ends up changing boots while protesting loudly. At 6.50 am, his mother drives us to the day-care institution.

Matthias's mother helps Matthias hang his jacket in the locker room and accompanies him to the common room, where a few other children are sitting at a table eating breakfast. Matthias kisses his mother goodbye and eats some breakfast. After breakfast, Matthias wants to colour more pictures in his colouring book, which he has brought with him from home. Gradually, more children arrive and a couple of hours later Matthias and the other children in his group are getting ready to go to a birthday celebration at Caroline's house.

This insight into the everyday life of Matthias illustrates that transitions are a regular part of his day. Not just transitions between places (home and day-care institution), but also between different activities and communities. To further explore the everyday transitions in Matthias's life, I will now situate them within a broader context, comprising knowledge about the communities and practices that he takes part in and, in turn, how his everyday transitions are shaped by his possibilities for connecting different life contexts.

Transitions in the day-care institution

The daily structure at the day-care institution alternates between adult-arranged activities and time for child-initiated 'free play'. (The amount of time allotted to these different pedagogical practices has been an issue for political debate, with a strong focus on adult structured activities with a learning purpose in recent years; see also Juhl, 2018.) As such, the day is organized with several transitions, where the children must disrupt their activities and start new ones. Coping with everyday transitions demands that children learn certain skills and understandings (Dreier, 2011, p. 14). In day care, this can be skills like putting on clothes and clearing up toys or understandings such as how transitions between activities are arranged during the course of the day. The possibilities for taking part and influencing what is going on in connection with these shifts and changes of activities vary.

Matthias actively engages in planning and forming transitions from one activity to another by inviting particular children to play, engaging in dialogues and disputes over rules, and initiating and leaving particular activities. Matthias must coordinate his attempts in relation to the interests and engagements of the other children, as well as to the day-to-day routines of the day-care institution. After lunch, for example, the children are supposed to play outside, often discussing what to play and making plans as they eat. Hence, where you sit during lunch can be significant as it allows you to talk to and make plans with other children you would like to play with afterwards. This can help in understanding children's sometimes very explicit emotional distress in relation to 'who to sit next to'. While this has to do with the concrete situation (having fun during lunch), it can also be understood in terms of creating transitions to new activities and influencing social possibilities. It is often in transition between locations (going inside from the playground or leaving on an excursion) that you see children eagerly calling out to certain other children and discussing plans for what they want to do later. Such plans often change; nevertheless, being part of the planning process and exploring common engagements with other children seem significant in relation to possibilities for taking part and contributing in a relevant way (see also Højholt & Kousholt, 2018 for similar examples of children during transitions between school and after-school centres). This is in line with previous research that has emphasized how children use each other in transitions and, consequently, how some children can find themselves in vulnerable positions due to exclusion from social coordination (Højholt, 2016; Stanek, 2014).

At the day-care institution, Matthias is considered part of a group of boys often referred to as 'the wild boys'. Most of the time, these boys play at the outer perimeter of the large playground or in the 'pillow room' (a small room with mattresses and pillows where the children can play without adult supervision). Among the boys, being tough, strong, fast and daring are considered valuable attributes. 'Let's be fast and furious', Matthias suggests, when we play. It is part of the boys' community to be in opposition to girls and grown-ups. The boys compete, challenge each other and have a lot of fun. However, frequently they end up fighting. They often argue about 'what to do' and 'who should decide'. The boys also come into conflict with the day-care professionals, who generally think the boys are too noisy and disruptive. They feel they too often have to reprimand them, separating them when they get into fights.

Even though the boys are often referred to as a group, they have different perspectives and possibilities for taking part in their shared activities. By including some examples that explore the boys' community from Jason's perspective, I will develop this point. Jason is often engaged in the same activities as Matthias, yet he does not seem to have the same possibilities for influence. In many situations Matthias takes the initiative and arranges joint activities, and he often directs the play. Jason, like Matthias, tries to influence and direct activities so that he can win or succeed in a game, but he often experiences what happens as 'unfair' and becomes frustrated and angry. The boys' collective way of arranging their community (e.g., giving importance to 'who can decide' and competition) has different meanings for the two boys. Jason's personal difficulties must be seen in relation to the social dynamics in the boys' community. The boys are conditions for each other; their possibilities for *changing* their participation are interwoven with the development of the communities they take part in.

I have outlined some aspects of Matthias's everyday life at the day-care institution he attends that appear significant in relation to his participation here, as well as his possibilities for connecting his different life contexts. The latter can be further explored by examining Matthias's life at home and his parents' perspectives. In addition, I include some examples from Jason's life at home and his mother's perspective to illustrate variations in possibilities for making transition between the day-care institution and family life.

Matthias at home and seen from his parents' perspective

Matthias's parents both prioritize being at home in the afternoon so they can help each other with the daily housekeeping and have time to take Matthias to recreational activities. This means they have to leave for work very early in the morning and that, during the morning routine, there is not much room for time together or conversation. Matthias tells me he finds it boring to get up in the morning, but it is not something that seems to bother him especially. In the morning, Matthias's parents place fewer demands on him. He is normally capable of getting dressed by himself, but this is not expected of him in the morning and he is allowed to watch cartoons. During the afternoon, there is more room for flexibility, and Matthias usually has a few hours in which to play before dinner. Matthias's parents appreciate that he is often good at playing on his own, and that he likes to be outside in the garden. Matthias's mother talks about Matthias as a 'typical boy' – meaning that he has a lot of energy, likes to be physically active, and is 'a bit hot-headed'. They think he is in many ways 'an easy child'; 'he is good at adapting to the daily routines'. Their conflicts with Matthias usually occur in the evenings. Matthias's parents do not adhere to strict bedtimes, preferring to adjust evening routines according to their children's wishes and moods (if they are playing happily, they consider it a shame to interrupt them). On the other hand, they do not want the children to be too tired in the morning. The different ways of organizing mornings and evenings mean that the demands placed on Matthias and his possibilities for influence vary – and the number of conflicts reflect this variation.

Matthias's mother describes how Matthias looks up to his big sister and how they engage in more sedate activities together, such as playing with dolls or building with Lego. She draws on such experiences when she becomes concerned that Matthias will have difficulties when he starts school because he is too 'restless and unfocused'. However, she also emphasizes that she is pleased that Matthias is so 'outgoing' – she thinks this will be an advantage for him when he starts school. How Matthias's parents understand Matthias is influenced by how he participates in family settings and at the day-care institution at the moment, but also by their expectations of how he will cope with the transition to school. This illustrates how parents' considerations of their child's development encompass anticipating future institutional transitions – the child's strengths and difficulties are understood both in relation to the present and to the anticipated demands and challenges in the future (Kousholt, 2011a, b).

Matthias's parents are of the opinion that Matthias likes attending the day-care institution, but he does not tell them much about what happens there. When they ask him, he will sometimes talk about getting into fights with the other boys. Matthias's parents do not approve of fighting; however, they do not consider such fights a 'serious problem' – the boys get into fights because they are boys and equally stubborn. Matthias's father says, 'I guess it is just boys who all want to be in charge'.

Jason's mother sees the boys' community differently. She thinks the boys fight too much and that Jason gets caught up in their destructive ways of relating to each other. She has talked with Jason about 'not hitting back' and trying to be nice to the other boys instead. However, it is her experience that her advice does not help Jason. Instead, it brings her into conflict with Jason, who claims she 'does not understand' and asks, 'why can the other boys hit when I can't'. The different parental perspectives on the boys' behaviour and different understandings of their social interplay influence how the parents view their own child's strengths and difficulties. The parents have different ways of talking with their children regarding the conflicts between the boys and have different views about the need for support for their own child and the group of boys as a whole. In this way, the different parental perspectives and approaches influence the boys' possibilities for connecting their different life contexts. The parents' different understandings of the boys' interplay also relate to the experiences they have when they drop their boys off at and pick them up from the day-care institution. This leads me to further consideration of home-institution transitions (arriving at and leaving the day-care institution) – what I refer to as *transitional time*.

Transitional time

Transitional time often has a certain intensity, despite the short duration: children crying or excitedly greeting each other, parents trying to leave without a commotion, remembering to give relevant information to the day-care professionals, checking their child has weather-appropriate clothing etc. During the interval when children and parents are coming and going, one can get a glimpse of different everyday practices and the way these practices are weaved together in the transition (Thorne, 2001, p. 360). The day-care professional's attention to transitions is most pronounced when the child first starts in day care. There are institutionalized routines for supporting the children (and their parents) during the 'settling-in period' (such as welcome letters, making a personalized nameplate with a photograph, practising saying goodbye, waving and so on).

One important skill enabling children to orientate themselves in relation to transitional time is knowing what time it is. Preschool children are typically not able to tell the time. Nevertheless, they often talk about what time they are going to be picked up, and what constitutes an early or late pick-up time (like Matthias, who talks about three o'clock being late, even though he is usually picked up around four). Time seems to be a more relevant topic for the children in the afternoon than in the morning. It does not seem particularly important whether they are right about the time; talking about and negotiating time is an important part of orientating themselves during the afternoon and the transition to home. The children develop their (still very unreliable) sense of clock-time by relating to the afternoon's routine activities and their parents' working hours (many institutions serve a healthy snack around three o'clock, so the term before or after 'fruit' is often used as a marker for what time it is).

Parents talk about how transitions are often vulnerable and associated with conflicts. Leaving a crying child in the morning or dragging a screaming child out of the day-care institution in the afternoon are associated with shame and insecurity in terms of being judged a bad parent – it 'follows you at work', as one mother said. The notable attention to the processes of being dropped off and picked up can be related to a cultural emphasis in Denmark on parent-child attachment as pivotal for child development, and, in turn, emotional attunement as a core priority in day-care institutions (Juhl, 2018). This places a focus on how children and parents part and reunite as a source of relevant information for the day-care professionals about the relationships in the family.

Children's everyday transitions are given most attention in proximity to vertical transitions, and there is some expectation that children will react in some way during such periods. Maybe that is why it seems parents can experience problems related to everyday transitions that are not immediately prior to or following a vertical transition as more difficult to understand (Kousholt, 2018). Transitional problems can raise concerns (among both parents and professionals) about the root of the problem: why does a particular child cry every morning or complain of stomach ache as pick-up time approaches? Are the child's actions related to conflicts with other children, changes among the staff, difficulties at home? Are they a temporary issue and part of normal development, or are they a symptom of more critical developmental problems? (See also Højholt, Juhl & Kousholt, 2018; Kousholt, 2012). Parents' accounts indicate that transitional time is something that is given a lot of thought and attention – in a way, it is the parents' 'window' into the institution and a basis for assessing how the child is doing. This excerpt from a dialogue between Matthias's parents is illustrative of such doubts concerning the well-being of one's child at the day-care institution.

> Mother: It is like, you have to say: no news is good news ... Matthias doesn't tell much ... there have been days where I have brought him to daycare and we have waved and said goodbye, and I have been in the car, and then he comes running out, crying, to get that last hug ... and then he is fine ...

Father: Well, we don't really know that …
Mother: No, but I think so, they [the day-care professionals] usually tell us if
something is wrong.

Several co-existing features shape the experience of the transition, such as the time of arrival, the practices and possibilities for saying goodbye and the social dynamics between the children. Matthias's parents both work full-time and they arrive at the institution early in the morning, when there are few other children and the day-care professionals' main priority is to provide a calm and welcoming environment. Jason's mother, on the other hand, is a student and, since her classes start late, she prefers to have a calm morning with plenty of time with her son and takes Jason to day care late in the morning. When Jason and his mother arrive, the children are playing and the day-care professionals are busy attending to practical activities. Compared to Matthias's mother, Jason's mother experiences the day-care institution and the relationships between the children quite differently, among other things due to their later arrival. Jason's mother is concerned about how the boys behave towards each other.

Mother: It is better if I arrive at the kindergarten earlier, I have noticed, because
if I get there later, then the children are all already engaged [in activities];
then it is harder for him [Jason] to join in, because they are very skilled at
shutting each other out. He gets so sad.

She tries to rearrange their everyday routine so as to arrive earlier, but since her classes end late, she often picks Jason up between 4.30 and 5.00 pm (which she considers late). This therefore constitutes a dilemma in relation to making their everyday life work, seen as a whole (Kousholt, 2011a).

The parents' knowledge of their child's well-being and development at the day-care institution is mostly indirect – in the sense that they are not usually physically present and must rely on the information they are given by the day-care professionals. Their experiences of how their child deals with transition time, what they can discern from the child's behaviour, and what he or she tells them at home are important spaces for gathering information. To grasp this indirect character of parents' knowledge, Thorne talks about how parents must 'read signs' (Thorne, 2001). Both parents and day-care professionals read signs to assess the child's well-being and development and can experience and interpret such signs differently. Transitions are significant in relation to such sign-reading processes and divergent interpretations are a source of misunderstanding and conflict in the collaboration between parents and professionals (see also Andenæs & Haavind, 2018).

Change in everyday transitions

Transitions between home and the day-care institution become a regular part of the child's everyday routines. When subjected to further scrutiny, however, such transitions are continuously in flux. Changes in transitions between home and the day-care institution are rooted in everyday practices as well as cultural practices for development – as exemplified by Matthias's desire to walk home on his own, facilitated by my presence that day. This indicates that, for children, being able to move between contexts on your own is an area to push for influence and autonomy. Children's spatial autonomy is evident as children grow up. This can be a topic of child-parent conflict and contestation (e.g., Thorne, 2001). However, it does serves as a sign of children's development.

Preparations for the transition to school are often accompanied by changes in the demands and expectations placed on the children in their everyday transitions (such as tying their own shoelaces or remembering their belongings without adult support, because they will be expected to manage such things at school). In Danish day-care institutions, it is common to organize adult-structured school-preparatory activities during the final six months of day care (see also Winther-Lindqvist in this book). Correspondingly, the day-care professionals' assessments of the child's behaviour at the day-care institution become increasingly related to how they view the child's ability to meet the demands of the school (such as being able to sit still and concentrate on a given task for a longer time span, and responding to a collective message). In this way, it is indicative that the day-care professionals' concerns that Matthias and the other boys are 'too wild and misbehave too much' become more pronounced when they consider that the boys are supposed to start school the following year. Hence, the demands of the school (as they are presented in the day-care institution) gain relevance for the children, as well as their parents, during the final months of day care. This, in turn, can change parents' views regarding their child's strengths and weaknesses.

Starting school can likewise result in changes to everyday transitions. The family's everyday practices are adjusted to meet the new demands and expectations (like being at school at a particular time, packing lunchboxes to last the whole school day, checking the contents of the child's school bag, and so on[2]). As part of children's vertical educational trajectory, an ever greater

---

[2]   In the majority of Danish day-care institutions, there is no exact start time (though many institutions recommend an arrival time no later than 9.00) and meals are included. This constitutes a difference from school where lessons start at 8.00 or 8.15 and children bring their own lunch (although in recent years, it has become possible to buy lunch in many schools).

number of everyday transitions occur (transitions between school subjects, classrooms, different teachers, between school and after-school centre etc.) and the children are expected to manage these varied transitions with less and less adult support (Kousholt, 2018). The demand that children are able to manage everyday transitions influences everyday life within the home and the ways in which parents support their child in dealing with these transitions.

Changes in the everyday practicalities of family life are one aspect of changes in the relationship between adult and child. Child-parent mutuality changes as the child becomes involved in new task, tackles expanded responsibilities and develops new ways of contributing to shared activities (Haavind, 1987, 2011). Changes in the mutuality among family members are thereby linked to child transitions (Højholt, Juhl & Kousholt, 2018) – this is most visible in the vertical transitions between educational institutions, but everyday transitions are also linked to changed mutuality due to the child's changing participation and engagements. The children's communities at the day-care institution change continuously and children change their participation in these communities, perhaps shifting their engagement towards other communities (for example, when a close friend moves away or develops a preference for a different type of play). During the child's time at the institution, there are changes in how the day-care professionals divide them into groups (the youngest children, those who will start school soon, those who want to play with Lego, and so on). In addition, what the child is engaged in might change, leading to changes in terms of what seems relevant for linking different life contexts (e.g., what the child brings or continues with from one context to another and what he or she leaves behind).

The focus on transitional time has shown the complexity of this time span and its significance in relation to children's development of their everyday conduct of life and to parents' insight and care. As such, transitional time can be considered a *conflictual space* due to its potential for disputes, frustration and (sensitive) negative assessments by parents and day-care professionals respectively.

Children's conduct of life across home and day-care institution

Following Matthias in his everyday life, I notice his engagement in the boys' community and his preoccupation with becoming skilled at climbing and drawing. It seems Matthias is engaged in 'getting good at things' – and that includes admiring the skills of older children. In this period in Matthias's life, the colouring book seems to be an important artefact for making connections between home and the day-care institution and for making connections to his older sister. This dimension is supported by research that has emphasized looking up to and imitating older children as significant in relation to children's development (Haavind, 2010; Hviid & Villadsen, 2018). In the excerpt from my field notes presented in this article, Matthias points to the vice-head and the head of the institution as having 'the secret keys'. These keys can be seen as an indication of being able to move freely in (and out of) the institution and of having access to the various rooms and cupboards. Matthias seems preoccupied with 'who can decide what', not least what and when he can decide for himself, and he seems to pursue this theme across his different life contexts. Matthias also engages in discussions about 'who can decide' at home, exploring the scope of possibilities available to him for deciding on his own (such as which boots to wear). This leads to a certain amount of conflict, both at the day-care institution and at home, but this does not seem to upset Matthias too much.

At home, Matthias's parents support him as an outgoing boy with a lot of energy and perseverance. In this way, there appear to be continuities between his home and day-care institution in relation to how he engages in conflicts (for example, related to having influence and being able to decide), but some discontinuity in relation to how he is perceived and the activities he can engage in. At home, Matthias plays with dolls together with his older sister, but at the day-care institution, girls are not allowed to take part in the boys' play and to have a girlfriend is something to be teased about. I later learned that Jason had a secret girlfriend at the day-care institution, whom he talked a lot about at home, but did not pay noticeable attention to at the institution. In contrast to Matthias, Jason talks a lot about his time in day care when at home – and often describes episodes that frustrate him. Jason's mother gets the impression that he is very fond of the other boys, but that he often feels left out. Jason's mother has tried to talk about this with the day-care professionals, as well as the other parents; however, she feels it has not helped much. She can see that her advice to Jason does not help him, and this contributes to conflicts and misunderstandings between them. This highlights how children's communities influence the support parents consider it necessary to offer their children in order to encourage a positive social life at the day-care institution. Furthermore, how children experience their parents' ways of engaging in their life in day care (as interference or support) also seems connected to what goes on between the children.

The boys develop their community in relation to a pedagogical practice emphasizing children's free play. In addition, stereotypical understandings of gender seem to reinforce the boys' physical conflicts and their opposition to girls and adults. Likewise, the categorization of 'wild boys' seems to simultaneously problematize and reinforce stereotypes about 'what boys are like'; a categorization that tends to narrow the understanding of the boys and hinder further exploration of what is at stake among them and what they are engaged in. This interpretation of the boys' community (which was also evident among the parents) can be seen as drawing on views on masculinity where physical activity, competitiveness and fighting are seen as linked to natural male characteristics (Frosh, Phoenix & Pattman, 2002; Haavind, 2010). This makes the boys competitiveness and fighting something 'natural' that adults can try to contain or minimize, but not fundamentally change. Still, such gendered understandings are not homogenous and have different meaning in the boys' lives across day care and home. Mutual exploration and collaboration between the professionals and parents could contribute to problematizing masculine stereotypes and help the boys develop a more inclusive community (cf. Brooker (2006) in relation to how peer cultures can transform children's beliefs about gender).

In their study, Lam and Pollard describe how children's 'family values and practices may be modified by the kindergarten or separated from the kindergarten classroom' (Lam & Pollard, 2006, p. 132). They relate these processes of modification or separation to the interplay between the children. Similarly, Vogler et al. (2008) point to the significance of children's communities in relation to educational transitions and underline how children's social activities enable them to contribute to experiences of change (p. 32). The analysis in this chapter, meanwhile, has underlined the significance of children's communities in relation to everyday transitions. At the day-care institution, the children share and discuss experiences from their family lives, including stories about their favourite toys at home, their siblings and so on. Through such dialogues, the children explore and relate their different life contexts to each other – they explore similarities and differences.

In relation to developing their conduct of everyday life, 'persons compare similarities and differences between their experiences and results in different social contexts and they take advantage of this in their pursuit of complex courses of change and learning' (Dreier, 2011, p. 12). This stresses how differences and similarities across different contexts provide possibilities for learning. Clearly, differences can lead to experiences of discontinuity or separation, but they can also be seen as opportunities for new and expanded possibilities. The analysis of how children experience *different configurations of continuity and discontinuity* can give a more nuanced account than comparing different social class backgrounds, which tends to emphasize contrast and differences between classes and pays less attention to variations within social groups (Tudge, 2008).

Employing the concept of conduct of life contributes knowledge about children's active engagement in everyday transitions and about how children pursue engagements across activities and contexts. By pursuing personal engagements, children create connections between the day-care institution and home. Some engagements and concerns can be more closely linked to one context than another, and some might need to be separated from certain contexts.

Exchange of knowledge and collaboration regarding transitions

For both Matthias and Jason (as well as for the other four children that participated in the study), further aspects of their participation and of what they were engaged in became visible to me when I followed them at home and interviewed their parents. This highlights that parents can contribute with significant knowledge about how their children act at home and what they are engaged in, and thereby to a more comprehensive understanding of the child's situation.

A study by Harkness and colleagues found that parents of children categorized as exhibiting 'problem behaviour', while acknowledging such problems, were more likely to also report positive social behaviour than these children's teachers (Harkness, Hughes, Muller & Super, 2005). The authors attribute poor communication between parents and teacher to the teacher not having access to a broader and more positive experience of the child's behaviour. Furthermore, they describe how this lack of access can create discontinuity between home and school. In relation to the case presented in this chapter, it seems that the day-care professionals lack insight into the different meanings of the boys' community for the boys themselves and the ways in which they can vary their participation and have other engagement at home. The parents, meanwhile, lack insight into how other children (than their own) experience the boys' social interplay and the meaning such interactions have for them across their life contexts. This points to the potential for not only exchanging different perspectives on the children, but situating differences and divergences in the different social practices the children take part in, and in relation to how continuity and discontinuity is experienced from the child's perspective. In this way, different perspectives and understandings (instead of a conflict about who has the right understanding) can contribute to a more *compound* understanding of the child's 'social situation of development' (Hedegaard, 2012). It also points to the possibilities if parents and day-care professionals explore their different views on the children's communities at the day-care institution and the different meanings these communities can have for the children. Such joint exploration can strengthen the collaboration between parents and professionals and support children's possibilities for connecting their different life contexts and, in turn, their conduct of everyday life.

References

Andenæs, A. & H. Haavind (2018), 'Sharing early care: Learning from practitioners', in M. Fleer & B. van Oers (eds), *International handbook of early childhood education* (Vol. 2, pp. 1483–1502). Dordrecht: Springer.

Brooker, L. (2006), 'From home to the home corner: Observing children's identity-maintenance in early childhood settings', *Children & Society*, 20(2), 116–127. doi:10.1111/j.1099-0860.2006.00019.x

Chaiklin, S., M. Hedegaard & U. J. Jensen (eds) (1999), *Activity theory and social practice: Cultural-historical approaches*. Aarhus: Aarhus University Press.

Corsaro, W. A., L. Molinary & K. Brown Rosier (2002), 'Zena and Carlotta: Transition narratives and early education in the United States and Italy', *Human Development*, 45(5), 323–348. doi:10.1159/000064646

Dreier, O. (2008), *Psychotherapy in everyday life*. New York: Cambridge University Press.

Dreier, O. (2011), 'Personality and the conduct of everyday life', *Nordic Psychology*, 63(2), 4–23. doi:10.1027/1901-2276/a000030

Fleer, M. & M. Hedegaard (2010), 'Children's development as participation in everyday practices across different institutions', *Mind, Culture, and Activity*, 17(2), 149–168.

Frosh, S., A. Phoenix & R. Pattman (2002), *Young masculinities: Understanding boys in contemporary society*. New York: Palgrave.

Haavind, H. (1987), *Liten og stor: Mødres omsorg og barns utviklingsmuligheter* [Small and big: Mothers' care and children's developmental possibilities]. Oslo: Universitetsforlaget.

Haavind, H. (2010), 'Masculinity by rule-breaking: Cultural contestations in the transitional move from being a child to being a young male', *NORA – Nordic Journal of Feminist and Gender Research*, 11(2), 89–100. doi:10.1080/08038740310002941

Haavind, H. (2011), 'Loving and caring for small children', *Nordic Psychology*, 63(2), 24–48. doi:10.1027/1901-2276/a000031

Harkness, S., M. Hughes, B. Muller & C. M. Super (2005), 'Entering the developmental niche: Mixed methods in an intervention program for inner-city children', in T. S. Weisner (ed.), *Discovering succesful pathways in children's development: Mixed methods in the study of childhood and family life* (pp. 329–358). Chicago, IL: The University of Chicago Press.

Hedegaard, M. (2012), 'Analyzing children's learning and development in everyday settings from a cultural-historical wholeness approach', *Mind, Culture, and Activity*, 19(2), 127–138. doi:10.1080/10749039.2012.665560

Hedegaard, M., K. Aronsson, C. Højholt & O. S. Ulvik, (eds) (2012), *Children, childhood, and everyday life: Children's perspective*. Charlotte, NC: IAP, Information Age Publishing.

Holzkamp, K. (2013), 'Psychology: Social self-understanding on the reasons for action in the conduct of everyday life', in E. Schraube & U. Osterkamp (eds), *Psychology from the standpoint of the subject: Selected writings of Klaus Holzkamp* (pp. 233–341). Basingstoke: Palgrave Macmillan.

Højholt, C. (2016), 'Situated Inequality and the conflictuality of children's conduct of life', in E. Schraube & C. Højholt (eds), *Psychology and the conduct of everyday life* (pp. 145–163). London: Routledge.

Højholt, C. & D. Kousholt (2018), 'Children participating and developing agency in and across various social practices', in M. Fleer & B. van Oers (eds), *International handbook of early childhood education* (Vol. II, pp. 1581–1598). Dordrecht: Springer.

Højholt, C., Juhl, P. & D. Kousholt (2018), 'The collectivity of family conduct of life and parental self-understanding', in E. E. Ødegaard & S. Gravis (eds), *Nordic perspectives of families and wellbeing* (pp. 13–26). Abingdon: Routledge.

Højholt, C. & E. Schraube (2016), 'Introduction: Toward a psychology of everyday living', in E. Schraube & C. Højholt (eds), *Psychology and the conduct of everyday life* (pp. 1–14). London and New York: Routledge.

Hviid, P. & J. W. Villadsen (2018), 'The development of a person: Children's experience within the cultural life course', in J. Valsiner & A. Rosa, *Cambridge handbook of sociocultural psychology* (pp. 556–574). Cambridge: Cambridge University Press.

Juhl, P. (2018), 'Early childhood education in Denmark: Contested issues', in S. Garvis, S. Phillipson & H. Harju-Luukkainen (eds), *International perspectives on early childhood education: Early childhood education in the 21st Century* (Vol. 1) (pp. 42–53). Abingdon: Routledge.

Jurczyk, K., G. G. Voß & Weihrich, M. (2016), 'Conduct of everyday life in subject-oriented sociology: Concept and empirical research', in E. Schraube & C. Højholt (eds), *Psychology and the conduct of everyday life* (pp. 34–64). London and New York: Routledge.

Kousholt, D. (2008), 'The everyday life of children across early childhood institution and the family', *Journal of Australian Research in Early Childhood Education*, 15(1), 98–114.

Kousholt, D. (2011a), *Børnefællesskaber og familieliv: børns hverdagsliv på tværs af daginstitution og hjem* [Children's communities and family life. Children's everyday life across day care institution and home] (1. ed.). Copenhagen: Dansk Psykologisk Forlag.

Kousholt, D. (2011b), 'Researching family through the everyday lives of children across home and day care in Denmark', *Ethos*, 39(1), 98–114. doi:10.1111/j.1548-1352.2010.01173.x

Kousholt, D. (2012), 'Family problems: Exploring dilemmas and complexities of organising everyday family life', in M. Hedegaard, K. Aronsson, C. Højholt & O. S. Ulvik (eds), *Children, childhood, and everyday life: Children's perspectives* (pp. 125–139). Charlotte, NC: Information Age Publishing, incorporated.

Kousholt, D. (2016), 'Collaborative research with children: Exploring contradictory conditions of conduct of everyday life', in E. Schraube & C. Højholt (eds), *Psychology and the conduct of everyday life* (pp. 241–258). London: Routledge.

Kousholt, D. (2018),Forældres samarbejde om børns fællesskaber i skolen. [Parents' collaboration about children's communities in school], in C. Højholt & D. Kousholt (eds), Konflikter om børns skoleliv [Conflicts about Children's School Life] (pp. 226–253). Copenhagen: Dansk Psykologisk Forlag.

Lam, M. S. & A. Pollard (2006), 'A conceptual framework for understanding children as agents in the transition from home to kindergarten', *Early Years*, 26(2), 123–141. doi:10.1080/09575140600759906

Rogoff, B. (1996), 'Developmental transitions in children's participation in sociocultural activities', in A. J. Sameroff & M. M. Haith (eds), *The five to seven year shift: The age of reason and responsibility* (pp. 273–294). Chicago, IL: University of Chicago Press.

Schraube, E. & C. Højholt (eds) (2016), *Psychology and the conduct of everyday life*. London: Routledge.

Stanek, A. H. (2014), 'Communities of children: Participation and its meaning for learning', *International Research in Early Childhood Education*, 5(1), 139–154.

Thorne, B. (2001), 'Pick-up time at Oakdale Elementary school: Work and family from the vantage point of children', in R. Hertz & N. Marshall (eds), *Working families: The transformation of the American home* (pp. 354–376). Berkeley and Los Angeles, CA: University of California Press.

Tudge, J. (2008), *The everyday lives of young children: Culture, class, and child rearing in diverse societies*. Cambridge: Cambridge University Press.

Vogler, P., G. Crivello & M. Woodhead (2008), *Early childhood transitions research: A review of concepts, theory, and practice*. Working paper No 48. The Hague: Bernard van Leer Foundation.

Winther-Lindqvist, D. & L. Svinth (2017), Early Childhood Education and Care (ECEC) in Denmark. *Oxford Bibliography*.

8

'A Darwinist at Our Dinner Table?': Discursive Transitions Between School and Home

Lucas Gottzén and Karin Aronsson

Introduction

The late German sociological theorist, Ulrich Beck (1997), has argued that a democratic society – a society that on all levels is pervaded by democratic values – is realized through what he calls 'self-socialization'. Self-socialization to the 'spirit of democracy' is accomplished in different institutions, such as the school and the family. But it is not primarily through teaching, reading books or through the written regulation of rights that the democratic spirit is realized, but through the experience and active exercise of political freedom in everyday life. According to Beck (1997), such an exercise shifts the 'power relationships of a society gradually into democratic reality' (p. 157). He argues that Sweden is the only country in the world that has taken the rights of children seriously and moved away from the 'private enslavement of children by their parents in the guise of care' (Beck, 1997, p. 161). This has been realized through the state's interventions in family life – a 'deprivatization of privacy' (p. 162) – and it has provoked a collision between the rights of the family and the rights of the child.

Whether Beck is right or wrong in his argument that the Swedish state – through its interventions in family life – has made possible an active exercise of 'the spirit of democracy', it is important to study *how* such an exercise is carried out, how adults and children negotiate, and how the state intervenes in the everyday lives of families through, for instance, the ideological influence of schools and other educational institutions. Family democracy is quite a complex and problematic affair (Jamieson, 1999; Smart & Neale, 1999; Solomon et al., 2002) and it might involve particular challenges in everyday discursive transitions between school and home, which might be related to different conflicting epistemologies that are at times in fundamental opposition to each other.

Everyday mealtime conversations form an important daily arena where family members discuss issues that have a bearing on the social order of the family and where family members negotiate not only specific topics, but also other matters, related to the framing of family politics (cf. Blum-Kulka, 1997; Ochs & Taylor, 1992). It may be depicted as the heart of family, but through everyday transitions between home and school children may bring with them and articulate discourses that are in conflict with the discourses of their family and, as a consequence, challenge the social order as well as test the 'democratic spirit'.

Evolutionist discourse in schools

In some Western countries such as the US, creationism is a widely-accepted belief system (Dennett, 1996). In contrast, Sweden is essentially a secular society, but there are religions with other understandings of the origins of man than the evolutionist one. A 'free church' is the generic definition of denominations that emerged as a parallel to the Swedish Lutheran church, which up until 2000 was a part of the state. During the nineteenth century there was an evangelical revival, and today there are a number of Pentecostal, reformed, and other free churches of protestant denominations.

In Sweden, most parents with confessional interpretations of the origins of life, including members of the free churches, have generally sent their children to municipal schools. The children in these families are thus introduced to two divergent models, two discourses, about the origins of life. One model, the evolutionary model, explains life as a result of time, chance and natural selection. The other argues that there is divine design, a divine agent, behind life.

In Swedish state schools, evolutionist theories constitute the privileged explanations of the origins of life. The syllabus of the Swedish school states that children should learn 'the worldview of the natural sciences with evolutionary theory as its basis' (Swedish National Agency for Education, 2011/2015, p. 148). The perspectives of the natural sciences of today are explicitly differentiated from the worldviews and explanations of other times and cultures. At the same time, Swedish schools endorse an orientation towards egalitarian ideas; all times and cultures are said to have a common ambition to understand and explain life.

Such a perspective can be found in biology schoolbooks for the first three grades of primary school. For instance, a reader (Enwall et al., 2001), acknowledges that people at all times have tried to explain the origins of life, but it simultaneously claims that most scientists today believe that the universe was created through the Big Bang (p. 8). Life on earth, as we now know it, is a result of millions of years of evolution (p. 14), and man has evolved from 'big apes' (p. 20). But this idea of man's relationship to apes is still a controversial one in many circles (e.g., in the US; on Darwin and his 'dangerous idea', see Dennett, 1996).

Evolutionism as hegemonic discourse

In this chapter, we argue that the state has an indirect influence on family relations through the educational system. It is indirect in the sense that school provides children with tools to challenge the authority of their parents; the relationship between master and novice is questioned. But children may also acquire knowledge in particular areas where they are introduced to a discourse that is in conflict with the discourse of their parents. This is especially the case when the discourse introduced to children has a hegemonic status (Laclau & Mouffe, 1985).

Discourses are to be understood as ways of representing the world – different ways of speaking about and understanding it (Edwards, 1997). They may also represent the world in widely divergent ways, in terms of 'contrasting versions' (Potter, 1996); something that might lead to open conflicts between proponents. Discourses differ in scale – how much of the world they include, and in stability – they could be more or less (but never completely) fixed.

The evolutionist discourse can, for instance, be seen as rather stable. In many contemporary Western cultures, it is the dominant and most common way of representing the world in important institutions such as schools and academic institutions, and it is a part of our taken for granted knowledge of how to understand the origins of life. It is also inclusive in the sense that it offers answers to existential questions. But the evolutionist discourse is not dominant in the sense that it is unchangeable or uncontested. Its position should rather be understood in terms of hegemony, where a particular representation of the world is claimed to have universal status but whose universal status can never be completely maintained (Laclau, 2000).

Since evolutionary theory has a hegemonic status in Swedish society at large, groups that do not agree with the evolutionist models of representing the world have to adjust, balance and explain their beliefs in relation to the dominant evolutionist discourse. This may be done in public debates, but also in everyday life interactions in schools and families. When children at school are faced with contrasting versions of reality (e.g., evolutionist versus religious ideas of the origin of life), they have to handle such divergent views of reality in some way. While teachers may be seen as yet another authority in children's lives, as Beck (1997) argues, school-based knowledge may be used to question parental authority. Children could therefore be seen not as passively being socialized to different values and beliefs by adults – they are agents of their own socialization, as they juggle and negotiate discursive transitions between school and home. This chapter will document and analyse family life strategies (by parents and children) for dealing with such transitions.

Data

The empirical data, mealtime family discourse in the interface of school and family, are taken from a large scale ethnographic study of family life in Italy, Sweden and the United States, where the overall goal has been to undertake a comparative analysis of the everyday lives of middle-class dual earner families in those countries (the projects were financed by the Alfred P. Sloan Foundation).

In each research site, a research team has documented a week in the lives of middle-class dual earner families that feature two or more children, where one is between 8–10 years old. The US data include thirty-two families. In Sweden and in Italy, sixteen families were documented with an array of ethnographic methods, including video-recordings and interviews. Each family has been filmed for up to forty hours, covering both mornings and evenings during weekdays as well as weekends (cf. Aarsand & Forsberg, 2010; Ochs & Kremer-Sadlik, 2013).

The data has then been classified in terms of so-called activity logs, which indicate type of activities (e.g., breakfast, dinner, homework, cleaning, watching television) in terms of time distribution. Based on these logs and repeated viewings of the original videos, it has been possible to identify target activities (mealtime conversations) and these have been transcribed in detail, and have then been analysed with microgenetic methods (Schieffelin & Ochs, 1996), in this case detailed analyses of social interaction. For ethical reasons, all names have been anonymized.

The present study is drawn from a collection of events that illuminate instances where the school is invoked during everyday family discourse. This chapter explores *home-school transitions*, as it documents educational challenges in cases where there are epistemological differences between the school's naturalist discourse and the parents' religious beliefs. In the following, we will document how parents and children handle such transitions.

Comets and satellites

As in many other Western cultures, dinner among Swedish middle-class families is often the only or primary time during the day when the entire family is gathered and has time for discussion. Family dinner talk has been studied by a number of scholars, illuminating ways in which it is a place of socialization to family values and social order (e.g., Aronsson & Cekaite, 2011; Aronsson & Gottzén, 2011; Aukrust & Snow, 1998; Blum-Kulka, 1997, 2002; Grieshaber, 1997; Ochs, Pontecorvo & Fasulo, 1996; Ochs & Taylor, 1992; Pan, Perlman & Snow, 2000; Pauletto, Aronsson & Galeano, 2017). The literature shows that dinner conversation is a rich activity type, involving different generations, and where much socialization to cultural values and ideologies takes place.

Our analyses of dinner discourse concern what Blum-Kulka (2002) calls explanatory discourse, that is, 'interactional moves emerging in natural discourse in response to some need or problematic state of affairs' (p. 87). A prototypical case would be an answer and the discussion that follows to a question about a problematic issue. In her study on American and Israeli Jews, Blum-Kulka (2002) found that the most frequent domains covered in explanatory discourse were explanations about social conventions and physical objects. Least common were explanations on metaphysics, but when they occurred these discussions tended to be elaborate and lasted for several minutes. Among the families we studied, a wide range of subjects were discussed – the events of the day, planning the rest of the week, physical objects, friends and family. Less frequent were discussions about politics and metaphysics.

The following sequence takes place while a Swedish middle-class family is having dinner in the kitchen on a Monday evening. The children, two daughters, Linnea (aged 10 years) and Emelie (8 years) are seated at the table, facing their parents, when Linnea introduces talk on comets and planets, invoking the subject of evolution.

Excerpt 1[1]

1   Linnea: Mom:

2   Mother: Mm

3   Linnea: Has it ever happened that a <u>come:t</u> (.) has destroyed

4   a: this a thing like this that spins around the Earth

5   such thing ((grinds with the arm))

6   Mother: Satellite?

7   Linnea: Yes (0.5) has it ever happened that a comet has hit

8   a satellite?

9   Emelie: Uaho auh a

10 Father: Do you know or do you ask?

11 Emelie: No I don't know

12 Father: Mm

13 Mother: No: I don't know that

14 Emelie: <u>YOU</u> ARE GREAT DAD!

15 Father: Well yes (.) thank you! Eh yes I think so (0.5) but I

16 have to say I think because I am not sure

17 Linnea: Mhm

18 Mother: Have you read about it (.)

19 you haven't read about it in school?

20 Father: Not anything not any with any person in it but=

21 Linnea: =No=

22 Father: =perhaps something that has spin around there (0.5) a satellite

23 that (.) feels something (.) measures something

24 Linnea: Mm yes

25 Mother: Mm

26 Emelie: Measures eh measures (.) mea:sures <u>yes</u> measures if there is any

27 <u>earthling</u> that can be put on our <u>PLANET!</u>

28 Father: Yeah

29 Mother: Yeah

30 Father: <u>Weather</u> satellite or (.) another satellite (.) very

31 xxx there are many xxx

32 Mother: Mm

33 Emelie: Yes weather satellite! (.) you can't listen to (xxx)

---

[1] Underlinings mark emphasis, (.) mark micro pauses and capital letters mark loud voice.

In this sequence, Linnea is asking for an explanation about comets and satellites (lines 3–5 and 7–8), which can indirectly be seen as an invitation of explanatory discourse on physical origin. But the objects discussed are far away and rather abstract, and the question seems to be difficult to answer for the parents. Mother admits her ignorance (line 13) while Father tries to produce an answer to his daughter's question about comets. He produces quite a guarded pre-sequence to his forthcoming explanation, downgrading his epistemic authority (Heritage & Raymond, 2005), including micro pauses and an explicit evidential 'I'm not sure' (lines 15–16). Thereby, he can be seen to position himself as someone who is not in the know or who at least does not wish to challenge other models of thinking. His uncertainty (or strategic ambiguity) is also expressed in his guarded response to the question (lines 22–23). Overall, his explanation is embedded in a series of pauses, hedges, hesitation markers, and other markers of uncertainty (Brown & Levinson, 1987: 'eh', 'I think so', 'but I have to say', 'I think', 'I am not sure', 'perhaps'; Heritage & Raymond, 2005). There might 'potentially have been something' that went around there. This explanation can be seen as a vague display of uncertainty. On another note, his somewhat jagged talk can be read as signs of mild discomfort or as signs of a strategically open or ambiguous position in relation to delicate issues that involve a potential divide or at least tension between school and home.

Mother introduces the issue of school into the discussion (line 19 'you haven't read about it in school?') in a way that might be seen as a way of disaligning with the school's (rather than the home's) set of beliefs and knowledge. Yet, even though Linnea states that she has not read about comets at school (line 21), the connection between school and the subject discussed (and later with evolutionism) forms an implicit framework for the present discussion. Along with the media, school is probably the primary source of scientific knowledge for these two children (as for many other children of school age). In any case, this is evidently Mother's assumption when checking whether they have read about it in school.

Life on Mars

In our prior excerpt, Linnea solicited her parents' explanations. In the next sequence, it is the father who positions the children as explainers (Blum-Kulka, 2002; line 37).

Excerpt 2
34. Linnea: But Emelie you must know that the:- (.)
35. that there is life in space above us

36 Emelie: Yeah:
37 Father: There is?
38 Emelie: On Mars.
39 Linnea: On Mars.
40 Emelie: I have heard that
41 Linnea: Small germs
42 Father: Ah well ((bows))
43 Linnea: Mm mm like this (.) there is a
44 Father: Xxxxx
45 Linnea: The question is as we know how life came to Earth.
46 Father: Mm
47 Linnea: That is the case you know.
48 Emelie: Well water xxxx=
49 Linnea: =Some believe that there are comets (.) from Mars (.)
50 with life (.) mm that has landed on the Earth (.) then the
51 question is how has life started on Mars then?
52 Emelie: Yeah yes it started to rain
53 Father: Mm hm
54 Linnea: Aha!
55 Emelie: And then did these germies come with the water
56 Father: Aha
57 Emelie: And the rain came from from a satellite an unknown satellite
58 they are unknown (.) they are the rain HAHAHAHA
59 Father: Yes that are questions difficult
60 Father: to answer
61 Emelie: I KNOW!

The two daughters, Linnea and Emelie apparently try to answer their father's question about whether there is life in space. In so doing, they are partly co-constructing a theory of life in space (lines 34–35, 38–41). But they have different strategies and goals, which have to do with the two girls' relation to knowledge and theories about the world. Emelie, the younger girl, elaborates on the subject at hand in a playful and performative way (lines 26–27, 48, 52, 55). In a lively and narrative style, she presents a hybrid theory of how life came to Earth: it started to rain (line 52) and 'germies' (*baskilusker*) came with the rain from an 'unknown satellite' (lines 55–57). Her hybrid account partly relates to scientific theories. Among astrobiologists it is, for instance, generally accepted that a considerable amount of organic molecules and water were imported to the early

Earth via asteroids and comets (Horneck et al., 2002). It is also believed that life on Earth emerged in water (Brack, 2002). Even so, Father does not align with Emelie's account. Instead, in lines 59–60 he is orienting towards Linnea's more downgraded and interrogative approach ('then the question is … '; lines 50–51). We may understand this as a matter of different generational alliances between the girls and their parents, where the elder girl Linnea can be seen to align with the adults by using their more downgraded way of presenting explanations, as well as subjecting to the causality of events that Emelie presents.

The by-product of an explanatory discourse, as of many other conversational genres, is implicit or explicit knowledge transmission. In contemporary Western family life, knowledge transmission is focused on modern scientific ways of thinking (Blum-Kulka, 2002). The guiding principles are rationality and verifiability. This sheds some light on the interaction between Emelie, Linnea and Father. We would argue that it is because Linnea is focusing on verifiability and logical criticism (lines 49–51), and the evidence of natural science and school that Father is taking up her account and not her younger sister's elaborate and playful approach to the same business.

The chicken or the egg?

Father then elaborates on Linnea's question about where life has come from, and he directs the discussion into more metaphysical aspects (lines 50–51; cf. Blum-Kulka, 2002).

Excerpt 3
62 Linnea: Mm (.) but hey you you think it was an unknown
63 satellite=
64 Father: Linnea=
65 Linnea: but you know it if you think it exists
66 Emelie: Yeah an unknown yes
67 Father: It is like answering (.) to the question=
68 Emelie: I can paint it
69 Father: What came first the chicken or the egg?
70 Linnea: Hm aha hm
71 Emelie: What?
72 Linnea: There has of course to be a chicken so there
73 can come an egg
74 Father: What came first the chicken or the egg?

75 Emelie: Well it was (.) a (0.5) the <u>egg</u>
76 Linnea: It has to be
77 Emelie: Man made so it became eggs
78 Father: Well mhm (aha)
79 Linnea: No it was the chicken that came first!
80 Emelie: (It came first)
81 Father: The chicken came first?
82 Linnea: That sounds the most plausible.
83 Father: That sounds the most plausible?
84 Emelie: NOHO how did the chicken come then?

Father here connects Linnea's criticism of the 'life from Mars theory', to a classical puzzle of origin: that of the chicken and the egg. The girls seem to enjoy the puzzle, but respond to his question in different ways. Emelie maintains that the egg came first (line 75), since man made the egg ('man made it into eggs'; line 77). In contrast, Linnea claims 'No it was the chicken that came first!' (line 79). But he repeats her conclusion in an interrogative tone, and she then produces a clarification: it sounds 'most plausible' that the chicken came first (line 82). Here Linnea is again approaching the problem in a scientific way. In line 70, she displays puzzlement ('Hm well hm'). In lines 72–73, she is then formulating an explanation for herself, thinking aloud as it were: 'Well there has to be a chicken so that there might come an egg'. Her hesitant, somewhat delayed response can be contrasted to Emelie's more immediate response (line 75).

We may understand Father's introduction of the chicken-egg puzzle as a philosophical comment on the fact that the question about the origins of life is impossible to solve. But it could also be understood as a critique of evolutionist theories. His puzzle bears a strong resemblance to Christian apologetics in general, and in particular the 'cosmological argument' presented by Thomas Aquinas (1225–1274), who in medieval times had already presented an evolutionist model that involved divine design. The cosmological argument is one of five arguments for the existence of God. In short, Aquinas argues that the chain of agent cause cannot go on forever, that there has to be a first cause at the end of the chain (Aquinas, 1998). The chicken-egg puzzle could therefore be interpreted as having the 'voice' (Bakhtin, 1986) of the cosmological argument, and thus an implicit critique of the naturalistic theories of life from space, as well as an alignment with Linnea's critique or question about agency (in lines 49–50). The question for both of them could be stated as follows: if life came from Mars or somewhere else in the universe, what (or who) was the cause of that life?

'Did we nourish a Darwinist at our table?'

Father's chicken-egg puzzle has introduced a discussion on the origins of life, where Linnea apparently assumes that the family's common ground is evolutionism.

Excerpt 4

85	Linnea: Yeah a lot of bird <u>species</u>
86	that have blended and like that and then out of a sudden
87	(.) it has become like (.) a <u>chicken</u> (.) because
88	you see it was that way men came to be (.) it became a lot of
89	these a:pe sorts
90	Emelie: Yes mm=
91	Linnea: and then in the end did we come
92	Father: ((to Mother)) Do we have a <u>Darwinist</u> here?
93	Ah? (.) Darwinist?
94	Mother: Hehe
95	Emelie: I answered xxxx xxxx
96	Linnea: Xxxx
97	Father: Did we nourish a <u>Darwinist</u> at our table ((in laughing voice))?
98	Mother: Hehe
99	Linnea: What?
100	Father: Did we nourish a <u>Darwinist</u> (.) at our table?
101	Mother: By my- by my <u>bosom</u>
102	Father: By our bosom he says that (.) Karl-Bertil Jonsson
103	Mother:Hehe Oh well
104	Father: Well yes we better talk about this Linnea.
105	Linnea: Because it can't be be that eh (.)
106	Father: hehe
107	Mother: hehe
108	Linnea: a chicken like <u>sort</u> (0.5)
109	Mother: Yeah
110	Father: Mm
111	Linnea: Mm eh mm eh eh mm gets an <u>egg</u>
112	Mother: Mm
113	Linnea: that out of a sudden becomes a <u>chicken</u>?
114	Mother: No
115	Linnea: That can't be possible. (.) of course it has to be
116	that the sort walks as we humans ((gesticulates))

117   Mother: Aha blended
118   Emelie: Like this like this
119   Father: One step at a time
120   Linnea: Yes
121   Emelie: Okay dad! Dad! Dad!
122   Linnea: One step at a ti:me
123   Emelie: Father
124   Father: Yes
125   Emelie: First (0.5) we are related to the apes
126   Father: Hehe okay
127   Mother: Hehe
128   Father: Yes

In an attempt to solve the problem of what came first, Linnea suggests that different bird species blended together, which all of a sudden resulted in something like a chicken, that we have emerged from the apes (lines 85–89), and it is likely that chickens have evolved like mankind, 'one step at a time' (line 122). She illustrates her theorizing with body posture and gestures (line 116), slightly bending her body and repeatedly putting one hand in front of the other, in a way that resembles classical illustrations of the evolution of man that are common in school textbooks – from Australopithecus to Homo Sapiens. In the nonverbal format of a mime, Linnea can thus be seen to formulate a basic theoretical assumption: evolutionist theory is a valid answer to the puzzle of origins. She is thereby formulating what could be called an 'existential assumption' (Fairclough, 2003) that man came to be through evolution (here implying that there is a common ground, that hers and her parents' shared belief is evolutionism). Through this assumption – by taking the common ground for granted – she is apparently drawing on what she sees as a hegemonic discourse.

However, if we look at Father's uptake, there is no such hegemony. Instead, he turns to Mother, asking 'Do we have a Darwinist here?' (lines 92–93). He repeats and elaborates his question (lines 97, 100 and 102), and Mother latches on, adding 'by my bosom'. He then includes 'by our bosom' in a mild complaint in the form of a rhetorical question 'Did we nourish a Darwinist at our table – by our bosom?' (lines 100–102).

His rhetorical question contains an 'intertextual reference' (Bakhtin, 1986) to *Karl-Bertil Jonssons julafton* ('The Christmas Eve of Karl-Bertil Jonsson'), a famous Swedish animated film, which has routinely been broadcast every Christmas Eve by Swedish public service television. This Christmas Eve story is about a fourteen-year-old boy Karl-Bertil Jonsson, who works at the Post Office during the Christmas holidays. His father is the manager of a department store and is very rich. Karl-Bertil's greatest hero is Robin Hood, and with the 'principle of lawless justice' as his motto, the youngster decides to take the parcel post from the rich and give it to the poor on Christmas Eve. Later, when his family has realized that the gift from their aunt has not arrived, Karl-Bertil confesses, and when his father hears about his son's Robin Hood actions, he cries out in dismay: 'What! I have nourished a communist by my bosom!' The narrator's voice comments in a sarcastic style, stating that he 'belonged to those who considered anyone who gave away anything for free as a communist'.

By invoking the nourishing of a communist 'by our bosom', Father places himself in a position of mock dismay: at discovering that his child is expressing an alien ideology. This could be interpreted as if he is offended by Linnea's evolutionist thoughts, positioning her as 'a Darwinist'. But the situation is more complex. Father is not only playing with the words of the film, he is laughingly imitating the rich father's angry voice and intonation in an ironic way (line 97). His telling the elder girl that, 'Well yes we'd better talk about this Linnea' (line 105) should be understood as another ironic statement (of being playfully stern). He invokes the rhetoric of mild discipline 'we'd better talk about this', but existential assumptions are not easily settled through disciplining talk. In any case, the parents align in warm laughter (lines 102–103 and 106–107). On a parenthetical note, their laughter has somewhat collusive qualities in that neither girl joins in or seems to understand the humour involved.

Likewise, both Father and then Mother react with laughter at Emelie's statement that they are related to the apes (lines 125–126) before the conversation turns to another topic. We do not know what happened after the team stopped filming, but there are no sequences during this dinner conversation or in our other data that suggest that Father or Mother had or were going 'to have a talk' about the elder daughter's evolutionist thoughts.

Simultaneously, Father seems to be orientated towards the fact that the evolutionist theory, as presented by the girls, is highly problematic. At no point in the discussion does he align with their evolutionist discourse; instead he repeatedly, but light-heartedly, reacts to Linnea's assumption that they have a common ground in evolutionist theory (the school's scientific model). But through referring to the animated film in a sarcastic way, Father is aligning with Mother in distancing himself from the girls. The girls do not seem to get the point of his irony, and therefore it becomes something (somewhat collusive) that aligns the two adults, but excludes the children. After Father and Mother's joint laughing, Linnea is displaying a high degree of epistemic uncertainty – she stumbles (lines 105 and 111) and modifies her statement ('because it can't be- be that eh (.)'; line 106), downgrading her epistemic authority (Heritage & Raymond, 2005). This, we argue, could be seen as her orienting to the complexity (and ambiguity) of navigating between the school's and the parents' belief systems.

When considering that the parents are members of a Swedish free church, their alignment could be interpreted as a conflict between evolutionism (represented by the daughters) and creationist theories. This is true to some extent, but we would argue that there is rather a conflict between evolutionist and what we could call 'divine causality'[2] discourse, in a rather complex way. Creationism, a more or less literary interpretation of Genesis, is fairly common among Swedish Christians, but far from the only way of understanding the origins of life. Among the more 'liberal' churches, like Father and Mother's congregational place of worship, most members interpret Genesis as a mythological text explaining *why*, not how, the world was created. This interpretation excludes naturalistic evolutionist models but suggests theistic evolutionist models, based on the idea of a divine origin. It is therefore most likely that Father does not have any major problems with the ideas Linnea is expressing, but he wants to point out the need for a first agent cause, preferably divine. On another note, the parents can also be seen to be engaged in 'doing democracy', allowing the children to choose between different epistemological models, or more precisely between the school's epistemology and that of their home.

In an attempt to show the complexity of the conversation, we would like to draw on Goffman's (1981) understanding of the different participant roles in conversations. In many multiparty conversations there is a speaker, an addressed participant and an unaddressed participant. But there could also be a non-ratified participant, a bystander who might be eavesdropping or unintentionally overhearing the conversation. In our case, Father is, for instance, addressing his wife in lines 92–93, while the daughters are at that moment unaddressed but ratified participants. In other instances, Father is primarily addressing Linnea, while Emelie is not addressed. There are also non-ratified participants: the researchers who are eavesdropping, and you – the readers of this chapter. In one way, the researchers videotaping and the scholars reading this are ratified, since

---

[2] The term 'divine causality' is used to define those philosophers arguing that the Big Bang had a supernatural cause. Thus, in a narrow sense, those arguing for divine causality are neither creationists, nor evolutionist.

the family has allowed the observation. But the researchers kept a low profile and seldom interrupted the business of the family, so their role in the conversations could be understood as 'ratified eavesdroppers'. Along with primary schools, universities are part of the educational system (and the hegemonic evolutionist discourse), and researchers from a university represent that very discourse. Thus, when Father is expressing a critique of evolutionist discourses he is not only in dialogue with Linnea and Emelie, he is also engaged in a dialogue with the educational system. Father's critique of Darwinism becomes a critique that is voiced (Bakhtin, 1986), not only in the private family realm, but, through the presence of the researchers, also at a public level.

Conclusion

It has been shown that children's ability to be ratified in an 'intellectual' conversation in the family is bound to the ways children align with an adult way of thinking. In this context, the adult way of thinking is characterized by logic, rationality and verifiability. We can distinguish a generational difference (linked to age or experience) between the ways that the two girls relate to the discussions on science and philosophy. While Emelie is oriented towards these issues as a way of storytelling and performance, Linnea aligns with Father's orientation towards logic and serious explanations.

Moreover, Linnea, by drawing on evolutionistic discourse (and the school's secular explanations), can be seen to challenge the creationism or divine causality discourse that Father indirectly advocates. When Linnea assumes that the family's common ground is evolutionism, Father reacts and, through the use of irony, he aligns with his wife in an implicit challenge to their daughter's evolutionist position. By drawing on an alternative hegemonic discourse, children may obviously challenge their parents' existential assumptions, and thereby also their status positions as privileged sources of knowledge. Along with the media, the school is a primary source of scientific theories about the origins of life. It could therefore be argued that contemporary schools may indirectly affect family relationships when children transition between school and home.

Democracy is not something that just happens, and as with all relations, family relationships are characterized by asymmetry and power imbalances. In order to understand how the family is, or is not, becoming more 'democratic' in Beck's (1997) use of the term, we have to analyse the relationship between the family members and society at large, how the private is deprivatized. We can distinguish different levels of democracy. Both girls' accounts are acknowledged by the parents, but only one account challenges existential assumptions and the relationships within the family. Obviously, a privileged family discourse and the authority of the parents might be challenged when the children draw on an alternative hegemonic discourse. But first, the children have to be ratified as 'competent' participants by aligning with the way that their parents present arguments. One aspect of such competence is the downplaying of epistemic authority (cf. Heritage & Raymond, 2005). By downgrading their certainty, both the father and the elder daughter can be seen to invite inter-generational negotiations about the family's existential assumptions versus the school's evolutionist epistemology. Any gap or transition between the two epistemological systems is made into a negotiable difference, rather than into an insurmountable divide.

Even in this liberal Christian middle-class setting, we can discern a conflict between two contrasting versions of the world. In the midst of this conflict are the children who have to balance between evolutionism, the discourse that school represents, and the creationist discourse of their parents' church. On the one hand, parents who instead send their children to confessional schools could argue that they protect their children from such conflicts and from painful transitions between home and school. On the other hand, it could be argued that the very handling of the transitions between school and home epistemologies introduces types of conflict that involve fundamental ways of exercising the spirit of democracy, in that children learn to handle divergent discourses and existential assumptions.

When Beck (1997) envisioned 'self-socialization', he saw it as part of a tendency towards increased individualization in Western societies, where individuals to some extent are forced to follow traditions but are able to more freely choose their relationships and construct their own biographies (see also Giddens, 1992). In line with critique from family and childhood studies (e.g., Jamieson, 1999; Smart & Neale, 1999), our findings rather suggest that children are still embedded in relational settings and that adult parents are still crucial agents of socialization. While children are far from passive in socialization practices (in this case socialization to 'the spirit of democracy'), they are not self-socializing but perhaps rather co-socializing with their parents as they also have to juggle and negotiate different discourses in the transition between school and home.

References

Aarsand, P. & L. Forsberg (2010), 'Producing children's corporeal privacy: Ethnographic video recordings as material-discursive practice', *Qualitative Research*, 10(2), 249–268.

Aquinas, T. (1998), *Selected Philosophical Writings*. Oxford: Oxford University Press.

Aronsson, K. & A. Cekaite (2011), 'Activity contracts and directives in everyday family politics', *Discourse & Society*, 22(2), 137–154.

Aronsson, K. & L. Gottzén (2011), Generational positions at family dinner: Food morality and social order. *Language in Society*, 40(4), 405–426.

Aukrust, V. & C. E. Snow (1998), Narratives and explanations during mealtime conversations in Norway and the US. *Language in Society*, 27(2), 221–246.

Bakhtin, M. (1986), *Speech genres and other late essays*. Austin, TX: University of Texas Press.

Beck, U. (1997), 'Democratization of the family', *Childhood*, 4(2), 151–168.

Blum-Kulka, S. (1997), *Dinner talk: Cultural patterns of sociability and socialization in family discourse*. Mahwah, NJ: Lawrence Erlbaum Associates.

Blum-Kulka, S. (2002), 'Do you believe that Lot's wife is blocking the road (to Jericho)?': Co-constructing theories about the world with adults', in S. Blum-Kulka & C. Snow (eds), *Talking to adults: The contribution of multiparty discourse to language acquisition* (pp. 85–117). Mahwah, NJ: Lawrence Erlbaum Associates.

Brack, A. (2002), 'Water, the spring of life', in G. Horneck & C. Baumstark-Khan (eds), *Astrobiology: The Quest for the conditions of life* (pp. 79–88). Berlin: Springer.

Brown, P. & S. C. Levinson (1987), *Politeness: Some universals in language usage*. Cambridge: Cambridge University Press.

Dennett, D. C. (1996), *Darwin's dangerous idea: Evolution and the meanings of life*. New York: Simon & Schuster.

Edwards, D. (1997), *Discourse and Cognition*. London: Sage.

Enwall, L., B. Johansson & G. Skiöld (2001), *Biologi med fysik och kemi*. Stockholm: Natur och Kultur.

Fairclough, N. (2003), *Analysing discourse: Textual analysis for social research*. London and New York: Routledge.

Giddens, A. (1992), *The transformation of intimacy: Sexuality, love and eroticism in modern societies*. Cambridge: Polity Press.

Goffman, E. (1981), *Forms of talk*. Philadelphia, PA: University of Pennsylvania Press.

Grieshaber, S. (1997), 'Mealtime rituals: Power and resistance in the construction of mealtime rules', *British Journal of Sociology*, 48(4), 649–666.

Heritage, J. & G. Raymond (2005), 'Indexing epistemic authority in talk-in-interaction', *Social Psychology Quarterly*, 66(1), 15–38.

Horneck, G., C. Milieikowsky, H. J. Melosh, J. W. Wilson, F. A. Cucinotta & B. Gladman (2002), 'Viable transfer of microorganisms in the solar system and beyond', in G.

Horneck and C. Baumstark-Khan (eds), *Astrobiology: The quest for the conditions of life* (pp. 57–76). Berlin: Springer.

Jamieson, L. (1999), Intimacy transformed? A critical look at the 'pure relationship'. *Sociology* 33(3), 477–494.

Laclau, E. & C. Mouffe (1985), *Hegemony and socialist strategy: Towards a radical democratic politics.* London: Verso.

Laclau, E. (2000), 'Ideology and hegemony: The role of universality in the constitution of political logics', in J. Butler, E. Laclau & S. Žižek (eds) *Contingency, hegemony, universality* (pp. 44–89). London: Verso.

Ochs, E., C. Pontecorvo & A. Fasulo (1996), 'Socializing taste', *Ethnos*, 61(1/2), 7–47.

Ochs, E. & C. Taylor (1992), 'Family narrative as political activity', *Discourse & Society* 3(3), 301–340.

Ochs, E. & T. Kremer-Sadlik (eds) (2013), *Fast-forward family: Home, work and relationships in middle-class America.* Berkeley, CA: University of California Press.

Pan, B., R. Perlman & C. Snow (2000), 'Food for thought: Dinner table as a context for observing parent-child discourse', in L. Menn & N. Bernstein (eds), *Methods for studying language production* (pp. 203–222). Mahwah, NJ: Lawrence Erlbaum Associates.

Pauletto, F., K. Aronsson & G. Galeano (2017), 'Endearment and address terms in family life: Children's and parents' requests in Italian and Swedish dinnertime interaction', *Journal of Pragmatics*, 109, 82–94.

Potter, J. (1996), *Representing reality: Discourse, rhetoric and social construction.* London: Sage.

Schieffelin, B. & E. Ochs (1996), 'The microgenesis of competence: Methodology in language socialization', in D. Slobin, J. Gerhardt, A. Kyratzis & G. Jiansheng (eds) *Social interaction, social context and language: Essays in honor of Susan Ervin-Tripp* (pp. 251–264). Mahwah, NJ: Lawrence Erlbaum Associates.

Swedish National Agency for Education [SNAE]. (2011/2015), *Läroplan för grundskolan, förskoleklassen och fritidshemmet 2011* (Revised 2015).

Smart, C. & B. Neale (1999), *Family Fragments?* Cambridge: Polity Press.

Solomon, Y., J. Warin, C. Lewis & W. Langford (2002), 'Intimate talk between parents and their teenage children: Democratic openness or covert control?', *Sociology*, 36(4), 965–983.

Children and Teachers Transitioning in Playworlds: The Contradictions Between Real Relations and Play Relations as a Source of Children's Development

Marilyn Fleer

Introduction

Back in 1984, Inge Bretherton researched how children move in and out of imaginary situations when playing (Bretherton, 1984). She found that in these situations children were both 'in frame' or 'out of frame'. Like El'koninova (2001a, b) and Schousboe (2013), she drew attention to the porous nature of the boundary between the real-world situation and the imaginary situation during play, showing how children sometimes solved problems from inside their imaginary play. However, these longstanding studies did not research the nature of the transition between the real role and play role of adults when playing with children inside imaginary situations. Rather, many studies and play researchers assumed that children's play can only really be play if adults are not involved (see critique by van Oers, 2013), even though some research shows that children have positive views on adult involvement in their play (Pramling Samuelsson & Johansson, 2009).

In contrast with the assumption that teachers should not be involved in children's play, is a cultural-historical conception of play where adults can, and do, take an active role in children's play. For instance, in her original research, Lindqvist (1995) has shown how teachers structure play situations to support the development of children's play. More recently, Hakkarainen (2010) in his empirical study of playworlds has identified the key pedagogical features of teachers that promote the joint development of a play narrative with children. What is common to these researchers is that they draw upon Vygotsky's (1966) cultural-historical conception of play, conceptualized as children creating an imaginary situation, and changing the meaning of objects and actions to give them a new sense. In playworlds, adults and children jointly create the imaginary situations and use objects and actions as pivots to develop their play narrative. These studies have given teachers a very different way of conceptualizing their work, and provided pedagogical guidance on how to create the play settings (Hedegaard, 2014) for supporting the development of play and thereby the overall development of children.

Although the pedagogical conditions and psychological characteristics of play development have been presented in these works (Hakkarainen, 2010), and related studies (Schousboe, 2013), we do not yet know enough about the effect of teachers as play partners transitioning between imaginary situations and real situations. What is missing from these studies of playworlds, is the child's perspective of observing their teachers transitioning between a real role of being a teacher to a play role of being a character or play partner in the imaginary situation. Consequently, the goal of this chapter is to fill this gap in understanding by holistically examining (Hedegaard, 2008) the transitions between real roles and play roles of children and teachers in playworlds. To achieve this goal, a theoretical discussion of what is already known about transitioning in play is presented as a backdrop to the current study, followed by the study design, findings, discussion and conclusion.

Background to the study: Psychological dimensions of transitioning in play

Studies that include the role of the teacher are based primarily in European and European heritage contexts, such as the original playworlds research of Lindqvist (1995) and those that have followed this line of inquiry (e.g., Hakkarainen, Brėdikytė, Jakkula & Munter, 2013). Lindqvist's (1995) research and theoretical conceptualization play in preschool settings, includes adults as play partners within the process of collectively created imaginary play situations. In playworlds children and their teachers physically enter into an imaginary situation using a cultural device, such as a large basket with a papier mâché hot air balloon to fly to distant lands (Lindqvist, 1995) or a wishing chair to go on adventures (stories of Enid Blyton) (Fleer, 2017). What is unique about playworlds is that all the children in the preschool and their teachers take a role in the play, and this means they must collectively transition into the playworld.

Hakkarainen (2010) has argued that there are different kinds of transitions into playworlds. Some transitions occur through physical borders, such as the cardboard box fixed to a door frame to act as the wardrobe when entering into and playing out the stories of Narnia. While other transitions are psychological, such as the example of Rumpelstiltskin (Brothers Grimm), where a character reads a coded letter (letters must be read backwards) that the children have to collectively solve, and collectively create a new play rule, such as putting their jackets on back to front, and walking backwards when in the playworld. Hakkarainen (2010) argues that, 'The transition rituals change children's mode of psychological activity and its logic' (p. 80). In this sense, playworlds create new conditions for children's development, acting as a psychological super tool (Hakkarainen, 2010). Of particular relevance to this chapter, is the change in logic by children when their teachers in reality are their teachers, but in the playworld they are their play partners. How this creates the developmental conditions for children is not well understood.

What is known, is that in playworlds the children and teachers are inside the problem situation, emotionally involved, and according to Hakkarainen (2010), are using narrative logic to maintain and develop the play plot. In line with Vygotsky's theory of development, and Hakkarainen's (2010) idea of the narrative logic of play, is the view that playworlds support developmental conditions because drama is created through the play plot (i.e., journeys, adventures, problem formulations), and this acts as the force for resolving the tension between real forms and ideal forms of development (Vygotsky, 1994). However, a study of this kind of relation has not yet been undertaken.

In line with the tension between real forms and ideal forms of development, Kravtsov and Kravtsova (2010) have drawn attention to the importance of the relations between the playworld and the real world through discussing a form of double subjectivity in spontaneous play. They refer to this as a dual positioning in play, where the child is both in the imaginary situation playing, while also being able to be above the play controlling their own play actions. They highlight play relationships and real relationships through illustrating how in, for example, the pretend play of playing hospitals, a child can be enjoying playing, but at the same time be frightened by the play actions. Important to the goal of this chapter is Kravtsov and Kravtsova's (2010) elaboration of dual positioning in play through drawing attention to how players are actively taking two positions by being 'simultaneously inside and outside of play' (p. 29). Children who take dual positions in play are logically framing their actions in the context of the play plot (*play relations*) while also taking into account the logic of reality (*real relations*). But how children transition between play relations and real relations is not explicitly discussed in their work.

Schouboe (2013) goes a step further and suggests that there are three interrelated spheres of reality in play that children deal with simultaneously. She says there are spheres of imagining, spheres of staging and spheres of reality. Although she does not show how children transition into these, she does give practical examples to illustrate psychologically how the spheres may simultaneously interact when enacted in practice. When imagining, children are inside the imaginary situation taking on a role in the play. However, when staging, they are in the process of making proposals and negotiating the play plot and roles. Here they are outside the imaginary play. The sphere of reality foregrounds the physical properties of materials and the children's environment in relation to the play themes. However, Schouboe (2013) argues that all three spheres are inseparable, because all three are needed to form and maintain the play. She says, 'The surfaces of contact between these spheres are penetrable, so that they both separate and unite the spheres' (p. 28).

Moller (2015) has also drawn attention to the relations between reality and imaginary situations, introducing the concept of a play scenario where transitions occur between play acts and play rules. She argues that 'encounters and experiences may change understandings of themselves [children], others, and aspects of the world' (p. 20). That is, children in play negotiate, recreate and explain the roles they observe in their real world, while also generating rules that can be reproduced outside the particular play setting. Development in play occurs between what she calls non-transgressive acts and transgressive acts, where the former is a reproduction of the established rules and the latter is where children change the rules of the play act. Development occurs because children agree to change the play rules to accommodate the new transgressive play act, transforming the play itself.

What is learned from these studies is that there are transitions in play, notably between the playworld and the cultural reality of everyday life. However, these ways of conceptualizing transitions in play say little about how these become successful transitions for children when adults enter into children's play.

In order to understand successful transition in play when adults are involved, it is important to study how adults support children in meeting new demands, and how potential conflicts between motives and the cultural content of everyday life is resolved. El'koninova (2001b) suggests that a key characteristic of children's play is repetition, and repetition helps children transition into purposeful and meaningful cultural content from the world in which they live. Cultural content is mediated by 'the process of "transference" of the motives of human activity', which El'koninova (2001b) described as 'the transition from an interpsychic to an intrapsychic form of play activity' (p. 31). In her research on children aged 4–7, she was interested in studying how in play children transition into these developed forms of human activity, and in drawing upon Elkonin's (translated in 2005) position, showed how motives change in the course of a child's development. She argued that children in different age periods reflect different aspects of the same reality in their play. That is, higher forms of play are found over the course of a child's development, and this becomes evident when studying their motive orientations to the same play situation, but where the play is reflecting different kinds of generalizations of the child's cultural world or real situation. The same motive orientation to play may be evident, but the cultural content is expressed through different forms of generalizations of reality in children's play.

El'koninova's results were gained through a study of children's re-enactment of fairytales at different ages, where little attention was given to what role the adult took in supporting the transition from an inter to an intrapsychic form of play. However, in a related study by El'koninova (2001b) into storytelling, she suggested that the teacher must take an active position in linking the two worlds for the child – the text of the tale, which includes the 'renewal and reproduction of the world depicted in it', with the real world of the child (p. 38). In this transitioning,

> the adult must skillfully bring the world of the listener and the world of the story together in such a way as not to frighten or terrify the child (i.e. equate the real world and the story world) or not to separate the two worlds from one another so much that the child loses interest (p. 38).

As such, the role of the adult appears to be pivotal in creating the conditions for children's development in storytelling, and potentially in the role-playing of fairytales and other stories. Playworlds includes both storytelling and the re-enactment of well-known fairytales (Hakkarainen, 2010), and like El'koninova's work, focuses on adults taking an active mediating role. However, in playworlds adults act as play partners mediating the cultural content of the play. When adults are a part of children's play this creates very different developmental conditions, because it places new demands upon children who do not expect teachers to take a play role. In the study reported in this chapter, we were interested to learn how children meet these potential contradictions and dramatic moments when adults enter the play, and also to identify how children dealt with, and transitioned into the playworlds with their teachers (Hedegaard, 2008).

Study design

The study sought to understand the contradictions between the play relations and real relations of teachers and children when acting as co-players in a jointly created playworld. To achieve the goal of this research, the children and teachers were followed as they became progressively engaged in the activities of the playworld of Robin Hood of Sherwood Forest.

Participants

A total of thirteen children consented to participate in the study. Of these, five were aged 5.9 years (5.5–6.4 years) and eight were aged 5.1 years (4.7–5.5 years). Australia is a culturally diverse community. The children were primarily from families who identified as only Australian (n=8), Australian-European heritage (n=4) and Australian-Asian heritage (n=1) backgrounds. Significantly, the group was made up of three girls and ten boys.

The children were from two classrooms located in a large city in eastern Australia. One classroom was known as the '4's' and the other as the '5's'. The children from each classroom came together for the project on playworlds. The four year olds moved from their classroom to the classroom of the five year olds for playworlds.

Two qualified teachers led the teaching programme across the two years of the study (Rebecca and Oriana), and they were supported periodically by a computer technician (Alex), who took a role inside the play as a castle engineer. Only the second year of the study is analysed and reported in this paper.

Data gathering

The study period ran over two years. The data from the second year of the study were gathered over thirty-seven weeks. Of this, a total of twelve weeks of digital observations of the teaching programme were made. Digital cameras were used to document the teacher's professional development and the teaching programme across the four terms of the school year. A total of thirty-five data gathering trips were made to the preschool and a total of fifty-two sessions were recorded from beginning to end.

The study gathered 123 hours of digital video data, of which twenty-five hours centred on teacher interviews, planning sessions between teachers, teacher reflections on the programme, and all the professional development sessions.

Two digital standard cameras and two GoPro cameras were used to gather data. One camera was placed on a tripod and positioned to capture an overview of group work or key project areas in the classrooms. The other camera was used to follow children and to capture small group and individual activities. The GoPro cameras were used inside the time machine – a small defined space that was difficult to film. One static GoPro captured the activities on a wide-angle lens, while a second GoPro was worn by a child on their forehead, capturing the moving actions and activities inside the time machine of one child – capturing their perspective.

Context and analysis

The teachers participated in professional development over the duration of the project, receiving regular support from the senior research assistant. The teachers created a playworld focused on Robin Hood from Sherwood Forest. The teachers used a time machine to move the children back in time. A tree house with a GoPro was used as the time machine. Another playworld prop was a log that lay in front of a gate that separated the classrooms. The children stood on this log, nominated the character they would be in the playworld, and then they would move across to either the other classroom or the time machine.

In order to effectively implement this playworld programme, the main teacher (Rebecca) was supported through participation in a postgraduate programme on cultural-historical studies before and during the delivery of the playworld.

In order to understand the intentions of the children, their motives (Vygotsky, 1998; Hedegaard, 2002; 2014) and the demands they meet (Hedegaard, 2008; 2014) in the context of the playworlds (Lindqvist, 1995), the digital data were analysed during moments of transition that were dramatic for children and teachers (Vygotsky, 1998).

Findings

The study found that there were many different transitions observed in the playworld as a result of the teachers' involvement in co-creating the imaginary play situations. Two key psychological dimensions and one pedagogical characteristic are presented as explanations of commonly observed practices in the playworld of the teachers and children. The cornerstones for understanding the relations between play roles and real roles were the following:

1. Genesis of the transitions between the real role and play role of the same person
2. Dramatic contradictions between the real role and play role of the same person
3. Teachers using role relations rather than real relations to help children's participation in the emerging playworld

Genesis of the transitions between the real role and play role of the same person

Over the period of the study, the children and teachers spent time engaged in a series of playworld adventures. In the example that follows, Oriana (teacher) enters and exits the classroom in role as Friar Tuck from Sherwood Forest.

Oriana in role as Friar Tuck enters and exits the classroom

The children are seated on a mat in the 5's classroom. Rebecca the teacher is with all the children from the 4's and 5's classrooms, and says, 'Where's Oriana?' The research assistant responds to her, saying, 'I don't know.' The children look around the room.

Oriana is positioned to enter into the classroom, using the outside door. She is about to walk into the classroom in role as Friar Tuck from Sherwood Forest. Several children look to the door and call out, 'I know where she is.' As they say this, Rebecca says, 'She must have … [pausing and noticing Oriana] Oh.' The children get excited as Rebecca cries out with enthusiasm, 'Quick, we must [inaudible].' The children squeal, laugh and quickly move up and down off the mat as Rebecca sings, 'Everybody sitting, sitting, sitting … it looks like we are going to have a surprise'.

Oriana enters the room. She is holding an A3-sized sheet of paper with writing on it scribed in old English text. The edges of the paper are burnt and frayed. The paper is textured and looks old. Oriana closes the door and then in a slow deep voice laughs, and in the same tone says, 'Hello children. How are you today?' Barny says, 'Good'. All the children are in a circle on the mat now, and look to Oriana in role as Friar Tuck. She says, 'Do you know who I am?' The children say in unison:

'Yes';

'It's you';

'No';

'Did you forget?'

Oriana in role as Friar Tuck looks to Rebecca and says, 'Hello' and then laughs as Rebecca replies 'Hello'. One child says, 'Are you Robin Hood?' Hugo says, 'Maid Marian'. Oriana as Friar Tuck says, 'I am a good friend of Robin Hood'. Hugo repeats, 'Maid Marian?' to which Oriana in role as Friar Tuck says, holding his chin, repeatedly saying and laughing, 'Oh she's a lovely girl.'

Oriana in role as Friar Tuck laughs and says to the children, 'I'm Friar Tuck. Hello everyone'. Thomas points to the paper in Friar Tuck's hand. Friar Tuck responds by saying, 'You're very clever. You noticed I've got something here'.

The children and Rebecca together inquire about the paper, commenting on both the old English writing and the texture of the paper. Friar Tuck explains that he wrote the letter for someone else. Rebecca asks, 'Is it some sort of old fashioned writing?' The children look closely, as Friar Tuck agrees. Rebecca suggests, 'It must be from another time'. Friar Tuck says, 'Yes it is', to which Rebeca responds by saying, 'From your time'. Friar Tuck agrees, and the children wriggle closer and closer. Friar Tuck switches momentarily to Oriana to begin controlling the children by saying, 'OK guys', then she catches herself, and goes into role and laughs in a deep slow voice saying, 'Why don't you sit down children', pointing to them and saying, 'You children are very funny, aren't you?' The children laugh and sit. Oriana in role as Friar Tuck invites two children to read the text in the letter (PRO36 H3 20161010 09 3:15–6:35).

Demands on the children

The teachers create an imaginary situation through Oriana going into role as Friar Tuck. In many preschools and schools in Australia, the teachers do not normally take a role in the imaginary play situation. This situation places a demand upon the children because they have to imagine the play situation, but also the role situation of Oriana. She is no longer a teacher (real relation they have with her), but is a character in the storybook she has been reading to them (play relation). The play relation is a new situation for the children.

Intentions

Both Rebecca and Oriana as Friar Tuck work together to develop the play narrative. They signal to the children that Oriana is not there, but that there is a visitor. Oriana in role says, 'Do you know who I am?' This gives the possibility for the children to enter into a playworld that has previously been established. But this is not straightforward, as suggested when some say, 'It's you'; and question, 'Did you forget?' However, the children appear to enter into the playworld as Oriana in role as Friar Tuck, laughs and talks slowly and in a deep voice. They begin to respond to the imaginary play situation, and begin to guess who Oriana is role-playing, suggesting, 'Are you Robin Hood?' or 'Maid Marian'. The children's relations with their teacher change from that of Oriana in the real situation, to Friar Tuck in the role situation.

Motives

Preschool children's leading activity is for play. By Oriana acting as Friar Tuck from Sherwood Forest, a playful situation is created for the children. The children appear to respond positively to the imaginary play situation, as it is motivating (Hedegaard, 2002), and draws upon their play motive (Vygotsky, 1966). It does not appear to be difficult for the children to enter into the imaginary situation of talking to Friar Tuck. Once the role is established, and the children appear engaged in the storyline, then the unfolding of the adventure emerges, and the children are swept away by the play narrative of rescuing the dragon in the castle in Sherwood Forest. However, at the end of the play situation, Oriana returns to her real role. In the segment that follows, Oriana as Friar Tuck has left the classroom, and re-entered from another door as Oriana. In switching back to the real situation of Oriana the teacher, an explicit contradiction is created between the 'real role' and the 'play role'.

Oriana enters the classroom

Oriana enters the classroom from an internal door. Rebecca notices and says, 'Oriana we had a visitor'. Oriana responds by saying, 'I'm sorry. I got caught up'. All the children look to Oriana. She is holding a large poster-sized sheet of paper. 'I got the paper that you needed. I will just go and get some pens'. The children follow her with a serious expression as Rebecca declares, 'Oriana always misses our best visitors'. The children watch Oriana, but do not comment.

All the children are now seated in a circle, as Oriana goes to sit down to join them. Rebecca is busy organizing the children, as Roger smiles at Oriana and says quietly, 'Friar Tuck came to visit us'. Oriana is now sitting, and Roger repeats more loudly, 'Friar Tuck came to visit us'. Oriana says, 'What do you mean?' Roger explains, 'He gave a special message [pointing to the letter], from his friend dragon'. Rebecca looks to Oriana and says, 'I know this is hard to believe [pausing], cause you're looking a bit confused …' to which all the children study

Oriana's face closely. Barny learns forward in order to glimpse her face better. The letter is read by Hugo to Oriana. She asks, 'Who is it from?' Hugo in role as a dragon calls out 'Me', followed by two other children who are also in role as dragons. The three children are seated together in the circle. Rebecca explains, 'Some of the children are dragons'. Oriana asks, 'Who delivered it?'. Crystal says, 'Friar Tuck'. Barny, in a soft but serious voice, says to Oriana, 'Do you know you look a little bit like him' (PRO36 H3 20161010 09 19:20:10–21:54:06).

Demands on the children

Changing the relation that the children have to Oriana from a play relation back to a real relation was supported through watching Friar Tuck leave and observing Oriana arrive from another door. This situation created new demands upon the children, as they needed to transition back from a play role to their real role with Oriana as their teacher. This transition between the play relation to the real relation was challenging for some of the children. For instance, Barny observes the similarities between Oriana and Friar Tuck. His serious and thoughtful expression of, 'Do you know you look a little bit like him', suggests he is not sure. Further, the play plot highlights for some of the children their own role as dragons.

No dress-ups or disguises were used by the teachers to support the children with either moving into role or moving back out of role. Oriana and Friar Tuck only differed in their voice quality, actions, and the play or real narrative they developed with the children. In order to better understand the transitions, further analysis of the dramatic contradictions was needed.

Dramatic contradictions between the real role and play role of the same person

A second finding of this study was the contradiction noticed by the children between the real relations and role relations of their teachers. In the example that follows, the children focus on trying to understand if the person who is standing with them is Alex the computer technician or Bob the engineer who lives in Sherwood Forest in the time of Robin Hood.

> Rebecca (teacher), Alex (computer technician for the school), and most of the children are standing on the special transition log in preparation for entering into the playworld. The usual practice in the playworlds' literature is for the children to decide upon what role they will take before entering into the playworld, to stay in role and to exit the imaginary situation by the same way they entered.

On this day, the 4's (children) are lined up on the log and waiting to enter the 5's classroom. One of the children in role (Maid Marian) runs up to Rebecca, as she wants to visit the bathroom, and this holds up the entry back into the classroom. While they wait, a discussion begins between four children about Alex. Alex is the sixth person standing on the log waiting. They are wondering if Alex is Bob the castle engineer or Alex the technician.

Cole smiles broadly and points at Alex, saying, 'That's Bobby'. Leo and Roger immediately look up at Alex and smile, with Roger laughing and forcefully saying, 'That's the same shoes as Bobby'. Cole then smiles and says, 'That's the same, that's the same hair as Bobby'. All four children look at Alex, smiling, but he does not respond. Cole looks intently at Rebecca, but she is still busy talking to Maid Marian about visiting the bathroom and does not hear the conversation between the four children. Roger holds his hat on his head with his arms, and swings from side to side, as he cheekily says, 'That's the same colour and the same beard'. Tom who is standing directly next to Alex, looks up, appearing to look at his beard, and then smiles broadly as Cole agrees. Roger also agrees, saying, 'Yeah' while smiling broadly. In a squeaky voice, Cole says, pointing at Alex and then back to Roger, 'He just looks like Bobby' (PRO40 H10 20161013 0.05–1.38).

In this first segment the children are standing on the transitioning log. This log is designed to support the children to physically enter into the playworld. Having Alex as the technician or Bob the Engineer with them creates a contradiction for them. They have previously visited Bob back in time and they have discussed engineering principles with him. But on the transitioning log, they wonder what role he is in.

Intentions

Alex is clearly not responding to the children, despite all four children looking at him, commenting on the physical features of Alex and Bob the castle engineer. The children smile each time they look at him or at each other. They appear to be emotionally engaged with the idea of the adult standing on the log as either Alex the technician or Bob the castle engineer.

Demands on the children

Alex does not respond to the children. He simply stands and shows no expression or even acknowledgement of the contradiction the children are facing. By not responding to the children he places an emotional and cognitive demand upon the children – they have to work out for themselves who he is. The children's expressions suggest that they are both happy and not sure at the same time. The confusion between Alex as the technician and Bob the castle engineer is maintained the whole time they are standing on the log. They do not know if this is an imaginary situation or the real situation.

Motives

The children appear to be highly engaged in the imaginary situation of Robin Hood of Sherwood Forest and their previous visit there to meet Bob the castle engineer. By going back in time, they learn about engineering principles from that time period that will support them in solving the problem situation that has emerged for them – to build a machine to help rescue the treasure, and later to also help rescue the dragon who is locked in the castle dungeon. Bob the castle engineer is a key player in their imaginary situation, and by being in role, he maintains the story plot and helps keep the playful narrative developing for the children. But as Alex the technician he has no role in the play narrative. The children's real relations with the adult standing on the log are motivated by their leading motive to play. The children's motive orientation to play is a strong force for how they relate to the adult called Alex.

Further, the contradiction between their real relation with Alex and their role relation with Bob is expressed through their referencing of this adult's features as being like that of 'Bobby' the castle engineer. This suggests they are transitioning into the imaginary situation as they are waiting to go from the 4's classroom to the 5's classroom where the playworld project is usually initiated.

In the next segment from the same day, the children have moved into the 5's classroom and are now seated in a circle on the floor. The teachers have not yet announced any movement into an imaginary situation. Rather they are primarily in the real situation of the classroom of the 5's. Alex is with them. He is in his real role as a computer technician visiting their classroom.

> Rebecca is seated on the mat with both Oriana and Alex, and all the children. They are all seated in a circle, so they can see each other. One girl is at the back reading a book, but she also comments from time to time, suggesting she is following the discussion. The children are chatting with each other, and a few of the children call out to Alex, 'Hey Bob' several times. Alex looks at them but does not respond. Rebecca turns to Alex and then back to all the children and says, 'Alex popped in to the classroom because he needed to update the software'. She then turns to Alex and asks, 'So was that what you were doing?' Alex nods in agreement. Rebecca continues, 'He was updating the software on my laptop and I started to tell him about the grabby hand machine, it's a bit like a crane,

with pulleys, isn't it? … and I asked him a couple of questions, and I realized, Alex knows a lot about simple machines, so he said he would come, because today team' … Rebecca is interrupted when Henry says, 'Can we go back in time?' In response to Henry, Rebecca turns to Alex and says, 'So we have got this friend, back in time…'. Alex responds by saying, 'OK'. Rebecca continues as Alex nods, '… called Bob, and he's a castle engineer in Sherwood Forest…'. Rebecca is interrupted by Roger, who says emphatically, 'He is that!' Rebecca looks to Roger and then continues, '… and so we are going to take our group…' Roger repeats 'He is that!' Oriana quickly interjects and says, 'No more interruptions'. Rebecca resumes, '… going to take our group plan back in time, and as soon as we do this…', Henry predicts and finishes the sentence, 'we go back in time'. Rebecca continues by asking, 'So shall we go round the circle and tell Alex some of our ideas? [before we go back in time to meet Bob the castle engineer]' (PRO40 H10 20161013 6.12–8.17).

Rebecca relates to Alex in his real role, explaining to him who Bob the castle engineer is. A number of the children appear to enjoy this contradiction, laughing and calling out 'Hey Bob', even though Alex is in his real role, rather than his play role. However, Roger appears worried by this contradiction, by pointing out that Bob is Alex, when he says emphatically, 'He is that!' He is not given an opportunity to clarify his perspective, as Oriana stops further interruptions so that Rebecca can continue.

Intentions

It would appear that the children mostly all respond to Alex in his role as the computer technician in the classroom – after declaring 'Hey Bob'. As Alex listens to the children's ideas that follow on from the excerpt above (PRO40 H10 20161013 6.12–8.17), the children stay in their real role and relate to Alex in his real role as the computer technician. Rebecca maintains the real relation between Alex and the children, rather than the play relation of Bob the castle engineer.

Demands on the children

Roger appears to struggle between the real relation he has with Alex, and the narrative that Rebecca gives about telling Alex about Bob the engineer. By Roger declaring, 'He is that', he foregrounds the contradiction he is facing between the real and play roles of the same person, while also trying to deal with the demands of going back in time in the playworld of Robin Hood where he met/ meets Bob. There is a further contradiction evident through the children sharing their ideas with Alex in the real moment while discussing ideas to take back to Bob in the time of Robin Hood. There appears to be contraction between the real time of their classroom and the role time of Sherwood Forest. This places a new demand upon the children.

Motives

The motive orientation for play and entering into the imaginary playworld appears to underpin the children's initial expressions of 'Hey Bob'. Their immediate response to Alex was as a play relation where he was Bob, rather than their real relations with him as Alex the computer technician. However, the contradiction was dealt with by the children as Rebecca focused their attention on learning principles. However, the contradiction was more difficult for Roger to deal with because the transition between the double role of play and reality for the character and context did not appear to be easily differentiated.

It also seemed that in playworlds there is a need for transitioning between the real relation and the play relation to be foregrounded in some way. Various perspectives on what was happening appeared to be evident for the children. All the children appeared emotionally engaged in the contradictions between the play relations and real relations with their teachers. This finding seemed to be related to the child's leading motive to play (Vygotsky, 1966). It is interesting to note that in this study, some children embraced the contradiction, enjoying it, while others were worried or intrigued by it, and this contradiction possibly creates a developmental condition for children as they work towards resolving this transition between the real role and play role of the teachers.

Teachers using role relations rather than real relations to help children's participation in the emerging playworld

In the study, it was repeatedly found that the teachers mostly used the characters and the story plot to help the children to solve social, behavioural and conceptual problems. It was common for the teachers to use their role in the story plot being enacted or discussed to guide behaviour. For instance, in the example below, Thomas has some difficulties staying with the storyline that is being introduced in the playworld by Mary, and he becomes disinterested. Rebecca uses her role as a mummy dragon in the playworld to invite Thomas as the baby dragon to be with her, and through this she is able to successfully transition Thomas back into the story plot.

The children are seated on the mat. Rebecca is seated with the children. Oriana is in role as Friar Tuck and is seated in front of the children, explaining a new problem that has arisen. Friar Tuck tells about the dragon being locked in the dungeon of the castle in Sherwood Forest. Mary says to Friar Tuck in a worried and questioning voice, 'Their houses burnt down?' Friar Tuck repeats, 'Their houses burnt down'. Many of the children nod and repeat the question, 'Their house burnt down?', waiting for Friar Tuck to respond. Rebecca explains to Friar Tuck, 'We've been learning a little bit about from your time, and we read that there were some fires, and we were so afraid about the villagers'. Many of the children nod. However, Thomas, who is seated diagonally opposite Rebecca, starts to hug the child next to him around the neck, smiling and laughing. He appears distracted from the storyline introduced by Mary and enthusiastically repeated by many of the children. Rebecca notices Thomas, and says to him, 'Little dragon, I need you over here with mummy dragon'. She motions to Thomas, who enthusiastically crawls and then walks across the mat and nestles comfortably into Rebecca's lap. Rebecca cradles Thomas, who now looks directly at Friar Tuck as she says, 'We have some problems. The dragon wants out'. In a squeaky baby dragon tone, Thomas says, 'Can we help?' Rebecca enthusiastically repeats and expands, 'Can we help? Yes, we can we help her?' Rebecca lifts Thomas's arms up and down enthusiastically, as though mummy and baby dragon are one. The discussion continues about how to rescue the dragon locked in the dungeon of the castle in Sherwood Forest (PRO36 H3 20161010 09 10–21:54:06–23).

Intentions

Rebecca and Oriana have planned their playworld on this day to introduce a problem scenario to the children, and to extend the play plot.

Demands on the teachers

Unexpectedly, Mary introduced into the playworld more content from the story they have been reading about Robin Hood of Sherwood Forest. Mary and the other children were worried about the fires potentially burning down the village and harming the villagers. Mary knew that Friar Tuck had come from Sherwood Forest and therefore might be able to deliver news about the villagers. However, Thomas did not respond to this new play plot, and started to distract another child. This created another demand upon the teachers to work out how to manage Thomas's behaviour. It was a demand because they were in the playworld as players and not teachers. To manage Thomas's behaviour they would normally have had to step outside of the playworld.

Demands on Thomas

The new demand upon the teachers was successfully resolved by the teachers using their play role to solve the problem. The behaviour management of Thomas was achieved through emphasizing the mummy dragon role of Rebecca, which in turn allowed her to call upon her baby dragon to sit with her. In role, Rebecca could stop Thomas from distracting another child. She could, from within the imaginary play situation, support Thomas to positively re-engage with the playworld. By taking this position within the playworld, Rebecca could successfully transition Thomas back into the playworld, where Thomas was able to contribute to the play plot as a competent player.

Discussion

The study identified that in the context of a playworld, where adults enter into children's play, contradiction is experienced by children. How children met these new demands, and how the contractions were dealt with by them (Hedegaard, 2008), were shown in this study to be consistently related to the children's play motive.

The central finding of the study was that when teachers entered into children's play, this created new developmental conditions for the children because of the new demands made upon the children that they needed to resolve. What became evident was, first, that the playworlds approach changed the relations between the children and teachers from real relations to play relations. What was observed, was that when teachers entered into children's play, a contradiction between their real role as teachers and their play role as characters in the playworld emerged for the children in this study. This contradiction only appeared when the teachers took on a play role in the playworld. The double position of being in a state of contradiction between the role relations and play relations, as we saw in the examples of Oriana/Friar Tuck and Alex/Bob, was disconcerting for some children, placing new demands upon these children. This suggests developmental moments in the playworld for these children.

Second, contradictions appeared to be successfully resolved when children changed their relations with their teachers from that of a real role to a play role. Importantly, the children's strong motive for play seemed to support the reconciling of these contradictions. That is, they wanted to engage in the play and therefore persisted in understanding the new play relations with their teacher. The children appeared to enjoy their teachers' participation in role. The dramatic and emotionally charged play situation created through the playworld can be explained by Zaporozhets's (2002) concept of an 'emotional image', which is in contrast to 'a purely rational image'. The emotional image acts as a 'special motiving, activating character and ensures their regulatory influence on the orientation and dynamics of the subsequent practical [play] activity' (p. 63). In our study, we found that the emotional image that is created by children with adults appears in the imaginary situation of the playworld. The narrative that is developed by the teachers and children, the special voice and gestures used by the teachers, and the continual revisiting of the story plot, together appeared to create the collective emotional image of the characters and play plot, connecting directly with the children's play motive. In this way, teachers appeared to successfully mediate the tensions between the real relations and role relations because of the children's strong play motive and the emotional image of the playworld being collectively formed.

Third, the contradiction of the teacher in a play role seemed to highlight for children a need to consciously consider their own role in the context of the rules of play associated with the collectively developing play plot in the playworld. That is, the children's focus of attention was related to not just the play plot, but also in relation to the child/adult characters in the play. The characters in the story of Robin Hood are known in advance through group story reading, and as such there are established rules and roles for playing Robin Hood. Changing the meaning of actions and objects appeared to always be in association with the rules of the storyline and the known characters. This foregrounds an ideal form (Vygotsky, 1994) of play action, that was shown in this study to be highly motivating for the children, and which the children drew upon when defining their own role in the play or what they would expect of other children when in the playworld. This 'emotional-cognitive reflection of the surrounding reality' (Zaporozhets, 2002, p. 63) possibly supports children to consciously consider their own role in the context of the rules of play associated with the collectively developing play plot. This creates different developmental possibilities associated with moving from changing the meaning of actions and objects in the imaginary situation to consciously drawing upon the roles in the play, where the focus is oriented towards the rules governing the play action of the character. This is a higher form of play practice (Vygotsky, 1966), which appeared to be supported in the playworld through the teachers being in role inside the imaginary play with the children.

Fourth, the new developmental conditions were also shaped through how the teachers responded to the children's play roles. It was found that when teachers were in role they supported the collective play of the children from within the play plot. The teachers used their role relations rather than their real relations with children to help children's participation in the emerging playworld. Being a part of an emerging play plot that includes all teachers and all children from a preschool setting is a new practice for teachers and children in early childhood education in Australia, and many European heritage contexts. This suggests that contrary to what dominates the play literature, teachers do have an important role in children's play in supporting the development of the play, and therefore the overall development of the children.

Fifth, a collective form of play created different developmental conditions for the children in our study. It was found that children needed to collectively imagine the play plot, the roles of the players and the rules for acting in the playworld. This collective rather than individually (or small group) oriented imagining, is different to what is currently the practice in many preschools in Australia. However, collectively oriented action with common rules and well understood roles is needed if children are to successfully play together in a playworld. Supporting this collective play activity from within role by the teachers appeared to be a successful pedagogical strategy for supporting the play development of the group, which in turn helped individual children stay with, and contribute to, the collective play in the playworld of Robin Hood.

Finally, a successful transition was evident for the children because the new play conditions changed the children's subsequent relationship with their teachers, where the new demand of teachers entering into children's play and the teachers support of children from within the play, iteratively positioned children within the new collective play practices as competent players. It is argued that these new play practices and the contradictions that emerge, can support the overall development of the children.

Conclusion

The study showed that there were many contradictions being experienced by the children as a result of the children and adults taking on a role in the imaginary situation created through reading the story of Robin Hood of Sherwood Forest. It is argued that the contradictions between the real roles and play roles of teachers created new developmental conditions for children, contributing to higher forms of play involving collectively established roles and rules, thus contributing to the development of the children and their play.

A study of the genesis of these transitions showed how new demands were being made on children to understand and fit within the new play situation. The demands arise because the children needed to respond to their teacher in a new way – in their role as a character, rather than in their role as the teacher. In addition, demands were also made upon children because they needed to determine when their teacher was in role. These new demands and play conditions appeared to generate a double subjectivity for the child – as both a player with their teacher and as a student with their teacher. Anticipation of these changing roles seemed to develop a new social motivation for both the play and the problem scenario that had to be solved in the playworld.

The differing psychological characteristics identified in this study appear to show how dramatic contradiction between the real relations and play relations of the teachers affords new possibilities for understanding how a child's play motive deepens, and this gives some insight into the key role of playworlds for supporting children's development. The contradiction between a play role and a real role creates new developmental possibilities for children, and this could potentially contribute to higher forms of collective imaginary play.

In conclusion, the study showed that a dramatic contradiction between the real relations and play relations of the teachers affords new possibilities and contributes to explaining the key role of teachers in supporting children's development. Successful transitions were found in the playworld because children were supported to become competent play partners in the context of the changing conditions of the real roles and play roles of their teachers. This gives insights into better understanding the developmental conditions of playworlds, and the key role teachers have in supporting children's development through being play partners in play for Australian early childhood contexts.

References

Bretherton, I. (ed.) (1984), *Symbolic play: The developemnt of social undertstanding.* Orlando, FL: Academic Press.

Elkonin, D. B. (2005), 'The psychology of play', *Journal of Russian and East European Psychology*, 43(1), 11–21.

El'koninova, L. I. (2001a), 'Fairy-tale semantics in the play of preschoolers', *Journal of Russian and East European Psychology*, 39(4), 66–87.

El'koninova, L.I. (2001b), 'The object orientation of children's play in the context of understanding imaginary space-time in play and in stories', *Journal of Russian and East European Psychology*, 39(2), 30–51.

Fleer, M. (2017), 'Digital playworlds in an Australia context', in T. Bruce, M. Bredikyte & P. Hakkarainen (eds), *Routledge international handbook of early childhood play* (pp. 289–304). Abingdon: Routledge Press.

Hakkarainen, P. (2010), 'Cultural-historical methodology of the study of human development in transitions', *Cultural-historical Psychology*, 4, 75–81.

Hakkarainen, P., M. Brėdikytė, K. Jakkula & H. Munter (2013), 'Adult play guidance and children's play development in a narrative play-world', *European Early Childhood Education Research Journal*, 21(2), 213–225, DOI: 10.1080/1350293X.2013.789189

Hedegaard, M. (2002), *Learning and child development: A cultural-historical study*. Aarhus: Aarhus University Press.

Hedegaard, M. (2008), 'A cultural-historical theory of children's development', in M. Hedegaard & M. Fleer (eds), *Studying children: A cultural-historical approach* (pp. 10–29). Maidenhead: Open University Press.

Hedegaard, M. (2014), 'The significance of demands and motives across practices in children's learning and development: An analysis of learning in home and school', *Learning, Culture, and Social Interaction*, 3, 188–194.

Kravtsov, G. G. & E. E. Kravtsova (2010), 'Play in L. S. Vygotsky's nonclassical psychology', *Journal of Russian and East European Psychology*, 48(4), 25–41.

Lindqvist, G. (1995), *The aesthetics of play: A didactic study of play and culture in preschools*. Uppsala: Acta Universitatis Upsaliensis, Uppsala Studies in Education, 62, 234.

Moller, S. J. (2015), *A developmental psychological perspective on creative imagination in play: How different toys influence children's play*. PhD Thesis. University of Copenhagen, Faculty of social Sciences, Denmark. ISBN 978-87-7611-875-4.

Pramling Samuelsson, I. & E. Johansson (2009), 'Why do children involve teachers in their play and learning?', *European Early Childhood Education Research Journal*, 17(1), 77–94.

Schousboe, I. (2013), 'The structure of fantasy play and its implications for good and evil games', in I. Schousboe & D. Winther-Lindqvist (eds), *Play and playfulness: Cultural-historical perspectives* (pp. 13–28). Dordrecht: Springer.

van Oers, B. (2013), 'Is it play? Towards a reconceptualisation of role play from an activity theory perspective', *European Early Childhood Education Research Journal*, 21(2), 185–198.

Vygotsky, L.S. (1966), 'Play and its role in the mental development of the child', *Voprosy Psikhologii*, 12(6), (62–76). Translated in *Soviet Psychology*, 1967, 5, 6–18.

Vygotsky, L. S. (1994), 'The problem of the environment', in R. Van Der Veer & J. Valsiner (eds), *The Vygotsky Reader* (pp. 338–354). Cambridge: Blackwell.

Vygotsky, L. S. (1998), 'Child psychology', in L. S. Vygotsky, *The collected works of L. S. Vygotsky*, *vol.* 5, trans. M. J. Hall, Robert W. Rieber (ed. English translation). New York: Kluwer Academic and Plenum Publishers.

Zaporozhets, A. V. (2002), 'Toward the question of the genesis, function, and structure of emotional processes in the child', *Journal of Russian and East European Psychology*, 40(2), 45–66.

Transition Between Child-initiated Imaginative Play and Teacher-initiated Activity: An Analysis of Children's Motives and Teachers' Pedagogical Demands in a Preschool Context

Anamika Devi, Marilyn Fleer and Liang Li

Introduction

In recent educational psychology research, inspired by Vygotskian cultural-historical theory, children's learning and development have been conceptualized in relation to their participation in different institutional settings such as family, preschool, school, community and play groups (Hedegaard & Edwards, 2014). Children are always in a transitional process, meeting social and institutional demands in their everyday lives. Transitional processes across different educational settings and across different countries have been examined by a growing number of researchers from the perspective of cultural-historical theory (Adams & Fleer, 2014; Bøttcher, 2014; Hedegaard, 2014; Sánchez-Medina, Macías-Gómez-Stern & Martínez-Lozano, 2014). However, transitional processes between two activity settings in one preschool setting have received less attention. Grounded in Vygotsky's cultural-historical theory, this chapter examines the demands that teachers' pedagogical practices make upon children as they transition from a child-initiated play activity to a learning activity in an Australian preschool. The aim of this chapter is to understand the transitional demands experienced by children who move between two activity settings (child-initiated play and adult-initiated activity) in a preschool context.

Wood (2014) states that child-initiated play has its own qualities and a child can choose his or her own activities, play partners and themes. But child-initiated play is always under the control of the early childhood teacher who organizes the space, time and resources for play. Therefore, child-initiated free play is shaped by institutional practices that are governed by policy frameworks, teachers' beliefs and values, parents' expectations and the pushdown effects from the primary curriculum that is becoming increasingly of concern in some Western heritage communities (Wood, 2014). In this sense, a child has the freedom to choose their play theme, play partner and play materials; however, the teachers prepare the play settings according to their own educational agenda (Wood, 2014). What is known is that adult-initiated activity is usually planned in accordance with curriculum goals, often structured, and resourced and managed by the adult to promote specific outcomes (Saracho, 2012). Importantly, the national frameworks for early childhood education in many countries, such as the UK and Australia, suggest that teachers should maintain a balance between child-initiated play and adult-guided activities through taking the role of an organizer, supporter and director in play-based learning (DEEWR, 2009; Department of Education, 2014).

According to Wood (2014), this means that the teacher should focus on organizing a learning activity that retains elements of play or playfulness, and where the pedagogical 'recipe' seeks to foreground a balance between child-initiated play and adult-initiated activity. Other approaches take into account children's perspectives in play-based learning, such as a dialectical model of conceptual play (Fleer 2010, 2011), which focuses on the child's motive for play and where the adult can take an active position to teach academic concepts to children in a playful manner, instead of giving direct instructions. The practical situation of pedagogical practice in preschools is different because 'pedagogic progression in play is framed as a transition from child-initiated play to formal, adult-initiated activities, which reinforces the point that play is valued not for what it is but for what it leads to in educational terms' as mentioned by Wood (2014, p. 153). This is an emerging tension in early childhood education, especially at the preschool level where children are in a transitional process from informal child-initiated play to formal educational activity initiated by teachers. This raises the dialectical problem of how teachers change playful activity settings to be about learning academic concepts, and how children change activity settings that support learning to make them more playful.

There are a number of cultural-historical studies that draw attention to the transition between activity settings. These studies focus on children's learning and development through researching the transition between different practice settings; for example, from home to school or from preschool to school (Corsaro & Molinari, 2000; Hedegaard & Fleer, 2013). However, the process of transition between activities and their relationship to learning are rarely studied and conceptualized (Hedegaard & Edwards, 2014). The national early childhood framework in Australia, within which the present study is located, focuses on children's transition from one institutional setting to another, for example, 'moving between home and childhood setting, between a range of different early childhood settings, or from childhood setting to full-time school' (DEEWR, 2009, p. 46). The framework emphasizes to educators that they should plan an effective transition between settings (home to preschool or preschool to school). However, this document does not address the need for successful transitions between activity settings within a preschool where academic learning is increasingly becoming an everyday practice for children. In addition, very few studies have looked at how a transition is experienced between two activity settings within a preschool (the exception is Fleer, 2014). As such, we were interested to know: 'How do children transition between activity settings within a preschool?'; 'What happens to the children's motive orientation when teachers make learning demands upon children in play-based settings?'; and 'What demands do children make upon teachers when their motive orientation is to play rather than to learn?'

The aim of this chapter is to address these questions. To achieve this aim, the chapter begins with a discussion of the conceptualization of transition and the concept of motives and demands from a cultural-historical perspective. This is followed by the presentation of the study, the findings of which are based on one case study and interview data of a teacher from one preschool, and concludes with a discussion of the results of this study.

The cultural-historical conceptualization of transitions

Elkonin (1999) showed how children's leading motive of play changes to the new leading motive of learning through the process of transition during different age periods, and as Hedegaard (2014) has elaborated in her research, as they move from kindergarten to school. They both point out that children's transition from one practice to another may create a crisis at a stable period of their development. Each stage of a crisis may change in relation to the dynamic changes in the developmental process of children, which in turn is related to social reality. According to Hedegaard (2014), when children move across different institutions their motive orientation may be changed by the demands and conditions that are constructed by different institutions in society. From the perspective of cultural-historical theory, these changing motives and demands can create a crisis in a child's life that is constructed by changeable social situations.

Vygotsky (1998) and Elkonin (1999) saw the transition as horizontal, where a child's entrance to a new practice is prescribed at the societal level. Inspired by cultural-historical theory, Hedegaard (2014) puts forward a view of transition in a vertical direction; as a zigzag transition where children move between different institutions (from school to after-school care or from home to school) in everyday life. Hedegaard also mentions that a child has social relations with his or her surroundings and enters into different activities in different institutional practices through multiple interactions with members of society. To understand how children learn and develop, Hedegaard (2014) stresses the need to conceptualize children and their environment as a unity and examine the changes of children's development in that unity where learning takes place.

In summary, studies have given attention to transition in relation to children's early learning and development from a cultural-historical perspective (Fleer, 2014; Hedegaard, 2014; Winther-Lindqvist, 2012; Zittoun, 2006). They have focused on young children's learning experiences in the context of moving between different practice settings from home to preschool or from preschool to school (Hedegaard & Fleer, 2013). Some studies have shown how children's emotional experiences are affected by the process of transitions as they move from one country to another (Adams & Fleer, 2014; Moore & Barker, 2012), and how children's learning can take place through '*microgenetic movements*' within one concrete activity setting (Fleer, 2014). Some studies focus on the age-specific nature of transitions (Hviid, 2008; Märtisin, 2010; Zittoun, 2006) and some studies pay attention to children's experiences when starting school in a new country (Ebbeck & Reus, 2005). However, these studies have not given attention to the transition between activity settings within a single preschool institution where the relations between children's motives and teacher demands upon children are the focus. Therefore, through a cultural-historical conception of transition, we can more holistically study the motives and demands made on children/teachers as they engage in learning activities within play-based settings.

Understanding motives and demands from a cultural-historical perspective

If we look at defining 'motive', we can see that, unlike other concepts in cultural-historical theory, there is no single standard definition of 'motive' in this theory. However, some key scholars have taken a step to define motives and demands through their empirical research. For example, Chaiklin (2012, p. 223) says, 'Motives should be defined and limited more rigorously in relation to societal needs'. Further, Fleer (2012, 2014) mentions that motive is not something that is internally driven but culturally developed and generated through observing or participating in an everyday activity. Also, it is pointed out by Hedegaard (2012b) that a motive captures a child's intentional actions and interactions with other members of the society in an activity setting. Motives are related to the practices and values in a society which are collectively structured rather than individually constructed (Hedegaard, 2012a). According to Hedegaard (2014), when children move from one institution to another, sometimes their transition can be smoother or sometimes not because different institutional demands can create different institutional conditions. The motive orientation of an individual is shaped by both the societal values and the institutional practices that are created through societal traditions (Hedegaard, 2012a).

To study a person's development and learning, we must also consider the institutional practices that a child experiences. In cultural-historical theory, the relation between the individual's motives and the demands of an institution is seen as a mediated relationship (Hedgaard, 2014). Hedegaard (2014) also mentions that development takes place when a child's motive orientation meets new institutional demands. For example, when a child enters into a school from a preschool, the child's motive orientation for play can be changed through a transitional process in order to deal with the new institutional demands of learning (such as reading, writing and counting). According to Hedegaard (2012b), a 'child's motives are related to what is meaningful and important for them' (p. 134) and 'an activity is only motivating for a child if the activity setting is linked with the child's already developed motives' (Fleer, 2014, p. 206). Preschool practices generally have foregrounded play-based practices, but in recent times this has started to change, and there is an expectation in some countries, such as Australia, for teachers to set up learning in line with new preschool curriculum demands. This means it has become increasingly important to study the motive orientation for play of preschool children in the new context of learning instruction (Fleer, 2010, 2012). Hedegaard (2012b) has argued that in an educational setting a teacher needs to be aware of the 'child's motive orientation as well as directing the introduced activities towards supporting new motive' (p. 135). However, the dominant leading activity of learning in a school curriculum can sometimes create a difficult transitional process for preschool children due to different demands (to play or to learn) in an educational setting.

Researchers, teachers and policymakers in early childhood education have focused on the broader transitional process from preschool to school. However, less attention has been directed to how young children meet the new learning conditions that teachers create during free play time where both children's initiated play is featured and learning activities are set up by the teacher. In these situations, children in small groups are called over to the tables to participate in the learning activity prepared by the teacher. Therefore, it becomes important to examine the transitional process between these two different activity settings.

Research design

To understand children's perspectives in a play setting through the lens of cultural-historical theory, we have to consider children's social relations to their environment and the surrounding circumstances. That means societal, institutional and activity settings cannot be ignored. According to Hedegaard (2008a), a researcher must consider three different perspectives when examining an individual child's development and learning within an activity setting – the societal, the institutional, and the individual perspective. Hedegaard (2012a, p. 18) states that 'These planes are interrelated: Society creates the conditions for institutions with its activity settings and persons do so with their specific biological conditions'. We have used Hedegaard's proposed perspectives during our data analysis and framed our research design in relation to her model.

The context of the preschool

In our research, the data were collected from a preschool (Leafy preschool – pseudonyms used), which is integrated with an early learning centre in Melbourne, Australia. State and federal government funding supported the establishment of this early learning centre. The Leafy preschool is situated in a small suburb in Melbourne where people are from European, Asian, African, South-Asian and Australian heritage backgrounds. Children at the preschool enjoy the spacious colourful room and outdoor play area designed and equipped to provide an engaging learning environment for them.

Participants

Children

A total of forty children including two focus children participated in the study. Both of the focus children are from an Indian cultural background and their parents migrated from India nearly five years ago. They both attend the preschool four days a week. In this chapter we present material related to one of the focus children, Apa (a pseudonym used), a four-year-old girl who has an older sister.

Teachers

Four full-time and two part-time teachers were in the room during the data collection periods. Most of the teachers in this preschool have a bachelor's degree in Early Childhood Education and have at least four years of work experience in the early childhood sector. They follow the Early Years Learning Framework (DEEWR, 2009) and the Australian national curriculum, to implement a play-based learning approach into their practice. They set up the activities and evaluate children's learning using the Early Years Learning Framework.

For this chapter, we have used only one video example as an illustration of the transition between two activity settings. The teacher, Bree (a pseudonym used), was interviewed using semi-structured interview techniques, and the results are also presented in this chapter.

Data gathering approach

To focus on the motive orientation of children and the pedagogical demands of teachers in relation to the ongoing and dynamic aspects of social interaction, it is essential to study the children and adults' verbal and nonverbal interaction. In this study, the visual digital methodological approach was adopted to collect the data in children's free play settings (Fleer & Ridgway, 2014). The data have been collected through a video camera, still camera, audio recorder, and field notes. Teachers' individual semi-structured interviews were captured by video camera and audio recorder. We used two cameras to capture the free play settings and transitional process between activities. One roaming camera was used by the first named researcher to capture the focus children's interactions with teachers and peers, and another camera was placed on a tripod to capture the play settings and children's transitional process from one activity to another. A total of 65 hours of video data were collected over the period of eight weeks. In addition, two and a half hours of semi-structured teacher interviews were collected in order to understand their perspectives regarding the pedagogical practice of the centres.

Data analysis

We have analysed video data, photographs, teachers' interview transcripts, and children's portfolios in order to gain a better understanding of the pedagogical practices of teachers and the transitional process of children from one activity setting to another. We used Hedegaard's (2008b) three levels of interpretations: common sense, situated practice and thematic interpretations to gain a broad understanding of the whole data set. This allowed for an analysis of the dynamic relationship between children's motives for play and the teacher's motive for learning noted during transitions between activity settings.

In the context of visual methodology, a common sense interpretation of the raw data allows for a holistic examination of the data set in order to compile moments of transition between child-initiated play and teacher-initiated activities. In our study, the video clips were explicitly described for understanding interactional patterns of teachers and children during the transitional process. The first named researcher then separated those video clips according to how transition took place in the two activity settings, and what the teachers' and children's perspectives were in each setting. For situated practice interpretation, we have linked a series of video clips related to the two activity settings (child-initiated play and instructional teaching), and looked closely at the children's transitional process. The multiple examples of the frequency of the transitional process between two activities and participants' individual perspectives from preschool helped the researcher to identify the patterns of transition at this level. In the thematic interpretation, Vygotsky's (1998) cultural-historical theoretical lens and Hedegaard's (2012b) theoretical concepts of motives and demands were used to answer the research questions with regard to how transition occurs between two activity settings, and what happens to the motives and demands of children and teachers during the transitional process as they move between activity settings.

Findings

There are two main findings from studying children's transitions between activity settings. First, the teacher's demand on children to learn subject-based knowledge was at odds with the children's motive orientation to play. Second, the teacher's pedagogical demands appeared to put on hold the children's imaginary play because the children had to follow the teacher-initiated activity exclusively, and no room was made for the children to continue their imaginary play in the instructional activity setting. These findings are discussed through the presentation of three episodes taken from the broader data set.

In the first episode, the children are followed during free play time where they initiate their own play activity. The second episode follows the children as they move from the free play setting to a mathematics activity at one of the tables in the preschool. The third episode follows both the children and the teacher as they negotiate the new practices for learning mathematics, in which the teacher seeks to make the mathematical experience more motivating by using a caterpillar puppet and paper leaves for the puppet to eat. We examine both the teacher's demands for learning mathematics, and the children's demands upon the teacher to continue their imaginary play.

Activity setting 1: Free play in the home corner

In the case example from Leafy preschool, the focus child Apa created an imaginative play with two other friends, Pippa and Vima (pseudonyms were used), in the dramatic play corner.

Episode 1: Child-initiated mummy-baby role play

> Apa (pretending to be a mummy) says 'night time … night time … nighting time' and her friends are pretending to be babies and lay down on the floor. Then Apa says again 'Cock-a-doodle-doo' (pretending to be a rooster). Her friends jump up from the floor and look for food on the shelf. Apa says 'Shh… she is sleeping'(pointing to a plastic doll that she is holding). Pippa says to Apa 'No, you gonna say the baby is sleeping'. Apa says again 'Yes, the baby is sleeping'.

In the first episode, the children were oriented towards setting up an imaginative play situation. They appeared to be bringing their everyday life experiences into their imaginative play and creating the role of mother and baby through the imaginary situation (Nicolopoulou, 1993; Vygotsky, 2004). They followed the 'rules' of the role of mother and babies, which are reflected in their actions and interactions in the play (Vygotsky, 1966). Apa was changing her role from mother to a rooster when it was necessary to extend the play. In their play, they also used imaginative dialogue like 'Cock-a-doodle-doo' (pretending to be a rooster) or 'Shh… she is sleeping'(pretending to be a concerned mother). According to Vygotsky (2004), the main aspect of imaginative play is the participant's need to simultaneously move between an imaginary situation and reality. In this play scenario, children were moving between an imaginary situation and reality through their interactions and actions to create the conditions of an imaginative mummy-baby role play, which supports Vygotsky's (2004) notion of imaginative play. For example, they collectively moved from the imaginary situation to reality while Pippa paused in the play to correct Apa's imaginative dialogue by saying 'No, you gonna say baby is sleeping'. Apa quickly agreed with Pippa and moved from reality to the imaginary situation again by saying 'Yes, baby is sleeping'. This play example simply shows how children were engaged and could extend the imaginative play by introducing everyday life experiences through their imaginary dialogues, shared conversations and actions. Although the play setting was prepared by the teacher, the children chose the play theme, play partners and materials by themselves.

Episode 2: Transitional moment

> Episode 2 is extracted from the same case example where Apa notices that Bree (their teacher) is putting some papers and a caterpillar soft toy on a small table. Apa walks towards the activity table from the dramatic play corner. Bree says to Apa 'I am going to set up a special game on the table. You should sit down to play. I am going to get something else' (Bree went to bring other resources to set up the activity). Apa runs to the dramatic play corner and announces loudly to her peers 'I am going to play a special game with Bree on that small table'. Then she runs back to the activity table and her friends follow her.

In the second episode, it appears from the data that there were three movements drawn by Apa between the mummy-baby imaginative play and the teacher-initiated special game. In the first phase, Apa found Bree setting up an activity on the table. Bree's activity motivated Apa to move from the dramatic play corner to the activity table. After asking Bree about the activity, she understood that Bree was setting up a special game for children, which stimulated her interest. In the second phase, Apa went back to the dramatic play corner from the activity table to let her friends know that she would join in Bree's special game. Her positive excitement (her facial and verbal expression 'I am going to play a special game with Bree on that small table') to join in the special game has been captured by the video camera and still photographs. Bree missed the opportunity to notice Apa's positive excitement at joining in the special game because she was focused on gathering all the resources in anticipation of teaching mathematical concepts. In the final phase, Apa came back to the teacher-initiated activity and all her other play partners followed. Her motive orientation to join in a special game also motivated her peers to leave the mummy-baby imaginative play and join in Bree's activity. It appears from the data that Apa's individual motive orientation of engaging in a special game motivated other children and created a collective transition from child-initiated play to a teacher-initiated activity.

In presenting the mathematical activity as a special game, Bree motivated the children to leave their imaginative play and be drawn into the new activity as a collective transitional process (she said to Apa 'I am going to set up a special game on the table. You should sit down to play'). Bree asked Apa to sit down to play. She used the word 'should' instead of inviting her to join in the new activity, which reflects the teacher's demands on Apa. However, Apa's interest and curiosity are not driven by internal instincts; rather, Bree's specially created game and Apa's motive orientation to play motivated her to join in the activity, which was externally constructed by the situation (Fleer, 2012). Apa's interaction with her teacher and peers, her interest in the caterpillar activity and her dynamic relationship with her external environment indicates the process of collective transition from the mummy-baby imaginative play to the special game created by the teacher (Fleer, 2012; Hedegaard, 2012a). If we analyse Apa's perspectives in these two episodes (1 & 2), it is easy to determine that Apa was emotionally and physically engaged in the imaginary play and her motive orientation was to join the playful environment. If we analyse Bree's perspective, her pedagogical motive was to set up a learning activity and then to have the children do the activity ('You should sit down to play'). Bree did not know what Apa and her friends had previously been playing and so could not transition the children into the new activity by drawing on the mummy-baby narrative. Additionally, Bree's intention was to create an interesting learning environment for children, naming the activity as a special game, which increased the children's interest in joining in her learning activity.

Activity setting 2: Mathematics task set up on a table

Episode 3: Teacher-initiated caterpillar activity

Apa, Pippa and Vima are now seated around a table. They are holding some soft toys that they bring from their role play. Bree asks them to move those toys from the activity table. Bree provides some leaves, papers, a punching machine and a soft caterpillar toy on the table to evaluate children's counting ability. Bree links the activity with the story of a very hungry caterpillar. She invites the children to consider how to use a punching machine to make a hole in the leaf. Bree said to the children that they could make many holes if they want to. Afterward they need to stick that leaf on the paper. Bree also asks children to count the number of holes and write the numbers beside each of the leaves. Apa asks Bree 'How is the caterpillar going to eat the leaf?' She said to Apa: 'We will only pretend that the caterpillar has eaten some leaves'. Vima is holding the caterpillar and pretending that the caterpillar is eating a leaf. She is moving the caterpillar prop around the leaf and saying 'Yum … yum'. Bree smiles at Vima and says, 'Is it eating? Yum… yum'. Apa is calling to Bree and trying to get her attention. Then Bree focuses on Apa and praises her for writing numbers.

At the end of this activity, Bree mentioned to the researcher that the parents put demands upon the teachers to teach academic concepts. When the researcher asked, 'Why did you set up the caterpillar activity for children?' Bree said:

> We will display these crafts on the wall to show parents. Parents always think children should learn academic concepts through the direct way of teaching. However, we always try to let them know, children are learning through play and we are trying to establish this approach in our care.

Episode 3 shows Bree's intention was to establish an educational agenda to evaluate children's literacy and numeracy ability through the caterpillar activity. She wanted to set up a play-based learning activity so she tried to create an imaginary situation by using the caterpillar prop and the story of *The Very Hungry Caterpillar* to make the learning motivating. Her teaching technique and innovative idea of trying to create an imaginary situation based on *The Very Hungry Caterpillar* story, using the punching machine and caterpillar prop motivated children to engage in her self-initiated activity. She tried to create a play-based learning situation by bringing the caterpillar prop and asked children to imagine that the caterpillar has eaten some leaves. The data shows that she was successful in motivating children to join in her activity by making it a special game. It appears from the data that the children brought their soft toys from the imaginary play to the teacher's activity while they transitioned collectively from their own play to the teacher-initiated activity. It therefore appears that they were in a collective imaginary situation during the transitional process. However, Bree asked them to move those toys from the activity table and could not notice the children's motivation was also linked to their soft toys, which could have afforded the opportunity for expanding their imaginary play into the new activity setting.

Bree's pedagogical demands in evaluating the children's literacy and numeracy abilities prevented her from understanding the children's play motive, but she was successful in moving children from their imaginary thinking to concentrate on her instructional learning approach (Fleer, 2014). The children were already in an imaginary world, which appeared through Apa's imaginative question ('How is the caterpillar going to eat the leaf?') and Pippa's imaginative action (she is moving the caterpillar prop around the leaf and saying 'Yum…

yum'). Bree smiled at Vima and did interact with her by saying 'is it eating?' However, her pedagogical demands to create learning conditions did not give her scope to understand the children's perspectives in wanting to create an imaginary situation with the soft toys; rather, she prompted them to follow her instruction. Bree proposed to the children to pretend that the caterpillar has eaten some leaves but could not develop the children's imaginary experiences in one creative endeavour (as suggested by Hakkarainen et al., 2014). She was not in line with the children's imaginary world where she could develop their learning experience through imaginative play because of her wish to engage the children in her own teacher-initiated, separate learning activity.

The instructional activity itself did not relate to the children's imaginative thinking at that moment; rather, it was simply a teacher-directed instructional activity where the teacher evaluated the children's counting and writing abilities. If we analyse this activity setting from Bree's perspective, her intention was simply to provide materials for supporting play-based learning; therefore, she tried to bring the concept of the caterpillar story and other resources deliberately to engage the children in her activity. If we analyse the entire situation from the children's perspective, they wanted to draw upon the materials for developing their imaginary situation through their imaginative question and action. In this case, Bree was successful in motivating the children to engage in the caterpillar activity, but her pedagogical practice could not bring together the children's interest with the teaching activity (Fleer, 2012).

In this example, the children's intentions were to bring to the new activity setting their own imaginary situation (through their action of pretending the caterpillar is eating a leaf and verbalization of 'How is the caterpillar going to eat the leaf?') and the teacher's intention was to set up a play-based activity (introducing a new technique for using the punching machine for counting numbers) that focused on learning. This meant the teacher and the children appeared to be in parallel worlds. This episode shows that the teacher changed the playful activity setting to be about learning academic concepts, while the children wanted to create an imaginary world. The data shows that the teacher did not capture the moment when children put demands on her (through their action and interaction) to go into the collective imaginary world together with them.

In episodes 1 and 2, we have found that the children's motive orientation to play and the teacher's pedagogical demands to set up learning conditions creates a transitional process between activity settings. In episode 3, children's motive orientation of engaging in imaginative play was disrupted by the teacher's pedagogical demand for learning. Her focus was to insist on the individual child's learning and development rather than connecting with the established collective imaginary situation or the emerging imaginary play situation that could have developed. She was more concerned about meeting the pedagogical demands for learning, influenced by parental demands for a more educational programme, and as reflected through her interview comments 'We will display these crafts on the wall to show parents'.

Bree's interview comment shows that parents are more interested in their children being involved in academic learning than being involved in child-initiated play (as she mentioned 'Parents always think children should learn academic concepts through the direct way of teaching'). The parents are putting demands on teachers to set up an educational agenda. On the other hand, early childhood pedagogical practice in Australia puts demands on teachers to set up play-based learning opportunities for children, which is reflected in Bree's comment 'We always try to let parents know children are learning through play and we are trying to establish this approach in our care'. We have found in the data set that the institutional and societal demands for educational programmes, mostly motivated the teacher to plan goal-oriented play-based teaching practice, but did so without considering the children's perspectives.

Discussion

Children's transition between child-initiated play and teacher-initiated activity

In preschools in Australia, the dominant practice tradition is play-based learning where the play is the leading activity for children. The teachers are responsible for creating learning activities that support the children's play motive (Fleer, 2014). The teacher from Leafy preschool was aware of implementing a play-based learning approach, therefore she created a separate caterpillar activity to teach writing and counting to children. As the first finding shows, the children's motive orientation to play and the teacher's pedagogical demand of teaching subject-based knowledge creates a transitional process between the child-initiated play to the teacher-initiated activity. Apa's personal motivation for joining in the special game and the teacher's pedagogical demand requiring Apa to sit down at the activity table motivated Apa and her friends to make a transition from their self-initiated imaginative play to the teacher-initiated activity. As a result, their transition was not internally driven; rather, it was promoted by their play motive and the teacher's demands for learning, which is promoted by the external situation. However, we suggest that the children put new demands upon the teacher to create a learning activity that was more playful for children.

It appears from the data that the children's motive for engaging in play makes the transition from play setting into a play-based learning activity setting possible. The new demands of literacy and numeracy in the preschool setting create new conditions for children's development. Bree was successful in establishing a teaching-learning nexus through introducing the caterpillar activity. She tried to create an imaginary situation though without involving herself in the children's imaginary play. She put the demands on the children to engage in a learning activity, but could not follow the children's perspectives in their approach to create an imaginary world inside the instructional activity setting (see episode 3). We have found that the children were engaged in the imaginary world during their transition (they brought their soft toys with them) but the teacher did not take the initiative to get involved in the children's imaginative play and to use their play narrative to create a collective learning environment through play (see Fleer, 2010). For instance, she could have drawn upon the mummy-baby narrative by positioning the caterpillar as a mummy caterpillar wanting to feed her babies, thus allowing the soft toys to join the imaginary play and to extend the play by suggesting they were visitors joining the caterpillar for dinner. The punching and counting of holes could have been used to support this expanded play narrative. However, Bree created a learning activity setting where the imaginary play was not related to the children's play narrative, even though she drew upon their play motive to make the learning more motivating.

The teacher's demands, through teaching academic content, holds back children's play motives

The case demonstrated that Bree was successful in motivating children to meet her pedagogical demands, but was unsuccessful in noticing the children's demands of creating a collective imaginary situation. The teacher focuses more on achieving the academic learning goal rather than developing the child-motivated play-based learning. Bree's pedagogical demand was giving instructions to the children in a playful manner, therefore she introduced a caterpillar storyline in her self-initiated activity. Bree was successful in implementing an educational agenda to teach subject-based knowledge; for example, evaluating children's writing and counting skills. However, the teacher did not consider how to fit the educational agenda into the children's existing imaginary play. In episode 3 it appears that Bree was busy implementing her programme, by noticing children's writing and counting skills through her instructional approaches (how to use a punching machine to make a hole or write numbers of the holes beside each of the leaves) and motivated children to engage in her instructions. Therefore, she could not tune into the children's imaginative thinking and missed the moment when Apa and Pippa showed their intentions to create an imaginary condition through their imaginative action and interaction. Instead, the teacher should have followed up on the child's question: 'How is the caterpillar going eat the leaf?' It does not mean that what the teacher did is wrong. Teachers need to teach something in order that children can learn the content of the curriculum. However, the teachers need to consider the child's perspective. The example shows that she lost the opportunity to build her understanding of that critical moment when children were in the imaginary situation. Rather, the teacher's pedagogical demands move the children from their imaginative thinking to the teacher's instructional approach, which actually did not help to develop children's learning motive. Her pedagogical demands of giving instructions to achieve her learning goal kept her away from the children's collective imaginary play.

The teacher's pedagogical demand was to establish an academic agenda for individual children, which was in turn framed by the parents' demands for academic learning. What the case demonstrated was that the demands from parents motivated the teacher to set up separate teacher-initiated learning activities for children, which sometimes put demands on children to be involved in the learning activity, and which ignores children's motive orientation to engage in play. Bree's interview comments show how parents evaluate teaching practice in a preschool setting, which actually frames a teacher's pedagogical demands in implementing their own separate learning activity. In adhering to the national curriculum, the teacher implements a play-based curriculum without considering children's play motives.

According to Hedegaard (2012a), society creates the conditions for the institution and this is evident in the activity settings that children enter into when in preschool. The data show that the teacher's pedagogical demands were motivated by societal demands, and that she was busy focusing on preparing children to be competent in subject-based knowledge (demand from parents) and at the same time was trying to develop a play-based learning activity in preschool (demand from the national curriculum). These demands actually motivated the teacher to create activity settings in such a way that it holds back children's play.

Conclusion

There are a number of scholarly articles showing how a person's motive orientation impels different types of transition in children's everyday life (Fleer, 2014; Hedegaard, 2014; Winther-Lindqvist, 2012; Zittoun, 2006). However, they are mostly focused on a broader view where the transition takes place from one institution to other institutions. This study gives new insight into transition, children's motive orientation to play and teacher's pedagogical demands on children to learn mathematical concepts, from one activity setting to another activity setting in a preschool. We have found in our data set that teachers created activities to fulfil the institutional and the pedagogical demands that appeared to hold back the children's play in a number of cases. Furthermore, the teacher could not follow the children's perspective, therefore the teacher missed opportunities to develop a learning motive. Additionally, the study shows how the teacher's pedagogical demands motivate her to set up a learning activity separately, which moved children from their imaginative play to the teacher's instructional activity setting.

A teacher tries to set up a balance between child-initiated play and teacher-initiated activity in their pedagogical practice, while at the same time trying to respect parental demands to teach literacy and numeracy in preparation for entrance into school (Crozier & Davies, 2007). Similar to Crozier and Davies's (2007) findings, our data demonstrated that the teacher created a separate learning activity, motivated by parental demands and tried to bring an imaginary situation into her activity. Furthermore, the teacher's intention to set up a teacher-directed activity did not allow her to notice children's motive orientation and motivational relationship with their environment is evident in our dataset. There were a number of ongoing learning possibilities that emerged in the children's imaginative play but the teacher could not follow up or perhaps did not try to understand the complexity of play involved in the children's play. Fleer's (2010) model of 'conceptual play' indicates that a teacher could implement a learning environment by considering children's perspectives if they take an active position in a playful manner. Our study shows that instead of creating a collective learning environment together with children, as proposed by Fleer (2010), teachers engage children in their own directed activities as part of evaluating children's literacy and numeracy competency, which dismisses the development of children's learning motives through play.

Hedegaard (2012b) argues that a teacher needs to be aware of the child's motive orientation while introducing activities that support a new motive. In line with Hedegaard's argument, this study is also arguing for thinking about how teachers could consider children's motive orientation to play when planning to teach academic learning in teacher-initiated activities. We also argue that a close look at the transitional process of moving between two activity settings is needed to understand how a teacher can become attuned to children's play motives, where academic demands are increasingly made on children by a teacher for teaching concepts. This chapter suggests that researchers need to consider studying transitional processes not only in institutional settings but also across activity settings (for example child-initiated play to teacher-initiated activity or vice versa).

References

Adams, M. & M. Fleer (2014), 'Moving countries: Belongings as central for realizing the affective relation between international shifts and localized micro movements', *Learning, Culture and Social Interaction*, 3, 56–66.

Bøttcher, L. (2014), 'Transition between home and school in children with severe disabilities: Parents' possibilities for influencing their children's learning environment', *Learning, Culture, and Social Interaction*, 3, 195–201.

Chaiklin, S. (2012), 'A conceptual perspective for investigating motive in cultural-historical theory' in M. Hedegaard, A. Edwards & M. Fleer (eds), *Motives in children's development: Cultural-historical approaches* (pp. 209–224). New York: Cambridge University Press.

Corsaro, W. A. & L. Molinari (2000), 'Priming events and Italian children's transition from preschool to elementary school: Representations and action', *Social Psychology Quarterly*, 63(1), 16–33.

Crozier, G. & J. Davies (2007), 'Hard to reach parents or hard to reach schools? A discussion of home-school relations, with particular reference to Bangladesh and Pakistani parents', *British Educational Research Journal*, 33, 295–313.

Department of Education, Employment and Workplace Relations (DEEWR) (2009), *Belonging, being and becoming: The early years learning framework for Australia*. ACT: Council of Australian Governments: Commonwealth of Australia. Retrieved from http://www.education.nt.gov.au/__data/assets/pdf_file/0018/20538/BelongingBeing-Becoming.pdf

Department of Education (2014), *The statutory framework for the early years foundation stage: Setting the standards for learning, development, and care for children from birth to five.* Department of Education, UK. Retrieved from http://www.foundationyears. org.uk/files/2014/07/EYFS_framework_from_1_September_2014__with_ clarification_note.pdf

Ebbeck, M. & V. Reus (2005), 'Transitions: Third culture children', *Australian Journal of Early Childhood Education,* 10(16), 10–16.

Elkonin, D. B. (1999), 'Toward the problem of stages in the mental development of children', *Journal of Russian and East European Psychology,* 37(6), 11–30.

Fleer, M. (2010), *Early learning and development: Cultural-historical concepts in play.* New York: Cambridge University Press.

Fleer, M. (2011), 'Conceptual play': Foregrounding imagination and cognition during concept formation in early years education', *Contemporary Issues in Early Childhood,* 12(3), 224–240.

Fleer, M. (2012), 'The development of motives in children's play', in M. Hedegaard, A. Edwards & M. Fleer (eds), *Motives in children's development: Cultural-historical approaches* (pp. 79–96). New York: Cambridge University Press.

Fleer, M. (2014), 'The demands and motives afforded through digital play in early childhood activity settings', *Learning, Culture, and Social Interaction,* 3, 202–209.

Fleer, M. & A. Ridgway (2014), *Methodologies for researching with young children: The place of digital visual tools.* Amsterdam: Springer.

Hakkaraninen, P., M. Bredikyte, K. Jakkula & H. Munter (2014), 'Adult play guidance and children's play development in a narrative play-world', *European Early Childhood Education Research Journal,* 21(2), 213–225.

Hedegaard, M. (2008a), 'Developing a dialectical approach to researching children's development', in M. Hedegaard & M. Fleer (eds), *Studying children: A cultural-historical approach* (pp. 30–45). New York: McGraw-Hill Open University Press.

Hedegaard, M. (2008b), 'Principles for interpreting research protocols', in M. Hedegaard & M. Fleer (eds), *Studying children: A cultural-historical approach* (pp. 46–64). New York: McGraw-Hill Open University Press.

Hedegaard, M. (2012a), 'The dynamic aspects of children's learning and development', in M. Hedegaard, A. Edwards & M. Fleer (eds), *Motives in children's development: Cultural-historical approaches* (pp. 9–27). New York: Cambridge University Press.

Hedegaard, M. (2012b), 'Analyzing children's learning and development in everyday settings from a cultural-historical wholeness approach', *Mind, Culture and Activity,* 19(2), 127–138.

Hedegaard, M. & M. Fleer (2013), *Play, learning and children's development: Everyday life in families and transition to school.* New York: Cambridge University Press.

Hedegaard, M. (2014), 'The significance of demands and motives across practices in children's learning and development: An analysis of learning in home and school', *Learning, Culture, and Social Interaction,* 3, 188–194.

Hedegaard, M. & A. Edwards (2014), 'Transitions and children's learning' (editorial paper), *Learning, Culture, and Social Interaction*, 3, 185–187.

Hviid, P. (2008), '"Next year we are small right?" Different times in children's development', *European Journal of Psychology of Education*, 23(2), 183–198.

Märtisin, M. (2010), 'Rupturing otherness: Becoming Estonian in the context of contemporary Britain'. *Integrative Psychological and Behavioural Science*, 44, 65–81.

Moore, A. M., & G. G. Barker (2012), 'Confused or multicultural: Third culture individuals' cultural identity', *International Journal of Intercultural Relations*, 36(4), 553–562.

Nicolopoulou, A. (1993), 'Play, cognitive development, and the social world: Piaget, Vygotsky, and beyond', *Human Development*, 36(1), 1–23.

Sánchez-Medina, J. A., B. Macías-Gómez-Stern & V. Martínez-Lozano (2014), 'The value positions of school staff and parents in immigrant families and their implications for children's transitions between home and school in multicultural schools in Andalusia', *Learning, Culture, and Social Interaction*, 3, 217–223.

Saracho, O. (2012), *An integrated play based curriculum for young children.* New York: Routledge.

Vygotsky, L. S. (1966), 'Play and its role in the mental development of the child', *Voprosy Psikhologii (Psychology Issues)*, 12(6), 62–76.

Vygotsky, L. S. (1998), 'Child psychology' (trans. M. J. Hall), in R. W. Rieber (ed), *The collected works of L.S. Vygotsky*, Vol 5. New York: Kluwer Academic and Plenum Publisher.

Vygotsky, L. S. (2004), 'Imagination and creativity in childhood', *Journal of Russian and East European Psychology*, 42(1), 7–97.

Winther-Lindqvist, D. (2012), 'Developing social identities and motives in school transition', in M. Hedegaard, A. Edwards & M. Fleer (eds), *Motives in children's development: Cultural-historical approaches* (pp. 115–132). New York: Cambridge University Press.

Wood, E. (2014), 'The play-pedagogy interface in contemporary debates', in L. Brooker, M. Blaise & S. Edwards (eds), *The Sage handbook of play and learning in early childhood* (pp. 145–156). Los Angeles, CA: Sage Publication.

Zittoun, T. (2006), *Transitions: Development through symbolic resources.* Greenwich, CT: Information Age Publishing.

Moral Imagining Through Transitions Within, Between and From Imaginative Play: Changing Demands as Developmental Opportunities

Jennifer A. Vadeboncoeur

Introduction

For the observer, imaginative play makes visible various learning and developing opportunities for participants who share, through continual negotiation, an imaginary situation with roles and rules for action (Vygotsky, 1933/1967). These opportunities for learning and developing include the dynamic relational sense of *moral imagining*, including how individuals see themselves in relationships, how relationships and relatedness are valued, and how meanings are created for the roles played in relation (Vadeboncoeur & Vellos, 2016). Moral imagining forms a compass for self-direction and context-based principles for acting in, on and with the world and, ultimately, for the physical and psychological actions that contribute to creating and transforming culture (Vadeboncoeur, 2017). It supports individuals to 'look at things as if they could be otherwise' (Greene, 1995, p. 76), and in seeing beyond the concrete context, becoming free from how things are to inquire into how things could be and, further, how they ought to be.

In this chapter, I theorize and describe moral imagining in relation to transitions within, between and from imaginative play. My interest is in how these transitions provide opportunities for moral imagining, as a relational sensibility of imagining, creating and acting together that is oriented towards a shared future. I draw on Hedegaard's (2012, 2014) framework for transitions, to bring these interests together with recent calls to examine how children initiate, maintain and terminate imaginative play (see Göncü & Vadeboncoeur, 2017). Of particular relevance are the concepts of motives and demands that emerge and change over time as activities shift and participants in activities orient in similar and different ways to changing requirements. Motives and demands are further shaped by each participant's social situation of development (Vygotsky, 1935/1994a), or their relation with their social environment. Central factors in social environments are participants' social relations as members of particular groups, such as children or parents, students or teachers. In turn, social relations are framed by social institutions, such as families or schools.

The chapter is organized into five sections. The first section defines moral imagining and central concepts that provide a useful foundation for examining features of imaginative play and, more specifically, the relational work of imagining social futures. The second section examines how twin sisters, Alex and Vivi, initiate imaginative play, including the motives and demands that form in the relation between children in play. Opportunities in their social situations of development change and, therefore, in the third section I describe transitions between enactments of imaginative play necessitated by a change in motives and demands and a desire to participate in a new activity. The fourth section highlights transitions as imaginative play shifts to dinnertime, from the perspective of the parents, as well as the continued negotiation and potential termination of play. The fifth section provides a discussion. Throughout each section, I locate moral imagining in the process of negotiating imaginative play in response to new motives and demands. The transcripts of videos used as the basis of this chapter were made in our home when Vivi and Alex were between 6.5 and about 7 years old; videotaping occurred several days a week for at least an hour a day. The chapter ends with a brief conclusion.

Moral imagining: Relational histories of shared experiences for possible social futures

A future, or proleptic, orientation is common to the work of parents and teachers, who draw from their own experiences and expectations to craft learning opportunities in the present with the intention that these opportunities will shape particular social futures for their children and/or their students (Cole, 1996; Panofsky & Vadeboncoeur, 2012; Vadeboncoeur & Murray, 2014). Playing and imagining are also future oriented activities that build upon prolepsis: they recombine participants' previous experiences and are enacted and performed in the present, thus creating a range of possible social futures (Vygotsky, 1933/1967, 1930/2004). The social futures made available in particular social environments, those that children readily have access to, are evident in the present environment (Vygotsky, 1935/1994a).

Defining imaginative play, Vygotsky (1933/1967) noted that participants are enabled to separate meaning from objects and actions given the flexible narrative of the imaginary situation and the accompanying roles and rules for action. Acting 'as if' a stuffed teddy is a baby, a child separates meaning from object and creates her own meaning for the teddy. The teddy becomes 'a baby' through the child's actions in this imaginary situation while she, simultaneously, becomes 'a mummy' or another adult figure. As participants create meanings for objects and actions to perform their roles, the imaginary situation may change from one moment to the next with the addition of various repurposed objects and symbolic actions.

Even if the narrative or content of play is an event that occurred in the past, playing and imagining are future oriented. For example, young children may move between playing parent to their stuffies and dolls, to playing parent and baby with each other. In the latter, and even for the child who plays the role of the baby, the physical and psychological action of playing the role creates developmental opportunities. By playing 'the baby' one way instead of another, the child remembers and enacts experiences in the present moment, through the creation of a 'fictitious "I"' (Vygotsky, 1933/1967). This enables a growing awareness of the difference between self and other – the child playing 'as if' a baby to the other child's 'as if' a mummy – and supports perspective taking. Performing as re-experiencing and/or remembering the past in the present carries forward significant and potentially new meanings into the future.

The imaginary situation holds promise not simply for the participant in the present moment of imaginative play, as a zone of proximal development (Vygotsky, 1933/1967), but also contributes to the creation of a world where what is played and imagined may become possible, or real (Lindqvist, 2001, 2003; Vygotsky, 1930/2004). Imaginative playing, imagining and creating provide enabling conditions for thinking, feeling and acting beyond the immediate, concrete context, in a sense untethering the participants from the weight of the concrete to play 'as if', imagine 'other than' and create a world, and objects and actions in the world, different from the one that currently exists. Playing, imagining and creating take on a moral valence when we inquire into the kinds of worlds imagined and what these worlds enable, as well as when participants' actions and the implications of actions are assessed in terms of relational qualities, for example, access, inclusion and equality.

Imaginative playing becomes an activity that links moral imagining to the creation of culture given considerations of the worlds created both in the present and, proleptically, as visions for particular social futures that may come into being (Vadeboncoeur, Perone & Panina-Beard, 2016). In general, inquiring into moral imagining in imaginative play acknowledges that some worlds created – again, both in play, in the present and the possible, or anticipated, worlds where future contributions may be realized – are more equitable than others. Yet, in a more immediate, experienced and present sense, moral imagining is an aspect of the lived experiences of participants-in-relation. Imaginative play includes creating roles for self and other, whether explicitly stated or merely oriented to, and thinking, feeling and acting through the imagined relations between roles (see discussion of sisters playing 'sisters', Vygotsky, 1933/1967). By empathetically entering into a role, participants enact an imagined relation and enable the contributions of other participants. Interpreting the role of baby or mummy, they work to create, negotiate and acknowledge their own identities in relation to the identities of others; identification and confirmation of others' interpretations of roles occurs as players both participate in and become an audience for each other's performance as a shared performance.

Moral imagining, as a psychological function, develops in relation, is grounded in and through the context of a relationship, and is made visible in a relational history of shared experiences that creates the possibility for a range of potential social futures. Relationships, and the relational histories that emerge from them over time, create a stage for future relationships not necessarily through abstract principles for relating, but as relationally grounded experiences that travel with participants on to other contexts in the future. In the context of imaginative play, moral imagining includes consideration of how an individual becomes a participant, how a participant interprets a role, and how the role is recognized by others. Moral imagining makes visible questions including, from a participant's perspective: how do I play this particular role when I am with you in your role? How do you and I grow into and become our roles in relation in this imaginary situation? This has implications for the particular relationships of participants outside of imaginative play as well: how am I 'me' when I am with 'you'? How do the two of us become 'we' in different activities in and, potentially, across contexts (Vadeboncoeur, 2011)?

The process of playing and imagining builds from lived experiences, expands through the experiences of others, is deeply felt and, therefore, grounded in emotion and memory, and becomes materialized or crystallized in the creation of a new practice, product, or something else (Vygotsky, 1930/2004). While a moral valence exists in considerations of how we are together, in imaginative play and otherwise, it also exists in and of itself in the theories that have contributed to this theorization. There is an explicit valuing of difference in Vygotsky's (1933/1967,

1930/2004) scholarship, and in the scholarship of Maxine Greene (1988, 1995) and Mary Warnock (1976, 1994), whose ideas are also foundational: it is the difference between what is and is not – or, in imaginative play, the real and the imaginary object, action, or situation – that provokes a growing awareness that actions can be 'as if' and objects can be 'other than' and, ultimately, enables participants to transform what exists into something new. Differences create a potential, an opening, for a new response or a new idea. While a new response or idea shared may be enacted in a variety of ways, in this particular moment and relation, the ways that support access, inclusion and/or equality, for example, ought to be preferred. Through empathy with the other (Greene, 2008) and/ or the sympathy for the other that moves us to act (Warnock, 1976, 1994), we imagine, create and act in ways guided by a dynamic sense of moral direction.

From imaginative play, to social relationships and relations in other contexts, how we are together in the present builds a range of potential social futures, as a family, as a school, as a community. Unique and collective contributions develop over time as thinking and imagining changes, yet the emerging unity of thinking and imagining remains (Vygotsky, 1932/1987). The recognition and valuing of difference provides an enabling condition, creating the potential and provoking a consideration, of a new response informed by the kinds of worlds we desire to contribute to and/or create. Imagining in play is central for participants to begin to recognize their own actions in the world as potentially agentic, as well as to recognize that particular social futures are shaped in the present. An assessment of the present, in a general sense, makes visible possible social futures, some more and others less desirable; yet more specifically, the imaginary situation created by children in play makes visible particular relational futures, some more and others less desirable from the perspectives of the participants.

Beginning with 'And … '

About halfway into their sixth year, Alex and Vivi began initiating imaginative play using the word, 'And … '. They had used 'tend … ', short for pretend, for several years and so the shift, captured on videos that have become a part of our household routine, was noticeable. They approached each other, sometimes with a stuffie in hand, and began creating an imaginary situation using what Göncü (1993) described as 'metacommunication': the sort of directorial speech that explicitly advances an imaginary situation and, with it, a potential invitation to play. They did this the majority of the time.

These interactions can be examined using Hedegaard's (2014) framework for the motives and demands that emerge in individuals' social situations of development and, more specifically, through participation in imaginative play as a particular kind of activity. While an individual's motive orientation may underlie the initiation of play, for play to continue it is likely that participants must come to share a goal, or at least be willing to assume that they share a common goal. Transitions within imaginative play occur as participants co-create new motives and demands, thereby changing the imaginary situation with and for the play partner. In the following, three excerpts of video transcripts illustrate both the initiation with 'And … ', and the movement of motives and demands in the beginning of the creation of an imaginary situation.

To provide some much needed context, in our household, stuffies are a part of our family. When the children receive them as gifts or they are purchased by us, we say, 'Welcome to the family!' Alex and Vivi routinely offer stuffies to comfort members of the family when they are hurt or sad. A favourite teddy may come on a trip with us to the grocery store in a bag with a water bottle, or be tucked away in a backpack to 'visit' school (although they are not allowed out of the backpack at school). The stuffies, favourite ones in particular, travel around the house, like nomads, from bed, to couch, to hallway floor, and sometimes even to the dining room table or a dining room chair. When a particular stuffie cannot be found, we build a narrative about how they wanted to go on holiday, where they might be, and when they are expected to return. This helps as they sometimes take a day or two to locate; once or twice, it was several months.

Over time, the twins' relations with their stuffies have changed. They favour different stuffies and narratives at times. Further, as other activities are learned, they are added to their repertoire, and enacted here and there, taking time away from the stuffies. From the monkey bars to learning how to ride a bike to writing lists of favourite books to badminton, new activities expand their landscapes of participation. Even so, Alex still asks me once in a while, at 9 years old, to leave her bedroom door closed while she goes to school 'so Old Teddy can nap'. If we are out the door before Vivi realizes that she's forgotten a stuffie who she planned to bring along, she quips, 'I think I can leave Teddy home, he's growing up'. Over time, although the stuffies do not grow, the children do, and they both get visibly older.

In each of the following three excerpts, 'And … ' is used to initiate imaginative play, to begin to create an imaginary situation, and it can also be seen as an initial demand, motivated by a player's interests.

Excerpt 1, from November 2014

Vivi meets Alex, who is returning from the kitchen after putting away her backpack, at their bedroom door with Poppin, a small stuffed penguin in her hand. She makes Poppin jump on Alex's shoulder, saying:

> Vivi: And she's sad today …
> Alex: [crying, as if she is Poppin] [then, in her own voice] Does … does she need … a friend?
> Vivi: Yes [in high-pitched voice for Poppin], where's Cutie? [a small stuffed cat]
> Alex: On my bed … [Alex collects Cutie and shows Cutie to Poppin] [in a high-pitched voice] Okay, now you're fine [to Poppin].

Excerpt 2, from January 2015

Alex's Black and Brown Puppy wants to play and Alex and puppy find Vivi and Billy Goat on the floor of the hallway:

> Vivi: And … you know why you can't act funny or silly around him? [Vivi is talking about Billy Goat who is resting]
> Alex: Why?
> Vivi: He might get up and chase you. Why don't you call him? [on the phone]
> Alex: Okay, what's his number?
> Vivi: 9–0–8–10-0-8-9-0-4–8
> Alex: [Alex dials the toy phone] Hello?

Excerpt 3, from March 2015

Alex and Viv are sitting at the dining table working in activity books. After a discussion about the maze they are working on, Alex lifts Old Teddy and says:

> Alex: And … his leg is broken …
> Vivi: Oh no! [coming around the table to Alex] We better get him to the … the blood sample hospital!
> Alex: Quick … his leg … wrap it … [Alex hands Viv a tissue] get the Band-Aid from the kit! [they run to their bedroom]

In the first and second excerpt, from November 2014 and January 2015, imaginative plays begins with 'And … ' offered by Vivi; Alex orients to and takes up what Viv offers to begin imaginative play and, without hesitation, shifts into her role. The offer presented is a new demand that reflects Vivi's interests and motive initially, but it is a motive that Alex is willing to share and this leads them into the co-creation of an imaginary situation. Each turn in the excerpts can be seen as an offer, or one form of demand in imaginative play, which creates the potential for a response, an elaboration, and/or a new direction. In the third excerpt, from March 2015, Alex makes the offer, a form of demand, and this initiates imaginative play and the opening for the transition from working together on activity books to playing. If Alex and Vivi orient to a new demand, offers and responses become a chain, also described as 'accept/build' (Holzman, 2009) or 'yes/and' (Perone, 2011). This pattern contributes to the ongoing narration of the imaginary situation (see Vygotsky, 1960/1997).

Examining the links in the chain of offers and responses highlights the ongoing relational work of initiating and maintaining imaginative play, alongside the potential dissolution of play. In a discussion of the development of ethical and moral behaviour in play, Vygotsky (1926/1997) emphasized the power of play to shape behaviour. Here, he noted that a child follows the rules in play not out of fear of punishment, failure in something, or loss of something, as might be utilized to teach students school rules, 'but only because observing the rules – which is a promise that he renews from one minute to the next – vouchsafes him the inner satisfaction that comes from playing a game, because here he *acts as part of the general enterprise that is formed out of a group at play*' (emphasis added, p. 233). Further, he argued '[n]owhere is the child's behavior so regulated by rules as in play, and nowhere does it assume such a free and morally instructive form as in play' (p. 233). This is so, Vygotsky (1926/1997) noted, because there are relational consequences to stepping away from or being excluded from the 'general enterprise'.

Becoming 'part of the general enterprise formed out of a group at play', for many children, may mean access to membership, inclusion, and, potentially, equality. The general enterprise may be seen as having created a vision for the future and enabled it to become real in the present. Thus, when 'we don't or can't' seem to play well together in general – or we don't or can't seem to play well with specific play partners – children may come to feel that they have failed at more than playing; they have failed at creating or contributing to the 'we', the general enterprise that builds a collective, a shared project, together. The dissolution of play may happen for a host of reasons, from waning interest or a new interest, to an offer that is not met, to a disagreement, to frustration, or exhaustion. Attending only to the apparent ease of imaginative play, without recognizing relational webs as foundational to it, may mean taking the accomplishment of this activity and the potential relational consequences of its termination for granted.

Negotiating in imaginative play

While the previous section examined the issue of transitions within imaginative play provoked by one kind of demand, an offer in play, this section describes changes in the children's social situations of development that give rise to new motives and demands, ultimately changing the character of play. As noted, Viv and Alex had been developing their relational history through imaginative play and, more often than not, they were able to successfully transition to other activities without abruptly terminating play through disagreement. During this time, I assumed that their shared motive was to remain in play, for as long as mutually desired, and that their offers and/or demands were made with a growing awareness of what would most likely be seen as meaningful and valued, and taken up within the narrative of the imaginary situation through a developing relational awareness.

The situation changed when Alex's and Vivi's grandparents came for a four-month visit in November 2014, a visit that occurs almost every year and is highly anticipated by everyone. The visit provided both children with the opportunity to colour with Nagymama, their grandmother, for extended periods of time, but this activity was of more interest to Alex than to Viv. Alex often appeared to prefer spending time sitting on the ottoman, comfortably nestled between Nagymama's outstretched feet. They both leaned in, from opposite directions, to colour either separate areas of the colouring sheets they had chosen or parts of the images on the pages of Nagymama's colouring book. They discussed colours, orchestrated their movements, and waited as one another completed an area as needed. This process was engrossing and yet it potentially excluded Viv who was happy to colour sometimes, but was not quite as taken with it as Alex.

Nagymama's arrival changed our routine activities, enriching our home in a number of significant ways. This change was experienced differently by the children. Although Vivi's offers to initiate play were the same, there were times when they were met with a different response from Alex. For Vivi, Nagymama's arrival created a new demand: she needed to allow Alex her time to colour with Nagymama. For Alex, the same change was a new opportunity, an opportunity for this special interaction, while Viv's continued interest in playing was a separate and competing demand, or an opportunity that was preferred less than usual. In this situation, Alex took up the opportunity to colour with Nagymama, when she was available, more often than not. At the beginning, Vivi maintained her motive – to play with Alex – yet their shared form of initiation, 'And … ' was not always successful. At times, I intervened and asked Vivi to read or play with me. Early on, I was not sure if and how Viv and Alex would negotiate their way through this change, and wanted to avoid what I thought might become either a conflict between them or feelings of exclusion for Viv.

These changes and, in particular, the opportunity for Alex, created new demands for both children and eventually resulted in a shift in motive for Viv: from playing with Alex, in general, to playing with Alex in a manner that enabled Alex and Nagymama to simultaneously colour together. Vivi enabled this situation by bringing stuffies over to Alex, laying them on the ottoman for her to use as needed, and moving like a satellite around Alex and Nagymama while they coloured. Sometimes Viv played on the floor next to the chair and ottoman, and other times she ran back and forth to the bedroom she shared with Alex to collect more or different stuffies to use. Alex responded by deftly balancing her colouring interactions with Nagymama while contributing the voice of her stuffie to Vivi's performance and, when a colouring break was needed to allow Nagymama to finish an area, Alex picked up and engaged with the appropriate stuffie to combine voice with embodiment. Both children appeared to balance their new demands and competing motives.

Excerpt 4, from January 2015

Nagymama is sitting in the big chair colouring. When the children enter the room and see her, Alex wants to colour, and Viv tries to maintain play with Alex. Alex invites Vivi to join her in colouring with Nagymama.

> Alex: [to Nagymama] Színezzünk! [Let's colour!]
> Vivi: [as Alex moves to Nagymama] Here's Old Teddy … [handing to Alex]
> Alex: [sits on ottoman, placing Old Teddy beside her] Mit színezel? [What are you colouring?]
> Vivi: Alex, … [looking at the seating arrangement, Alex is already settling in, looking through coloured pencils] we can do Elmo and Glover … hockey … I'll get a book … [she runs to their room and gets the large book they use as the hockey rink, as well as small stuffies Elmo and Glover who wear homemade equipment made from cut ping pong balls and fridge magnets (helmet, backpack and skates), she sets the book on the floor next to Alex and Nagymama, handing Elmo to Alex]
> Alex: [taking Elmo and placing him on the ottoman] [to Vivi] Nagymama is doing a mandala. Színezzünk!
> Vivi: And … look I can … [taking Elmo] here they go … [she moves both Elmo and Grover around on the surface of the book] … It's your turn! [in

high-pitched voice for Grover, she continues with both for about a minute
then says] Oh, a goal, you try now …

Alex: [not looking up from her colouring] Okay … it's my turn now [Vivi is
moving both Elmo and Grover] … I'll try for a goal … Goal! [Vivi makes
Elmo take the shot] … I've got a goal now!

Vivi: Good for you, Elmo, you have a goal now! [in high-pitched voice for
Grover]

Nagymama: [smiling] Ki az? [Who is that?]

Vivi: Grover és Elmo.

Alex: Do another, Vivi!

[about a minute passes while Vivi moves the stuffies around and adjusts their gear]

Nagymama: [to Vivi] Mit gondolsz a narancssárgáról? [What do you think
about the orange?]

In this excerpt, Vivi creates the possibility for play to continue by offering a
new imaginary situation and willingly allowing play to revolve around Alex.
She physically brings the offer to where Alex is sitting with her grandmother
colouring and plays the roles of both Elmo and Grover, as well as the set director
and props manager. For her part, Alex invites Viv to colour and when this
is not taken up, she contributes the voice of her stuffie while colouring with
Nagymama. Later, when the demands of colouring allow it, she picks up Elmo
and helps him move around the rink a few times before returning to colouring. In
this instance, imaginative play is maintained by expanding it to include another
activity – colouring with Nagymama – and being responsive to the motives and
demands that emerge from the activity of colouring.

Excerpt 5, from July 2015

Alex, with her activity book, pencil and eraser in hand, sits down on the floor
where she and Viv have just been playing with their New Teddies. Alex begins to
work in the activity book.

Viv: Pretend you are New Teddy.

Alex: [eyes still on the activity book, slips into New Teddy's voice] So … how
was your day?

Vivi: [takes on responsibility for moving both of the teddies] [in a high voice]
Okay. Where's your baby?

Alex: [in her own voice] Who's the baby, Vivi?

Vivi: I'll get … [running to bedroom] … look the baby is Poppin … [returning
from the bedroom]

Alex: Okay, but …

Vivi: I'll get Cutie [running to the bedroom] you … here's yours [gently plopping Cutie next to Alex] …

Alex: [in a high voice] Thanks Viv [although this appears to have been from her own speaking position], [soft crying] Where's my Mummy? [continuing to focus on the activity book]

Vivi: [in her own voice speaking to Cutie] Here she is Cutie … [placing Cutie in New Teddy's arms up against her own knees so Alex can see them]

In Excerpt 4, from January 2015, when their social situations of development changed creating new opportunities and demands, both children collaborated to shift the character of imaginative play to allow Alex to participate while colouring with her grandmother. Alex offered her voice and played an embodied role when she could, while Viv provided Alex with options of stuffies to play with and maintained play within arm's reach. This practice continued well into the summer months even after their grandparents had left, as shown in Excerpt 5, from July 2015.

With new demands, the imaginative play in Excerpt 4 expands to bridge another activity and, at times, includes a third participant as when Nagymama asks about the stuffies or requests feedback about a colour. At different times, Nagymama includes both children, comfortably affirming what they are doing, making room for Viv, and supporting Alex in her dual role. This creates potential new demands and motives yet again. However, it also confirms the value of their new form of play, given the acknowledgement from Nagymama, and honours the complexity of the hybrid activity. Responding to changing motives and demands requires that Viv, Alex and Nagymama create and enact new roles in relation to each other; that they negotiate to maintain these relations, rather than allowing imaginative play to terminate, is embodied evidence of what they value in their relationships, as well as the activities through which they build their relational histories. The location of this activity, within a particular home and family, may have provided conditions consistent with the expansion of imaginative play, rather than its dissolution; play grows to include a grandmother and her grandchildren in two different, and potentially contradictory, activities.

Once imaginative play is initiated, the negotiations that occur in order to maintain play when new motives and demands emerge become a pathway of potential transitions and opportunities to maintain or terminate play. Rather than a clean line demarcating one activity from the next, which may, at times, characterize some transitions between activities, particularly in contexts where the demands are numerous and the motives are competing, it is possible to observe imaginative play as a potentially expanding and hybrid activity. Indeed, for some participants, imaginative play itself may form a sort of adhesive, or relational bond, based on the shared purpose provided from the imaginary situation. Negotiating in play provides an experience of a shared commitment to both the activity and the relationship, contributing to the creation of relational histories. More specifically, imaginative play is what Vivi and Alex 'do together'; it forms the basis for their relationship with one another, including how, why, and when they join together in goal directed activities.

Transitions from imaginative play

Transitions may most obviously occur in the movement between distinct activities, such as between homework time and dinner time, and between social institutions, such as home and school (Hedegaard, 2014). In these examples, transitioning to a new activity may include several features. One feature may be the shared preparation of participants for new motives and demands, as when a participant announces she's almost done with homework or another announces that it is almost time to 'wash up'. Both announcements highlight that some form of completion is close at hand and, depending on the words chosen and the intonation, they can be experienced as more or less urgent demands. In some environments, one activity must be terminated for a new activity to begin. For example, in the transition from homework time to dinner time, if a family table is the setting for both, this might require quickly completing as much homework as possible, adding bookmarks and closing books, organizing papers, stacking both together with pencils and erasers, and carrying them to another area of the home. In this example, the transition is made visible in social speech, the actions of the participants, and the changes to the objects in the physical space.

Sometimes, for better or for worse, transitions between activities are not experienced with such distinct markers of change as when a change of activity is heralded by a visible change in space. For example, sometimes in our home, the character of imaginative play changes to 'fit' new demands in each child's social situation of development, rather than being terminated by these new demands. This leads to a less clearly delineated and, potentially, more confusing hybrid activity when imaginative play may include dinner time or the reverse. Typically stuffies do not come to the dinner table, we try to keep it clear, but I frequently have papers on the table at my place. Less frequently, small stuffies come to the table with the children and are not a distraction. The rule is that Alex and Vivi can engage in play as long as they eat and as long as their play is not a disruption. Occasionally, it is.

Excerpt 6, from April 2015

Viv and Alex have been playing and arrive at the dinner table with a small monster stuffie each. They begin eating and simultaneously continue to speak to each other as their stuffies, sometimes moving the stuffies, who are facing each other across the table, and sometimes just using their voices. About three minutes into 'dinner time', the following occurs:

> Alex: [giggling quietly] … he just looks so funny … see what happens when I squeeze his face … [squeezing the stuffie's face and giggling, then making the stuffie walk across the table]
> Vivi: [picks up her stuffie, she tries it] … wait, the skate came off [giggling, she pulls off the other skate, then tries again] … it's funny … [continuing to giggle]
> Mum: Okay, time to focus on your food … let's leave those on the table …
> [the children begin eating again, about two minutes later, as their parents are talking, Viv and Alex continue]
> Viv: Alex, … [pushing and pulling the face] can you see? It's so … wait … different … [looking at the stuffie and pulling it]
> Mum: If they [the stuffies] can't sit quietly on the table, then they will need to wait for you on the couch.
> [the children seem enthralled by the faces of their stuffies and don't seem to hear her]
> Mum: Do you want them to go to the couch?
> [the children begin eating again, about four minutes later, and after some shared dialogue, as their parents are talking, Viv and Alex begin whispering the voices of the stuffies]
> Alex: Vivi, my face hurts [high voice].
> Viv: Mine too [high voice], what's hap … [happened?] … did someone pull your face?
> Alex: No [high voice], … this is a mask … a Halloween mask … [she reaches for her stuffie] …
> Dad: [in a quiet, but serious tone] It's time to eat, you need to focus on your food … so we're not here all night, don't pick it up again, Alex … Vivi …

In Excerpt 6, from April 2015, the motive of the children, which appears to be to play and to eat, seems to work intermittently, at least initially. The stuffies are not always a distraction and the parents are willing to let them stay as long as the children are focused on eating. Yet, when play involves handling the stuffies and appears to take precedence, the parents begin to articulate their demands more explicitly. The children are told that the stuffies will need to wait for them on the couch if, it is implied, they cannot eat their dinner. Later, after eating, shared dialogue, and when the parents are engaged in several exchanges, the children whisper the voices of their stuffies, leaving them on the table. The father intervenes when Alex reaches to pick up her stuffie. Play continues to be interwoven at the dinner table, reemerging periodically, until the final demands are clarified: 'It's time to eat, you need to focus on your food ... don't pick it up again'. After this, they focus on their dinner, share stories about their day, sometimes inquiring and other times giggling, as they eat.

In this excerpt, imaginative play emerges periodically over the course of dinner then becomes deemphasized. It is terminated with their father's demand when the pace of eating becomes too slow, and/or progress through dinner appears to be hindered. Imaginative play changes in relation to new demands and motives; however, this change may not be automatic when a new activity, such as dinner time begins, but may be required only when the children cannot attend to the central demand or demand(s) of the new activity – in this case, eating dinner in a timely fashion. How this transition – moving from play to dinner – occurs both reflects and develops how we relate to each other, the extent to which we prioritize each other's interests, motives and demands, and balances these (sometimes well, sometimes less well).

It is interesting to note that when the children are offered a demand that competes with play, but appears no less interesting in its own right – such as to engage in dialogue with their parents directly – the children willingly leave their imaginary situation and join their parents. Offering a competing demand and potentially shifting their motive from participating in play to participating in a dialogue, may have been an alternative and additive strategy to end the play at the dining room table that evening. Rather than telling the children to stop playing, engaging them in an alternative option or offering an alternative motive may have had a similar outcome to the direct demand (but it may have required that the parent's motive to engage in dialogue be an inclusive one).

Given the children's participation in play at the table, to the point of distraction, it is possible that, for them, playing becomes a form of relating to each other that is especially useful when they are not included in their parents' conversation. Without shared topics of concern that are recognizable to their parents, they relate, share and converse through an imaginary situation and through stuffies that have a particular role to play in the imaginary situation (unlike, the children may feel, their own absent role in their parent's conversation).

Discussion

Across the six excerpts, whether the participants are siblings, as in Excerpts 1, 2, 3 and 5, or grandchildren and their Nagymama, as in Excerpt 4, or children and their parents, as in Except 6, imaginative play, at least in this home, is an activity that is more than one of many activities: it is the central activity forming the foundation of the twin's relationship, acknowledged as significant and valued by the parents, and supported by Nagymama. Here, imaginative play is flexible and expandable. It is potentially responsive to new demands, rather easy to hybridize, and the preferred activity when alternative activities or topics of conversation are not on offer for the children. It is one of the primary ways in which we work to form our 'general enterprise' as a family, and Viv and Alex form their specific 'we'.

Clear across each of the excerpts, is the commitment of participants to make play work and, through imaginative play, to make relationships work. For example, in Excerpts 1–3, offers are continually made and taken up, without hesitation. Requests for clarification are voiced using metacommunication over the top of the imaginary situation to negotiate its direction and balance the roles of the participants. In Excerpt 4, imaginative play is expanded to maintain play and, in a sense, to maintain the relationship between Vivi and Alex, while supporting Alex's interests and the demands that she willingly orients to. Invitations from Nagymama for information and advice in this hybrid activity seem to both normalize it and acknowledge its value. In Excerpt 6, the children are required to commit to the new demands of eating dinner. When those are not addressed, play must be terminated, and is by the father; attention is focused on eating.

New demands within imaginative play (Excerpts 1, 2, 3), the exposure of competing motives and attempted negotiations in play (Excerpts 4, 5, 6), and the complex relational work of initiating, maintaining and terminating imaginative play, is highlighted across the excerpts. The character of imaginative play in this home environment may expand to include new activities; Alex can colour in play, the rules bend, the boundaries expand and narrow as needed for the twins to continue to play. This may not be the case in other social institutions or settings when play time is initiated or terminated more abruptly, for example, when it is 'time to' engage in an activity that is not compatible with play or when it is 'time to' go home. Changes foregrounded in transitions, or the potential changes in offers and demands, provide an opening for considerations of what could be and/or ought to be enacted.

Concluding thoughts

Over time, in transitions within, between and from imaginative play, moral imagining as a psychological function evident in relational histories of shared experiences begins a creative process of making real what participants value as 'good' relationships, as well as expectations for roles in relationships and how to renegotiate them as/when interests, demands, motives and activities change. Taking up a new offer or a demand exemplifies a commitment to the 'general enterprise', to being together in relation. Agreeing to an offer may reflect more than the general affirmation, 'I want to play', and instead may specify, 'I want to play *with you*', and further, with who and what I 'know', think, feel about you now.

Thus, terminating play has relational consequences that should be acknowledged. Though not always dire, and not of the same kind of consequence as failing in the social institution of schooling, terminating play, stepping away and/or being excluded all have the potential to highlight the fragility of relating and doing 'we'. While children are imagining their roles in relation, and creating imagined worlds in relation, in initiating and maintaining imaginative play, they will also have to eventually imagine – and experience – the termination or dissolution of play. It may be important, therefore, to introduce children to ways of ending play alongside encouragement to initiate play. In this way, play may end in ways that soften the likelihood of hurt feelings or feelings of failure in the relationships that constitute the 'general enterprise'.

Transitions may be experienced by participants differently, and offers to initiate, maintain and terminate play may not always be clear. Participants learn how much to demand, how far to push boundaries, but this does not mean that demands are perfectly articulated, consistent with the motives of any or all participants and/or that participants themselves do not create disagreements out of frustration and/or exhaustion. A significant feature of imaginative play and examinations of transitions in imaginative play is the shared motive provided by an imaginary situation. A shared motive may enable a common vision, a shared purpose and, perhaps, for the participants a 'general enterprise', at least for the time being. For Alex and Viv, it is almost 'as if' by playing they are relating, imagining future relationships with others and with each other as well. How they play and relate, and the direction of their contributions, is shaped by their moral imaginings.

Further, imaginative play may become an activity through which participants become more individuated given the actions and choices that become visible through play that were not visible before. Empathizing to feel one's way into a role, imagining worlds that have not been experienced as possible worlds, and sympathizing with others in ways that foster collective action towards possible social futures – in these ways imaginative play may be said to leave both collective and individual traces on children who play.

References

Cole, M. (1996), *Cultural psychology: A once and future discipline*. Cambridge, MA: Belknap Press of Harvard University Press.

Göncü, A. (1993), 'Development of intersubjectivity in social pretend play', *Human Development*, 36: 185–198.

Göncü, A. & J. A. Vadeboncoeur (2017), 'Expanding the definitional criteria for imaginative play: Contributions of sociocultural perspectives', *Learning and Behavior*, 45(4): 422–431.

Greene, M. (1988), *The dialectic of freedom*. New York: Teachers College Press.

Greene, M. (1995), *Releasing the imagination: Essays on education, the arts, and social change*. San Francisco, CA: Jossey-Bass.

Greene, M. (2008), 'Education and the arts: The windows of imagination'. *Learning Landscapes*, 1(3): 17–21.

Hedegaard, M. (2012), 'Analyzing children's learning and development in everyday settings from a cultural-historical wholeness approach', *Mind, Culture, and Activity*, 19(2): 127–138.

Hedegaard, M. (2014), 'The significance of demands and motives across practices in children's learning and development: An analysis of learning in home and school', *Learning, Culture, and Social Interaction*, 3(3): 188–194.

Holzman, L. (2009), *Vygotsky at work and play*. New York: Routledge.

Lindqvist, G. (2001), 'When small children play: How adults dramatise and children create meaning', *Early Years: An International Journal of Research and Development*, 21(1): 7–14.

Lindqvist, G. (2003), 'Vygotsky's theory of creativity', *Creativity Research Journal*, 15(2): 245–251.

Panofsky, C. P. & J. A. Vadeboncoeur (2012), 'Schooling the social classes: Triadic zones of proximal development, communicative capital, and relational distance in the perpetuation of advantage', in H. Daniels (ed.), *Vygotsky and sociology*, 192–210. New York: Routledge.

Peleprat, E. & M. Cole (2011), '"Minding the gap": Imagination, creativity, and human cognition', *Integrative Psychological and Behavioral Science*, 45(4): 397–418.

Perone, A. (2011), 'Improvising with adult English language learners', in R. K. Sawyer (ed.), *Structure and improvisation in creative teaching* (pp. 162–183). Cambridge: Cambridge University Press.

Vadeboncoeur, J. A. (December, 2011), '*"How am I me when I'm with you?": Identity as mediated memory*', Deconstructing achievement: A sociocultural perspective colloquium. Hong Kong Baptist University, Hong Kong.

Vadeboncoeur, J. A. (2017), *Vygotsky and the promise of public education*. New York: Peter Lang.

Vadeboncoeur, J. A. & R. J. Collie (2013), 'Locating social and emotional learning in schooled environments: A Vygotskian perspective on learning as unified', *Mind, Culture, and Activity*, 20(3): 201–225.

Vadeboncoeur, J. A. & A. Göncü (2018), 'Playing and imagining across the life course: A sociocultural perspective', in P. Smith & J. L. Roopnarine (eds), *Cambridge handbook of play: Developmental and disciplinary perspectives* (pp. 258–277). Cambridge: Cambridge University Press.

Vadeboncoeur, J. A. & D. Murray (2014), 'Imagined futures in the present: Minding learning opportunities', *National Society for the Study of Education*, 113(2): 633–652.

Vadeboncoeur, J. A., A. Perone & N. Panina-Beard (2016), 'Creativity as a practice of freedom: Imaginative play, moral imagination, and the production of culture', in V. P. Glăveau (ed.), *The Palgrave handbook of creativity and culture research* (pp. 285–305). London: Palgrave Macmillan.

Vadeboncoeur, J. A. & R. E. Vellos (2016), 'Recreating social futures: The role of the moral imagination in student-teacher relationships in alternative education', *International Journal of Child, Youth, and Family Studies*, 7(2): 307–323.

Vygotsky, L. S. (1933/1967), 'Play and its role in the mental development of the child', *Soviet Psychology*, 5(3): 6–18.

Vygotsky, L. S. (1932/1987), 'Imagination and its development in childhood', in R. W. Rieber & A. S. Carton (eds), *The collected works of L. S. Vygotsky, Volume 1: The problems of general psychology, including the volume thinking and speech* (pp. 339–349). New York: Plenum Press.

Vygotsky, L. S. (1935/1994a), 'The problem of the environment', in R. van der Veer & J. Valsiner (eds), *The Vygotsky reader* (pp. 338–354). Cambridge, MA: Blackwell.

Vygotsky, L. S. (1931/1994b), 'Imagination and creativity of the adolescent', in R. van der Veer & J. Valsiner (eds), *The Vygotsky reader* (pp. 266–288). Cambridge, MA: Blackwell.

Vygotsky, L. S. (1926/1997), *Educational psychology* (trans. R. Silverman). Boca Raton, FL: St. Lucie Press.

Vygotsky, L. S. (1960/1997), 'Genesis of higher mental functions', in R. W. Rieber (ed.), *The collected works of L. S. Vygotsky: Volume 4 The history of the development of higher mental functions* (pp. 97–119). New York: Plenum Press.

Vygotsky, L. S. (1998), 'The problem of age', in R. W. Rieber (ed.), *The collected works of L. S. Vygotsky: Volume 5 child psychology* (pp. 187–205). New York: Plenum Press.

Vygotsky, L. S. (2004), 'Imagination and creativity in childhood', *Journal of Russian and East European Psychology*, 42(1): 7–97.

Warnock, M. (1976), *Imagination*. Berkeley, CA: University of California Press.

Warnock, M. (1994), *Imagination and time*. Oxford: Blackwell.

Index

Lightning Source UK Ltd.
Milton Keynes UK
UKHW021148190821
389106UK00009B/304